THE EXETER
ENGLISH-RUSSIAN DICTIONARY
OF CULTURAL TERMS

THE EXETER
ENGLISH-RUSSIAN DICTIONARY
OF CULTURAL TERMS

Roger Cockrell

UNIVERSITY
of
EXETER
PRESS

First published in 1998 by
University of Exeter Press
Reed Hall, Streatham Drive
Exeter, Devon EX4 4QR, UK
www.ex.ac.uk/uep/

British Library Cataloguing in Publication Data
A catalogue record for this book is available
from the British Library

ISBN 0 85989 504 1

Printed in Great Britain by
Short Run Press Ltd, Exeter

CONTENTS

ACKNOWLEDGEMENTS

I would like to thank all those who helped in the compilation of this dictionary. I am particularly indebted to Nadya Keenan and Peter Scorer of the Department of Russian, William Hanson of the Department of German, Alexey Zadorojnyi of the Department of Classics, and other colleagues in the School of Modern Languages and the Faculty of Arts at Exeter. I am also very grateful to Professor Viktor Kabakchi of St Petersburg for all his helpful comments and assistance. Finally, I would like to record my appreciation of the unfailing support and encouragement given me throughout by Simon Baker, Richard Willis, Anna Henderson and their colleagues at the University of Exeter Press. The responsibility for all errors, whether of omission or commission, lies with me.

Roger Cockrell
Exeter
September 1998

INTRODUCTION

The Exeter English-Russian Dictionary of Cultural Terms is an interlingual and directional work of reference. Its aim is to provide the Russian equivalent for some 7,000 foreign and cultural words, terms and phrases to which English speakers with a knowledge of Russian might need to refer. Although the dictionary can be used in a whole range of non-academic as well as academic contexts it is designed to be of particular use to English speakers writing in, or translating into, Russian. As will be explained below, furthermore, it is not just a matter of *translation*: transfer from one alphabet to the other, from the Roman to the Cyrillic, entails the quite separate issue of *transliteration*, an issue which is compounded by the fact that the Russians have yet to adopt a single generally accepted system.

Many of the terms in this dictionary will of course be found in other dictionaries and, indeed, all the terms that appear here can be found in *some* work of reference or other, though not necessarily in works easily available to English speakers; this book is the only one of its kind to bring such words and phrases together in a single volume. Since the dictionary's range of references is wide, embracing the social and natural sciences as well as the humanities, it follows that it is primarily intended not for the specialist in any one particular field, but for a much wider readership.

Indeed, 'cultural' is to be interpreted here in its broadest sense to include names, titles, words and expressions with which 'un citoyen du monde civilisé' might be expected to be familiar. The main categories of the terms included in this dictionary are as follows:

the ancient and classical worlds: Babylon, Sumer, ancient Egypt, the Seven Wonders of the World, the Greeks and Romans, Greek and Roman gods, the Fates, the Muses, the Labours of Heracles, Roman Emperors, writers and books

art (architecture, painting, sculpture): artists and works, general terms

astronomy: the solar system, signs of the Zodiac, constellations, stars, general terms

the bible: books of the Old Testament, Old Testament names, books of the New Testament, New Testament names

culinary terms (including wine and viniculture)

foreign words and phrases: the term 'foreign' is used here to indicate words, terms and phrases which are part of the English vocabulary but which could be classed as 'cosmopolitan' or 'third-culture', i.e. neither English nor Russian. Despite the fact that the overall approach of this dictionary is, for the reasons given below, inclusive rather than exclusive, foreign terms in the following categories have been omitted:

(i) Non-specialist terms which are very rarely used in everyday English. *The Penguin Dictionary of Foreign Terms and Phrases*, for example, lists over thirty entries under the head word 'coup', but whereas terms such as 'coup de grâce' or 'coup d'état' have an obvious place in a dictionary of this sort, others such as 'coup de boutoir' or 'coup de malheur' have not been included.

(ii) Terms such as 'défense de fumer' or 'è pericoloso sporgersi' which will of course be familiar to English-speakers who travel abroad but which nonetheless cannot be considered as part of English vocabulary.

(iii) Phrases such as 'homme de paille' or 'fortuna favet fortibus' possessing a direct English equivalent which is in normal usage.

(iv) Words originally of foreign derivation which have been fully assimilated into English (e.g. chalet, cravat, salon, sauna).

geographical names and terms

history: early history, Middle Ages, early modern and modern history, twentieth-century history

INTRODUCTION

legends and myths

linguistic and literary terms

literature: writers and books

mathematical and scientific terms

music and opera: composers and works, musical terms

philosophy: writers and works, philosophical terms

political terms

prehistory: geological eras and periods, prehistory

psychology: writers and books, psychological terms

religion: general terms, the Disciples, orders of monks and friars, Christian Church Calendar, canonical hours, the liturgy

theatres, concert halls, museums etc.: theatrical terms; names of theatres, concert halls, museums

Cultural terms emanating from Russia itself have been included only when (a) they are in reasonably widespread use in English and (b) the Russian original for such terms may not be familiar or obvious, even to those with a knowledge of the language (e.g. *Nutcracker Suite, Rite of Spring*).

The most important question confronting the

compiler of a work of this nature is where to draw the boundary between what to retain and what to omit. Why, for example, include a word such as 'lento', when its Russian equivalent is a letter-by-letter transliteration (ленто)? Or what is the point of including, say, 'haricots verts' when the 'obvious' Russian equivalent is зеленые бобы? Certainly at first sight the justification for including these particular instances, amongst others, might seem to be small. Yet further examination of the dictionary's contents will show that there are sufficient variations from the expected to warrant an inclusive rather than exclusive approach. The following points should be noted in particular:

(i) There are many instances in which a letter-by-letter transliteration is either not possible or inconsistently realized. This point will be discussed more fully below, under Transliteration.

(ii) There may often be small but real changes in the Russian version, such as the addition of a hyphen where there is none in the original language, or the inclusion of a perhaps unexpected soft sign.

(iii) The Russian term used may often not be the obvious one, or there may be alternative versions; these may, in some cases, be fully synonymous or there may be differences in register or tone.

(iv) Russian biblical or historical names may differ from their modern counterparts: compare for example the biblical Далида (Delilah) with the generally accepted modern form of Далила, as in Saint-Saëns' opera Самсон и Далила. Conversely, the distinction in English between the biblical 'Israelites' and modern 'Israelis' is not followed in Russian, which uses израильтяне for both.

(v) Whereas some terms are translated, others are transliterated. If, for example, 'The Rockies' appear as Скалистые горы and 'Lake Superior' as озеро Верхнее, then it might seem reasonable to assume that 'der Schwarzwald' would be Черный лес, but the generally accepted Russian term is in fact Шварцвальд.

(vi) For those who are speaking Russian rather than writing it, there is the question of where to place the stress: it will become clear that when foreign words are transferred into Russian they quite often fail to retain the same stress pattern. Not all American states, for example, are stressed as in English.

(vii) There is a third way of rendering foreign words and phrases: as a direct transfer in their original (i.e. non-Cyrillicized) form. In some cases indeed all three renderings are possible: 'de facto', for example can be rendered as «de facto», де-факто, or фактически/на деле. During the Soviet period this direct transfer option was used relatively rarely, certainly in the public, non-specialist domain; but Russia is now witnessing a return to the situation before the 1917 revolution, when for the educated public the use of such terms, particularly Latinisms, in their original form was far more widespread (a full list is given in Babkin and Medvedev, *Slovar' inoiazychnykh vyrazhenii i slov*, three volumes, Moscow, 1995). The forms given in this dictionary reflect current usage as far as possible, but it should be kept in mind that *all* such terms can theoretically be used in their non-transliterated form, and that whether or not they are will depend at least partly on the context and the implied readership.

More generally, in connection with this final point, it should be noted that one of the most remarkable features of post-Soviet Russia has been the disappearance of the linguistic and cultural barriers which were erected for ideological reasons during the years of the Soviet regime. Since 1991 the Russian language has been flooded with foreign borrowings, and there has been little active or effective resistance to this process. It is of course true that there are many Russians who regard the use of *any* 'westernism', whether in Cyrillic or Roman letters, as a betrayal of their Slav heritage. The chief proponent of this viewpoint, expressed with all the zeal of a French *académicien* defending the virtues of his native tongue against the incursions of English, is one of Russia's most celebrated living nationalists, the writer and former dissident Aleksandr Solzhenitsyn. In the introduction to his dictionary of words which are derived from Slavonic roots Solzhenitsyn deplores the use in Russian of terms such as 'weekend' (уик-энд), 'briefing' (брифинг), 'establishment' (истеблишмент) and 'image' (имидж); the use of such vocabulary is tantamount, in his view, to 'saying farewell to one's own native language' (A. Solzhenitsyn, *Russkii slovar' iazykovogo rasshireniia*, Moscow, 1990, p. 3). Nevertheless such views, however powerfully expressed, are unlikely to prevail; even if a communist-led goverment were to come to power in Russia it is difficult to foresee a return to the cultural and linguistic isolationism which characterized the worst years of the Cold War.

CONVENTIONS

Since this dictionary is not intended to perform an encyclopaedic function, contextual information has been provided only when it has been considered necessary to do so. See the list of abbreviations below.

Entries are in a single alphabetical order, with the exception of certain entries which form natural groupings rather than individual items. There are seven such entries: *Beaufort Scale; Calendar, French Revolutionary; Disciples, the Twelve; Fates, the Three; Heracles, the Labours of; Muses, the; Seven Wonders of the World.*

cross-references
Cross-references from English to foreign terms and titles are given whenever appropriate (e.g. 'Storm and Stress' to 'Sturm und Drang'; *Magic Flute, The* to *Zauberflöte, Die*; *Six Characters in Search of an Author* to *Sei personaggi en cerca d'autore*). A few titles are given in their original language only (*L'Après-midi d'un faune, Così fan tutte*; conversely and exceptionally, the English title is preferred when it would seem to be the more familiar in a British context (Mendelssohn's *Calm Sea and Prosperous Voyage*, for example).

CONVENTIONS

grammar
Grammatical information has been kept to a minimum and is confined to an indication of the gender of nouns ending in a soft sign, whenever that is not obvious, and the occasional construction using a preposition.

hyphens
A repeated hyphen at the end of one line and the beginning of the next indicates a compound that is always hyphenated, as distinct from a single hyphen marking a split at the end of a line.

italics
The italicisation of foreign words and phrases conforms to the usage in *The Oxford Dictionary for Writers and Editors*.

oblique stroke
Used to indicate synonymous alternatives, often in the form of a transliterated term together with its Russian translation: лимерик/шуточное выражение.

proper names
Names are listed according to surname, except where the first name is the most natural lead word for an entry: Maria Stuart, Marcus Aurelius, Robert the Bruce. In such cases cross-references are not given. Surnames only of artists, authors and composers are given immediately after the entries referring to their works.

CONVENTIONS

quotation marks(«..»)
Used only for terms in Russian, such quotation marks indicate (a) all titles of literary, musical and artistic works, newspapers and journals etc.; (b) a phonetic, as opposed to a conventional, transliteration; (c) terms used in their non-transliterated form; (d) quotations.

semi-colon
Used to distinguish between (a) homonyms; (b) different grammatical forms of the same term, with nouns preceding adjectives and adjectives preceding adverbs.

square brackets
Used to indicate a paraphrased translation when there is no exact rendering available in Russian (see, for example, *enfant terrible*).

stress marks
Cyrillic words are stressed throughout in the reference section of the Dictionary.

TRANSLITERATION

The hyphen in «де-факто» is a reminder that the transfer from one system to another is not always as straightforward as it might appear (other examples would include «нотабена» and «проформа»). This problem becomes particularly evident with the transliteration of proper names and titles from the Roman alphabet into the Cyrillic. All transliteration systems of course are flawed in one way or another: transliterating the other way round, from Cyrillic to the Roman alphabet, is a notorious problem, with no single system able to resolve the conflict between familiarity and consistency (Leo Tolstoy or Lev Tolstoi? Maxim Gorky or Maksim Gor'kii?). *The Oxford English Dictionary*, as Viktor Kabakchi notes, transliterates щи, Russian cabbage soup, as shchi but it also adds the following variations: tschee, stchi, stchie, stchee, shtchee, shtchi, shtshi and schtschi (Kabakchi, V.V., *Angliiskii iazyk mezhkul'turnogo obshcheniia*, St Petersburg, 1993, p. 53).

For Russians, however, who have to deal with the phonetic challenges posed by English and French, to name only two languages, the problem is compounded. With English, for example, there are particular difficulties associated with the transliteration of a 'w' or an 'h'. In the case of the former, Russian usage nowadays seems to favour 'y' rather than 'в' so that 'William' for example is nowadays almost always rendered as Уильям (with the German 'Wilhelm' as Вилгельм). The latter case, however – the transliteration of the 'h' sound – is not so clear-cut. 'Hitler' remains Гитлер and 'Heath' Гит (although Emily Brontë's hero Heathcliff is Хитклифф). But whereas the Nazi leader who fled to Britain during World War II is known in Russia as Гесс, the author of *Steppenwolf* appears as (Герман) Хессе. Heidelberg is Гейдельберг, whereas another German city, Heilbronn, is Хейльбронн. 'Hardy' is now usually transcribed as Харди, but the Russian habit of referring to H.G. Wells as Герберт Уэллс often surprises English speakers. In some instances, transliterated forms (with English 'h' equalling Russian г) appear together with phoneticised forms: on many Russian maps of the British Isles Hastings appears as Гастингс (Хейстингс), and Hull as Гулл (Халл), as distinct from Гул for Goole. With this dualism in mind, the reference, in English, in the *Great Soviet Encyclopedia* (vol. 13, p. 174) to a newspaper entitled *The Korea Gerald* seems more understandable.

Other transliteration points to note include the following:

(i) English 'aw', as in Shaw, is generally 'oy' (Бернард Шоу). Note, however, that Evelyn Waugh, in whose name the 'augh' is phonetically identical, becomes Ивлин Во. 'Lawrence' oscillates seemingly at random between Лоренс and Лоуренс, with the former being used for D.H. and the latter for T.E.

(ii) German 'ö/oe' becomes ё (Мёрике, Гёте).

(iii) The two quite distinct German dipthongs 'eu' and 'ei' are both usually rendered by ей (Фрейд, Гейне); note, however, Хайдеггер and Бернштайн (also possible as Бернштейн). Strictly phonetic transliteration is used with titles of newspapers, such as «Зюддойче цайтунг».

(iv) The conflict between appearance and phonetics is also apparent in the use of ей for English names with quite different phonetic values, such as Reynolds (Рейнолдс) on the one hand, and Gainsborough (Гейнсборо), on the other.

(v) Mute consonants at the end of French proper nouns are generally omitted (Мане, Дюма), although Марат reminds us that even here there is not total consistency.

(vi) 'Superfluous' consonants are sometimes omitted, particularly with German names (Гофман, Гауптман, for example).

(vii) Use of the Cyrillic э at the beginning of names is straightforward and as one might expect – Элиот, Эванс, Эйзенхауэр. Its phonetic role within a name or word, however, is more complex: Мэн, for example, does double duty for both the

TRANSLITERATION

American state of Maine and for the (Isle of) Man.

(viii) Hyphens are often used in compound titles where they are not present in the original language: Нью-Йорк, Ковент-Гарден, Энигма-вариации, Вайльдфелл-Голл.

ABBREVIATIONS

adj.	adjective
anthrop.	anthropology
Arab.	Arabian
archaeol.	archaeology
archit.	architecture
Arthur.	Arthurian legend
astron.	astronomy
Aust.	Austrian
bibl.	biblical
bio.	biology
chem.	chemistry
Chin.	China/Chinese
cont.	continued
cul.	culinary
dat.	dative
eccles.	ecclesiastical
f.	feminine
gen.	genitive
geog.	geography
geol.	geology
Germ.	German
herald.	heraldry
hist.	historical
hort.	horticultural
Jap.	Japanese
leg.	legal
ling.	linguistics

ABBREVIATIONS

lit.	literature
m.	masculine
math.	mathematics
meteor.	meteorology
milit.	military
mus.	music
myth.	mythology
nat.soc.	National Socialist
philat.	philately
philos.	philosophy
phys.	physics
polit.	political/politics
prehist.	prehistory
psych.	psychology
relig.	religion
Rom.	Roman
sci.	science
tech.	technology
theatr.	theatre
US	United States/American
vers.	versification
vin.	viniculture
zod.	zodiac

A

Aarhus (Denmark) : Óрхус

Aaron (bibl.) : Аарóн

Aaron's rod (bibl.) : жезл Аарóнов

Aaron's Rod (Lawrence) : «Флéйта Аарóна»

Abaddon (bibl.) : Аваддóн

à bas! : долóй!

Abbasides (hist.) : Аббасúды

abbé : аббáт

Abbey Theatre (Dublin) : «Э́бби Тиэтр»

Abbildung : иллюстрáция

abbreviatura (mus.) : аббревиатýра

ABC (American Broadcasting Company) : Эй-Би-Си
(«Амéрикан бродкáстинг кóмпани»)

Abel (bibl.) : А́вель

Abélard, Pierre : Пьер Абелáр

Abel Sánchez (Unamuno) : «А́бель Сáнчес»

Abhandlung über den Ursprung der Sprache (Herder) :
«Исслéдование о происхождéнии языкá»

Abhandlungen : трудь́

Abigail (bibl.) : Авигéя

Abimelech (bibl.) : Авимелéх

ab initio : с начáла

Abitur : выпускнь́е экзáмены в срéдней шкóле

Ablaut (ling.) : аблáут

Abner (bibl.) : Авенúр

abomination of desolation (bibl.) : «мéрзость
запустéния»

ab ovo : с сáмого начáла

aborigine : аборигéн

abracadabra : абракадáбра

Abraham's bosom (bibl.) : лóно Авраáмово

Abram/Abraham (bibl.) : Аврáм/Авраáм

Absalom, Absalom! (Faulkner) : «Авессалóм,
Авессалóм!»

1

ABSALOM AND ACHITOPEL

Absalom and Achitopel (Dryden) : «Авессало́м и
  Ахитофе́ль»
abseil : спуска́ться на кана́те
Abu Hassan (Weber) : «А́бу Гаса́н»
Abu Simbel (archaeol.) : А́бу-Си́мбел
Abwehr (hist.) : а́бвер/неме́цкая контрразве́дка
Academic Festival Overture (Brahms) : акаде́мическая
  торже́ственная уверти́юра
académicien : акаде́мик
Académie française : Францу́зская акаде́мия
a cappella (mus.) : а капе́лла
Accadian *see* **Akkadian**
accelerando (mus.) : ускоря́я темп
accidie : лень; хандра́
Achaean League (hist.) : Ахе́йский сою́з
acharnement : остервене́ние
Acharnians (Aristophanes) : «Ахарня́не»
Achenar (astron.) : Ахена́р
Acheron (myth.) : Ахеро́н/Ахеро́нт
Achilles : Ахи́лл
Achilles' heel : Ахилле́сова пята́
Achtung! : внима́ние!
Acis and Galatea (myth.) : Аки́д и Галате́я
Acropolis : Акро́поль (m.)
Across the River and into the Trees (Hemingway) : «За
  реко́й в тени́ дере́вьев»
Actaeon (myth.) : Актео́н
acte gratuit : беспричи́нный посту́пок
Action Française (hist.) : «Акьсо́н Франсе́з»
Acts of the Apostles, The : «Дея́ния святы́х
  Апо́столов»
actualité : действи́тельность
acute accent/accent aigu : о́строе ударе́ние/аку́т
AD : н.э. (на́шей э́ры)
adagio (mus.) : ада́жио
Adam (bibl.) : Ада́м
Adam Bede (George Eliot) : «Ада́м Бид»
Adelaide : Аделаи́да

Adenauer, Konrad : Ко́нрад Аденáуэр

à deux : вдвоём

ad hoc : для да́нного слу́чая

ad hominem : примени́тельно к челове́ку

adieu : проща́й(те)

ad infinitum : до бесконе́чности

Adler, Albert : Альбéрт А́длер

ad lib : экспро́мпт

ad libitum (mus.) : по жела́нию

ad nauseam : до тошноты́

Adonis (myth.) : Адо́нис

Adoration of the Lamb (Van Eyck) : «Поклонéние а́гнцу»

Adoration of the Magi (Leonardo) : «Поклонéние волхво́в»

Adoration of the Trinity (Dürer) : «Поклонéние Тро́ице»

a due voci (mus.) : в два го́лоса

Advent : предрожде́ственское вре́мя

Adventurer, The (periodical) : «Иска́тель приключéний»

Adventures of Augie March, The (Bellow) : Приключéния О́ги Ма́рча»

Adventures of Huckleberry Finn, The (Twain) : Приключéния Гéкельберри Фи́нна»

Adventures of Sherlock Holmes, The (Conan Doyle) : «Приключéния Шéрлока Хо́лмса»

advocatus diaboli : адвока́т дья́вола

Aegean Sea : Эгéйское мо́ре

Aegisthus (myth.) : Эги́сф

Aeneas : Энéй

Aeneid (Vergil) : «Энеи́да»

Aeolian : эоли́йский

Aeolus (myth.) : Эо́л

Aeschylus : Эсхи́л

Aesculapius (myth.) : Эскула́п *see also* **Asclepius**

Aesop : Эзо́п

Aesopian language : Эзо́пов язы́к

AFFAIRE D'HONNEUR

affaire d'honneur : де́ло че́сти

affettuoso (mus.) : ла́сково

afflatus : вдохнове́ние

aficionado : стра́стный боле́льщик/ покло́нник

a fortiori : тем бо́лее

African National Congress *see* ANC

Afrikaans : африка́анс

Afrikaner : африка́н(д)ер

After Many a Summer (Huxley) : «По́сле мно́гих лет умира́ет ле́бедь»

Aga Khan : А́га-Хан

Agamemnon : Агаме́мнон

agape : ага́пе/дру́жеская трапе́за; христиа́нская любо́вь

agent provocateur : провока́тор

Age of Bronze, The (Rodin) : «Бро́нзовый век»

Agesilaus : Агесила́й

Agincourt, battle of : би́тва при Азенку́ре

agitato (mus.) : ажита́то

Agnes Bernauer (Hebbel) : «А́гнес Берна́уер»

Agnes Grey (Anne Brontë) : «А́гнес Грей»

Agnus Dei : «А́гнус де́и»

à gogo : в изоби́лии

agon : состяза́ние

agora : аго́ра/ры́ночная пло́щадь

AGR (Advanced gas-cooled reactor) : графи́то-газовый реа́ктор

Agricola : Агри́кола

Agrippa : Марк Випса́ний Агри́ппа

Ahab (bibl.) : Аха́в

Ahaziah (bibl.) : Охозия

Ahriman : Арима́н/А́нхра-Ма́йнью

à huis clos : закры́тый

Aida (Verdi) : «Аи́да»

aide-de-camp : адъюта́нт

aide-mémoire : па́мятка

AIDS : СПИД (Синдро́м Приобретённого Имму́нного Дефици́та)

4

Aisne, River : Эна

Aix-la-Chapelle : Áхен

Aix-la-Chapelle, Peace of : Áхенский мир

Aix-les-Bains : Экс-ле-Бéн

Ajax : Аякс

Akkad : Аккáд

Akkadian : аккáдский

Aktiengesellschaft (AG) : акционéрное общество

Alabama : Алабáма

à la carte : по вы́бору

Aladdin's magic lamp : волшéбная лáмпа Аладди́на

à la guerre comme à la guerre : на войнé — как на войнé

Alain-Fournier, Henri : Анри́ Алéн-Фурньé

à la mode : мóдный

à l'anglaise : на англи́йский манéр

À la recherche du temps perdu (Proust) : «В пóисках утрáченного врéмени»

à la russe : на ру́сский манéр

Alaska : Аля́ска

Albacete : Альбасéте

Albany (US) : Óлбани

Albee, Edward : Эдуáрд Óлби

Albeniz, Isaac : Исаáк Альбéнис

Alberta : Альбéрта

Albert Herring (Britten) : «Áльберт Хéрринг»

Albigensians (hist.) : альбигóйцы

Alcaics (vers.) : алкéева строфá

Alcatraz : Алкатрáз

Alcestis : Алцéст

Alchemist, The (Jonson) : «Алхи́мик»

Alcibiades : Алкивиáд

Alcools (Apollinaire) : «Алкогóли»

Alcuin : Áлкуин

Aldebaran (astron.) : Альдебарáн

Aldeburgh : Óлдбро

al dente : не развáренный

Aldermaston : Óлдермастон

Aldwych Theatre (London) : «Óлдуич»

alea jacta est : «жрéбий брóшен»

Alexander's Feast (Dryden) : «Пи́ршество Алекс-а́ндра»

Alexander the Great : Алексáндр Македóнский

Alexandrine (vers.) : александри́йский стих

Alfieri, Vittorio : Витто́рио Альфьéри

al fine (mus.) : до концá

Alfred the Great : Альфрéд Вели́кий

alfresco : на вóздухе

Algeria : Алжи́р

Algerian women (Delacroix) : «Алжи́рские жéнщины»

Algol (astron.) : Áлгóль

Algonquian : алгонки́нский

Algonquin : алгонки́н

Alhambra : Альгáмбра

alias : он/онá/они́ же

Ali Baba and the Forty Thieves : «Али́ Бáба и сóрок разбóйников»

alibi : áлиби

Alicante : Аликáнте

Alice's Adventures in Wonderland (Carroll) : «Али́са в странé чудéс»

aliquot (math.) : крáтное числó; крáтный

aliquot part (math.) : дели́тель

Alkor (astron.) : Алькóр

alla breve (mus.) : [исполнéние мýзыки, напи́санной в четырёхчетвертном размéре, «на два»]

Allah : Аллáх

allegretto (mus.) : аллегрéтто

allegro (mus.) : аллéгро

allemande (mus.) : аллемáнда

Allende, Salvador : Сальвадóр Альéнде

Allies (hist.) : сою́зники/сою́зные держáвы

All Saints' Day : прáздник Всех Святы́х

All's Well that Ends Well (Shakespeare) : «Всё хорошó, что хорошó кончáется»

6

Almagest (astron.) : Альмагéст

Alma Mater : áльма-мáтер

Almayer's Folly (Conrad) : «Каприз Олмéйера»

Almería : Альмерия

Almohades (hist.) : Альмохáды

Alemanni (hist.) : алемáнны

alpenhorn : гóрный рожóк

alpenstock : альпенштóк

Alpes-de-Haute-Provence : Áльпы Вéрхнего Провáнса

Alpes-Maritimes : Áльпы Примóрские

Alpha and Omega : Áльфа и Омéга

Alsace-Lorraine : Эльзáс-Лотарингия

Also sprach Zarathustra (R. Strauss) : «Так говорил Заратýстра»

Altair (astron.) : Альтаир

alter ego : «вторóе я»/единомышленник

Althusser, Louis : Лýи Альтюссéр

altocumulus (meteor.) : высокó-кучевые

Alton Lock (Kingsley) : «Óлтон Лок»

altostratus (meteor.) : высокó-слóйсты

AM (amplitude modulation) : амплитýдная модуляция

amabile (mus.) : лáсково

Amahl and the Night Visitors (Menotti) : «Амáль и ночные гóсти»

Amalekites (bibl.) : амалакитяне

amanuensis : помóщник/помóщница

Amazon, River : Амазóнка

Amazon women (myth.) : Амазóнки

Ambassadors, The (James) : «Послы»

ambience : окружáющая обстанóвка

ambrosia : амбрóзия

amen : аминь

American Legion : Американский легиóн

American Tragedy, An (Dreiser) : «Америкáнская трагéдия»

Amharic (ling.) : амхáрский язык

Amis, Kingsley : Ки́нгсли Э́мис

Ammonites (bibl.) : аммонитя́не

Amnesty International : организа́ция
  Междунаро́дная Амни́стия

Amorites (bibl.) : амори́ты/аморе́и

amoroso (mus.) : любо́вно

Amos (bibl.) : «Кни́га Проро́ка Амо́са»

amour-propre : самолю́бие

ampere : ампе́р

Ampères's law (sci.) : зако́н Ампе́ра

amphibrach (vers.) : амфибра́хий

Amphitryon (Kleist) : «Амфитрио́н»

Amsterdam : Амстерда́м

Amundsen, Roal : Руа́ль А́мундсен

amuse-gueule (cul.) : лёгкая заку́ска

Anabaptists : анабапти́сты

anacoluthon (ling.) : анаколу́ф

Anacreon : Анакрео́нт

anacrusis (vers.) : анакру́за

Ananias (bibl.) : Ана́ний

Anatomical Lesson, The (Rembrandt) : «Уро́к
  анато́мии до́ктора Тю́лпа»

Anaxagoras : Анаксаго́р из Клазоме́н

Anaximander : Анаксима́ндр Миле́тский

Anaximenes : Анаксиме́н Миле́тский

ANC (African National Congress) : АНК (Африка́н-
  ский национа́льный конгре́сс)

ancien régime : короле́вский строй

Ancient Mariner, Rime of the (Coleridge) : «Поэ́ма о
  ста́ром моряке́»

Andalucía : Андалу́сия

andante (mus.) : анда́нте

andantino (mus.) : анданти́но

Andersen, Hans Christian : Ханс Кристиа́н
  А́ндерсен

'An die Freude' (Schiller) : «К ра́дости»

Andorra : Андо́рра

Andrew *see* **Disciples, the Twelve**

8

Andrews, Mr and Mrs (Gainsborough) : «Портре́т Р. Эндрюса с жено́й»

Androcles and the Lion (Shaw) : «Андро́кл и лев»

Andromache (Euripides) : «Андрома́ха»

Andromaque (Racine) : «Андрома́ха»

Andromeda (astron., myth.) : Андроме́да

Andromeda nebula (astron.) : тума́нность Андроме́ды

Angelico, Fra : Фра Анже́лико

Angevin (hist.) : анжу́йский *see also* **Plantagenet**

Angles (hist.) : а́нглы

Anglican Church : Англика́нская це́рковь

Anglicanism : англика́нство

Anglo-Catholicism : англокатолици́зм

Anglo-Saxon Attitudes (Wilson) : «А́нгло-саксо́нские по́зы»

Anglo-Saxons (hist.) : а́нгло-са́ксы

Anglo-Sikh Wars : а́нгло-си́кхские во́йны

Anglo-Zulu War : а́нгло-зулу́сская война́

Angry Young Man : «рассе́рженный молодо́й челове́к»

angst : страх

Ångström unit : а́нгстрем

Animal Farm (Orwell) : «Ско́тский ху́тор»

anima mundi : мирова́я душа́/душа́ ми́ра

animato (mus.) : анима́то

Anjou : Анжу́

Annales (Tacitus) : «Анна́лы»

Anne of the Five Towns (Bennett) : «А́нна из пяти́ городо́в»

Annunciation/Lady Day : Благове́щение

annus mirabilis : год чуде́с

Another Country (Baldwin) : «Чужа́я страна́»

Anouilh, Jean : Жан Ану́й

Anschluss (hist.) : аншлю́сс

Anselm : Ансе́льм

Antaeus (myth.) : Анте́й

Antares (astron.) : Анта́рес

ANTE MERIDIEM

ante meridiem **(a.m.)** : утра́; у́тром

anthroposophy : антропосо́фия

Antic Hay (Huxley) : «Шутовско́й хорово́д»

Antichrist : Анти́христ

Antigone : Антиго́на

Antioch : Антиохи́я

antipasto (cul.) : заку́ски

Antiquary, The (Scott) : Антиква́рий»

antistrophe (vers.) : антистрофа́

Antoninus Pius : Антони́н Пий

Antony and Cleopatra (Shakespeare) : «Анто́ний и Клеопа́тра»

Antwerp : Антве́рпен

à outrance : до го́рького конца́

Apache : апа́чи

apartheid : апарте́ид

Ape and Essence (Huxley) : «Обезья́на и су́щность»

Apennines (geog.) : Апенни́ны

aperçu : кра́ткое изложе́ние (summary); проница́тельное замеча́ние (insight)

aperitif : аперити́в

apfelstrudel : я́блочный пиро́г (из слоёного те́ста)

Aphrodite : Афроди́та

Aphrodite of Cnidus (Praxiteles) : «Афроди́та Кни́дская»

Apocalypse : Апока́липсис

Apocrypha : Апо́крифы

Apollinaire, Guillaume : Гийо́м Аполлине́р

Apollo : Аполло́н

Apollo and Daphne (Bernini) : «Аполло́н и Да́фна»

Apollonian : аполло́новский

apologia pro vita sua : самозащи́та

a posteriori : апостерио́ри

Apotheosis of Homer (Ingres) : «Апофео́з Гоме́ра»

Appalachians (geog.) : Аппала́чи

Appalachian Spring (Copland) : «Аппала́чская весна́»

'Appassionata' sonata (Beethoven) : «Аппассиона́та»

appassionato (mus.) : аппассиона́то

Appeasement (hist.) : поли́тика умиротворе́ния

Appian Way (Rom.) : А́ппиева доро́га

Apple Cart, The (Shaw) : «Теле́жка с я́блоками»

apples of the Hesperides *see* **Heracles, the labours of**

Appleton layer (meteor.) : слой Э́плтона

appoggiatura (mus.) : аподжату́ра

Après-midi d'un faune, L' (Mallarmé) : «Послеполу́денный о́тдых фа́вна»

après nous le déluge : «по́сле нас хоть пото́п»

après-ski : о́тдых по́сле лы́жного спо́рта

a prima vista : на пе́рвый взгляд

a priori : априо́ри

apropos/*à propos de* : кста́ти; в связи́ с

apud : по/у

Apuleius, Lucius : Лу́ций Апуле́й

Aquarius (zod.) : Водоле́й

à quatre mains (mus.) : в четы́ре руки́

Aquila (astron.) : Орёл

Aquinas, Thomas : Фома́ Акви́нский

Aquitaine : Аквита́ния

Arab Legion (hist.) : Ара́бский легио́н

Arachne (myth.) : Ара́хна

Aragón, Luis : Луи́ Араго́н

Aramaic (ling.) : араме́йский язы́к

Arcadia : Арка́дия

Arc de Triomphe, L' : Триумфа́льная а́рка

Archimedes : Архиме́д

Archimedes lever : Архиме́дов рыча́г

Archimedes principle : зако́н Архиме́да

Arcturus (astron.) : Аркту́р

Ardennes : Арде́нны

Areopagitica (Milton) : «Ареопаги́тика»

Ares (myth.) : Аре́с

Argenteuil (Manet) : «Аржанте́й»

Argonauts : Аргона́вты

Argos (myth.) : А́ргос

argot : арго́/жарго́н

argumentum ad hominem see ad hominem

ARIA

aria : а́рия

Ariadne (myth.) : Ариа́дна

Ariadne auf Naxos (R. Strauss) : «Ариа́дна на На́ксосе»

Ariel, ou la Vie de Shelley (Maurois) : «Арие́ль, и́ли Жизнь Ше́лли»

Aries (zod.) : Ове́н

arietta (mus.) : арие́тта

Arion (myth.) : Арио́н

arioso (mus.) : арио́зо

Ariosto : Людови́ко Арио́сто

Aristides : Аристи́д

Aristophanes : Аристофа́н

Aristotelian : аристо́телев

Aristotle : Аристо́тель

Arizona : Аризо́на

Arkansas : Арканза́с

Ark of the Covenant (bibl.) : ковче́г открове́ния

Armada, Spanish (hist.) : Непобеди́мая Арма́да

Armageddon : Армагеддо́н/Армагеддо́нская би́тва

Armagh : Арма́

arme Heinrich, Der (H. von Aue) : «Бе́дный Ге́нрих»

Arminius : Арми́ний

armoire : шкаф

Armorica (myth.) : Армо́рика

Arms and the Man (Shaw) : «Ору́жие и челове́к»

Armstrong, Louis : Луи́ А́рмстронг

Arnim, Elisabeth von : Бетти́на А́рним

Arnold, Matthew : Мэ́тью Арно́льд

Arouet, François-Marie *see* **Voltaire**

arpeggio (mus.) : арпе́джио

Arrhenius, Svante August : Сва́нте А́вгуст Арре́ниус

arrière-pensée : за́дняя мысль

arriviste : карьери́ст(ка)

arrondissement : о́круг

Ars Amatoria (Ovid) : «Нау́ка любви́»

Art Deco : стиль в декорати́вном иску́сстве

Artemis (myth.) : Артемида
Arthur, King : король Артур
Art Nouveau : новое искусство/модерн
Art poétique, L' (Boileau) : «Поэтика»
Ascanius (myth.) : Асканий
Ascension Day : Вознесение
Asclepiad (vers.) : асклепиадов стих
Asclepius : Асклепий   *see also* **Aesculapius**
ASEAN (Association of South East Asian Nations) :
  Ассоциация наций юго-восточной Азии
Asher (myth.) : Асир
Ashmolean Museum (Oxford) : Музей Ашмола
Ashtaroth *see* **Astarte**
Ash Wednesday : Пепельная Среда
As I Lay Dying (Faulkner) : «На смертном одре»
asphodel : асфодель/асфодил
assegai : ассегай/дротик
Associated Press : «Ассошиэйтед пресс»
Assommoir, L' (Zola) : «Западня»
Assumption of the Virgin, The (Titian) : «Вознесение
  Марии»
Assyrians : ассирийцы
Astarte (myth.) : Астарта
Asturias : Астурия
Astyanax (myth.) : Астианакт/Астианакс
Aswan Dam : Асуанское плотина
asyndeton (ling.) : асиндетон
As You Like It (Shakespeare) : «Как вам это понрав-
  ится»
Atatürk, Kemal : Мустафа Кемаль Ататюрк
atelier : ательé
a tempo (mus.) : в прежнем темпе
Ather.aeum : Атеней/Афиней
Athene, Pallas (myth.) : Афина
Athos, Mount : Афон/Святая гора
Atlantic Charter : Атлантическая хартия
Atlantis : Атлантида
Atlas (myth.) : Атлас

À TOUT PRIX

à tout prix : любо́й цено́й

Atreus (myth.) : Атре́й

Atropos *see* **Fates, the Three**

attacca (mus.) : ата́ка

attentat : покуше́ние/преступле́ние

Attila the Hun : Атти́ла, вождь гу́ннского сою́за

Attlee, Clement : Кле́мент Э́ттли

aubade (mus.) : у́тренняя серена́да

Auckland : О́кланд

au contraire : напро́тив

au courant de : в ку́рсе (+ gen.)

Auden, W.H. : Уи́стан Хью О́ден

au fait : в ку́рсе (+ gen.)

au fond : в глубине́

Aufklärung : эпо́ха Просвеще́ния

Aufstieg und Fall der Stadt Mahagonny, Der (Brecht, Weill) : «Возвыше́ние и паде́ние го́рода Махаго́нни»

Aufzeichnungen des Malte Laurids Brigge, Die (Rilke) : «Заме́тки Ма́льте Лау́ридса Бри́гге»

Augeian stables *see* **Heracles, the labours of**

au gratin (cul.) : запечённый по́сле посы́пки тёртым сы́ром

Augures (Rom.) : Авгу́ры

Augusta (US) : Авгу́ста

Augustine, St : Августи́н Блаже́нный

Augustus/Octavian : Гай Окта́вий А́вгуст

au lait (cul.) : с молоко́м; моло́чный

au naturel : без припра́вы (cul.); в есте́ственном ви́де

au pair : ня́ня-иностра́нка

au revoir : до свида́ния

Auriga (astron.) : Возни́чий

Aurora (myth.) : Авро́ра

aurora australis : ю́жное сия́ние

aurora borealis : се́верное сия́ние

Auschwitz : Осве́нцим

Aus dem Leben eines Taugenichts (Eichendorff) : «Из

жи́зни одного́ безде́льника»

auslese (vin.) : отбо́рное вино́

Austen, Jane : Джейн О́стин

Austerlitz, battle of : А́устерлицкое сраже́ние

Austin (US) : О́стин

Australopithecus (anthrop.) : австралопите́к

Austrian Succession, War of the : война́ за Австри́йское насле́дство

Austro-Hungarian Empire : Австро-венге́рская мона́рхия

aut Caesar aut nihil : «ли́бо Це́зарь, ли́бо ничего́»

auto-da-fé : аутодафе́

autobahn : автостра́да

Autolycus (myth.) : Автоли́к

autres temps, autres moeurs : «други́е времена́, други́е нра́вы»

Auvers Landscape after Rain (Van Gogh) : «Пейза́ж в Ове́ре по́сле дождя́»

Auxerre : Осе́р

avant-garde : аванга́рд; передово́й

avant la lettre : не вполне́ зако́нченный

avant-propos : предисло́вие

Avare, L' (Molière) : «Скупо́й»

Avars (hist.) : ава́ры

ave! : здра́вствуй

Avebury (arch.) : Э́йвбери

ave, Caesar! morituri te salutant : «здра́вствуй, Це́зарь, иду́щие на смерть приве́тствуют тебя́»

Ave Maria : моли́тва Богоро́дице «А́ве Мари́я»

Avenarius : Ри́хард Авена́риус

Avercamp, Hendrick : Хе́ндрик Аверка́мп

Averroës/Ibn Rushd : Аверро́эс/Ибн Рушд

Avicenna/Ibn Sina : Авице́нна/Ибн Си́на

Avignon : Авиньо́н

Avila : А́вила

Avogadro constant (sci.) : число́ Авога́дро

Avogadro's law (sci.) : зако́н Авога́дро

à volonté : по жела́нию

avoué : пове́ренный
Axis (hist.) *see* **Berlin-Rome axis**
ayatollah : аятолла́
Azazello : Азазе́ль
Azores : Азо́рские острова́
Azores high (meteor.) : Азо́рский антицикло́н
Aztecs : ацте́ки
azure (herald.) : лазу́рь (f.)

B

BA : бакалавр гуманитарных наук
Baal (bibl.) : Ваал
Ba'ath Party : партия Баас
Babbitt (Sinclair Lewis) : «Бэббит»
Babel, tower of : Вавилонская башня
Babeuf, François : Франсуа Бабёф
Babylon : Вавилон
baccalaureate : степень бакалавра
baccarat : баккара
Bacchae (Euripides) : «Вакханки»
bacchanalia : вакханалия
Bacchant(e) (myth.) : вакханка
Bacchus (myth.) : Вакх (Greek)/Бахус (Latin)
Bacchus and Ariadne (Titian) : «Вакх и Ариадна»
Bach, Carl Philipp Emanuel : Карл Филипп
Эмануэль Бах
Bach, Johann Christian : Иоганн Христиан Бах
Bach, Johann Sebastian : Иоганн Себастьян Бах
Bach, Wilhelm Friedemann : Вильгельм Фридеман
Бах
Back to Methuselah (Shaw) : «Назад к Мафусайлу»
Bacon, Francis : Фрэнсис Бэкон
Badajoz : Бадахос
Baden-Powell, Robert : Роберт Баден-Пауэлл
Baden-Württemberg : Баден-Вюртемберг
badinage : шутливый разговор
Badlands (US) : «Бэдленд»
Badoglio, Marshall : Пьетро Бадольо
Baha'i (relig.) : бехай; бехайстский
Baignade, Une (Seurat) : «Купание»
Baiser, Le (Rodin) : «Поцелуй»
Baiser au Lépreux, Le (Mauriac) : «Поцелуй, даров-
анный прокажённому»
baksheesh : бакшиш

BALAAM

Balaam : Валаа́м

Baldassare Castiglione (Raphael) : «Балдасса́ре Кастильо́не»

Balder (myth.) : Ба́льдр

Baldwin, James : Джеймс Бо́лдуин

Baldwin, Stanley : Стэ́нли Бо́лдуин

Balearic Islands : Балеа́рские острова́

Balfour Declaration (hist.) : деклара́ция Ба́льфура

Ballad of Reading Gaol, The (Wilde) : «Балла́да Ре́д-ингской тюрьмы́»

Ballo in Maschera, Un (Verdi) : «Бал-маскара́д»

Baltimore : Балтимо́р

Balzac, Honoré de : Оноре́ де Бальза́к

bambino : ребёнок

banderilla : бандери́лья

banderillero : бандерилье́ро

Banquet of the Officers of the St George Militia Company (Hals) : «Банке́т офице́ров стрелко́вой ро́ты св. Гео́ргия»

Baptists : бапти́сты

Bar at the Folies-Bergère, A (Manet) : «Бар «Фоли́-Берже́р»

Barabbas (bibl.) : Вара́вва

Barbarossa : Барбаро́сса

Barber of Seville, The (Rossini) see *Barbiere di Siviglia, Il*

Barbican Centre (London) : Барбика́нский культ-у́рный центр

Barbiere di Siviglia, Il (Rossini) : «Севи́льский цирю́льник»

Barbizon School (art) : Барбизо́нская шко́ла

barcarole (mus.) : баркаро́ла

Barcelona : Барсело́на

Barchester Chronicles (Trollope) : «Барче́стерские хро́ники»

bar mitzvah : бар-ми́цва

Barnaby Rudge (Dickens) : «Бе́рнаби Рэдж»

Baroja y Nessi, Pio : Пи́о Баро́ха-и-Не́си

baroque : баро́кко; в сти́ле баро́кко/баро́чный

Barque of Dante, The (Delacroix) : «Ладья́ Да́нте»

Barrack Room Ballads (Kipling) : «Пе́сни каза́рмы»

Barrie, James : Джеймс Ба́рри

Bartered Bride, The (Smetana) : «Про́данная неве́ста»

Barth, Karl : Карл Барт

Barthes, Roland : Рола́н Барт

Bartholomew (bibl.) : Варфоломе́й

Bartholomew Fair (Jonson) : «Варфоломе́евская я́рмарка»

Bartholomew, Night of St (hist.) : Варфоломе́евская ночь

Bartok, Bela : Бела Ба́рток

Basel : Ба́зель (m.)

Basque : баск/баско́нка; ба́скский

bas-relief : барелье́ф

Bas-Rhin : Рейн Ни́жний

basso (mus.) : ба́ссо

basta! : хва́тит!

Bastien und Bastienne (Mozart) : «Бастие́н и Бастие́нна»

Bastien-Lepage, Jules : Жюль Бастье́н-Лепа́ж

Bastille, storming of the : взя́тие Басти́лии

bateau-mouche : речно́й трамва́й

Bathsheba (bibl.) : Вирса́вия

Baton Rouge (US) : Ба́тон-Руж

Battle of Cascina (Michelangelo) : «Би́тва при Каши́не»

Battleship Potemkin, The (Eisenstein) : «Бронено́сец «Потёмкин»

Batu (hist.) : Баты́й

Baudelaire, Charles : Шарль Бодле́р

Bauhaus (art) : «Ба́ухауз»

Bavaria/Bayern : Бава́рия

Bay of Pigs (hist.) : Пла́я-Хиро́н

Bayeux Tapestry : ковёр из Байё

bayou : прото́к

BAYREUTH FESTSPIELHAUS

Bayreuth Festspielhaus : Байрёйтский театр

BBC : Би-Би-Си (Британская радиовещательная корпорация

BC : до нашей эры

Beaker people (prehist.) : культура колоколовидных кубков

Beardsley, Aubrey : Обри Бёрдслей

béarnaise sauce (cul.) : беарнский соус

Beatitudes (bibl.) : блаженства

Beatles : «Битлз»

Béatrice et Bénédict (Berlioz) : «Беатриче и Бенедикт»

Beauchamp's Career (Meredith) : «Карьера Бьючемпа»

beau-fils : зять (son-in-law); пасынок (step-son)

Beaufort Scale (meteor.) : шкала Бофорта

  0 Calm : штиль (m.)
  1 Light air : тихий (ветер)
  2 Light breeze : лёгкий
  3 Gentle breeze : слабый
  4 Moderate breeze : умеренный
  5 Fresh breeze : свежий
  6 Strong breeze : сильный
  7 Near gale : крепкий
  8 Gale : очень крепкий
  9 Severe gale : шторм
  10 Storm : сильный шторм
  11 Violent storm : жестокий шторм
  12 Hurricane : ураган

beau geste : великодушный поступок

Beaujolais : божоле

beau monde : бомонд

Beautiful and Damned, The (Fitzgerald) : «Прекрасные и обречённые»

Beauvoir, Simone de : Симона де Бовуар

beaux-arts : изящные искусства

béchamel sauce (cul.) : бешамель (f.)

Becket, Thomas à *see* **Thomas à Becket**

Beckett, Samuel : Самуэ́ль Бе́ккет
becquerel (sci.) : беккере́ль (masc.)
Bedouin : бедуи́н
Beecher-Stowe, Harriet *see* **Stowe, Harriet Beecher**
Beelzebub : Вельзеву́л
Beerbohm, Max : Макс Би́рбом
Beerbohm Tree, Henry : Ге́нри Би́рбом Три
Beethoven, Ludwig van : Лю́двиг ван Бетхо́вен
begum : бегу́ма
behaviourism : бихевиори́зм
Beheading of St John the Baptist, The (Caravaggio) :
  «Казнь Иоа́нна Крести́теля»
Behemoth : Бегемо́т
Beijing : Пеки́н
bel air : изы́сканные мане́ры
Bel Ami (Maupassant) : «Ми́лый друг»
bel canto (mus.) : бель ка́нто
bel esprit : остря́к
Belfast : Бе́лфаст
Belfort : Бельфо́р
belladonna : белладо́нна
Belle Epoque, La (hist.) : «бель эпо́к»/нача́ло XX
  ве́ка во Фра́нции
belle-fille : неве́стка (son's wife); сноха́ (daughter-in-
  law); па́дчерица (step-daughter)
Bellerophon (myth.) : Беллерофо́нт
belles lettres : беллетри́стика
belle-soeur : золо́вка (husband's sister); неве́стка
  (brother's wife); своя́ченица (wife's sister); сво́дная
  сестра́ (step-sister)
Bellini, Giovanni : Джова́нни Белли́ни
Bellini, Vincenzo : Винче́нцо Белли́ни
Bellow, Saul : Сол Бе́ллоу
Belshazzar (bibl.) : Валтаса́р
Belshazzar's Feast (Walton) : «Валтаса́ров пир»
bend (herald.) : пе́ревязь (f.)
Benedictine (liqueur) : бенедикти́н
Benedictines : бенедикти́нцы

BENEDICTUS

Benedictus (eccles.) : Бенедиктус
Benelux : Бенелюкс
Bengal : Бенгалия
Ben-Gurion, David : Давид Бен-Гурион
Benjamin (bibl.) : Вениамин
ben marcato (mus.) : хорошо подчёркнуто
Bennett, Arnold : Арнольд Беннетт
Bentham, Jeremy : Иеремия Бентам
Beowulf : «Беовульф»
berceuse (mus.) : колыбельная
Berchtesgaden : Берхтесгаден
Bérénice (Racine) : «Береника»
Berg, Alban : Альбан Берг
bergamasque (mus.) : бергамаска
bergère : глубокое кресло
bergschrund : горная трещина
Bergson, Henri : Анри Бергсон
Berkeley, Bishop : Джордж Беркли
Berkeley (California) : Беркли
Berlin : Берлин
Berlin Philarmonic Orchestra : Берлинский филармонический оркестр
Berlin—Rome axis (hist.) : ось (f.) Берлин-Рим
Berlioz, Hector : Гектор Берлиоз
Bermuda : Бермудские острова
Bermuda Triangle : Бермудский Треугольник
Bernardin de Saint-Pierre : Бернарден де Сен-Пьер
Bernard of Clairvaux : Бернар Клервоский
Bernini, Giovanni : Джованни Лоренцо Бернини
Bernoulli numbers (math.) : числа Бернулли
Bernouilli's theorem (math.) : теорема Бернулли
Bernstein, Leonard : Леонард Бернштейн
bersagliere : берсальер
Berwald, Franz : Франц Бервальд
Besançon : Безансон
Bessemer process (tech.) : Бессемеровский процесс
Besuch einer alten Dame, Der (Dürrenmatt) : «Визит старой дамы»

Betelgeuse (astron.) : Бетельге́йзе

bête noire : предме́т осо́бой не́нависти

Bethany : Вифа́ния

Bethel : Ве́филь

Bethlehem of Judaea : Вифлее́м Иуде́йский

Bethlehem, Star of : Вифлее́мская звезда́

Bethphage : Виффа́гия

Bethsaida : Вифсайд

bey : бей

Beyle, Henri *see* **Stendhal**

Beyond Good and Evil (Nietzsche) *see* *Jenseits von Gut und Böse*

Bhagavadgita (Hindu relig.) : Бхагава́д-ги́та

Biedermann und die Brandstifter (Frisch) : «Бидер-ма́н и поджига́тели»

Biedermeier (lit.) : Бидерме́йер

bien cuit (cul.) : отва́ренный

Biennale (Venice Art Exhibition) : бienна́ле

big-bang theory (sci.) : тео́рия Большо́го Взры́ва

Big Sur (Kerouac) : «Биг Сур»

bijou : пре́лесть; преле́стный

Bildungsroman (lit.) : рома́н воспита́ния

Bild-Zeitung : «Бильд-ца́йтунг»

billet-doux : любо́вная запи́ска

Bill of Rights (US hist.) : Билль (m.) о права́х

Billy Budd (Britten) : «Би́лли Бадд»

Bird in Space (Brancusi) : «Пти́ца в простра́нстве»

biretta : ша́почка

Birth of Tragedy, The (Nietzsche) *see* *Geburt der Tragödie, Die*

Birth of Venus (Botticelli) : «Рожде́ние Вене́ры»

Biscay, Bay of : Биска́йский зали́в

Biscayan : биска́ец; биска́йский

Bismarck, Otto : О́тто Би́смарк

bisque (cul.) : ра́ковый суп

Bizet, Georges : Жорж Бизе́

Black, Joseph : Джо́зеф Блэк

Black Arrow, The (Stevenson) : «Чёрная стрела́»

black body radiation (sci.) : излуче́ние чёрного те́ла

Black Death (hist.) : чёрная смерть

Black Forest : Шва́рцвальд

black hole (astron.) : чёрная дыра́

Blackshirts (hist.) : чернору́ба́шечники

blague : шу́тка; брехня́

Blair, Eric *see* **Orwell, George**

Blake, William : Уи́льям Блейк

Blanc, Louis : Луи́ Блан

blanc de blanc (vin.) : бе́лое вино́ из бе́лого виногра́да

blanquette (cul.) : рагу́ из бе́лого мя́са

Blanqui, Louis : Луи́ Бланки́

blasé : пресы́щенный

Bleak House (Dickens) : «Холо́дный дом»

Blechtrommel, Die (Grass) : «Жестяно́й бараба́н»

Blenheim : Бленхе́йм

Blenheim, battle of : би́тва при Го́хштедте

Blériot, Louis : Луи́ Блерио́

Blinding of Samson, The (Rembrandt) : «Ослепле́ние Самсо́на»

Blithedale Romance, The (Hawthorne) : «Бла́йтдейль»

Blitzkrieg (hist.) : бли́цкриг/молниено́сная война́

Bloemfontein : Блу́мфонтейн

Bloody Sunday (hist.) : «Крова́вое воскресе́нье»

Bloomsbury Group : кружо́к «Блу́мсбери»

Bluebeard's Castle (Bartok) : «За́мок Си́ней Бороды́»

Blue Danube, The (J. Strauss) : «Голубо́й Дуна́й»

blues (mus.) : «блю́зы»

Blut und Eisen (hist.) : «желе́зо и кровь»

B Minor Mass (J.S. Bach) : «Ме́сса си-мино́р»

Boadicea *see* **Boudicca**

Boanerges (bibl.) : Воанерге́с

Boaz (bibl.) : Воо́з

bocage : бока́ж

Boccaccio, Giovanni : Джова́нни Бокка́ччо

Bodas de sangre (Lorca) : «Крова́вая уса́дьба»

Bodensee *see* **Constance, Lake**

Bodhisattva (relig.) : бодисха́тва

Bodleian Library (Oxford) : библиоте́ка Бо́дли

Boeing : «Бо́инг»

Boeotia : Бео́тия

Boeotus (myth.) : Бео́т

Boer War : А́нгло-бу́рская война́

Boethius : Ани́ций Боэ́ций

boeuf bourguignon (cul.) : говя́дина по-бургу́ндски

Bogomils : богоми́лы

Bohème, La (Puccini) : «Боге́ма»

Boileau-Despréaux, Nicolas : Никола́ Буало́-Депре́о

Bois de Boulogne : було́нский лес

Boito, Arrigo : Арри́го Бо́йто

bolero : болеро́

Boleyn, Anne : А́нна Боле́йн

Böll, Heinrich : Ге́нрих Бёлль

Bologna : Боло́нья

Boltzmann constant (sci.) : постоя́нная Бо́льцмана

Bombay : Бомбе́й

bona fide : че́стный; че́стно

bon-chrétien (cul.) : бонкретье́н

Bonduca *see* **Boudicca**

Bonhoeffer, Dietrich : Ди́трих Бонхо́ффер

bonhomie : добродушие

Boniface, St : св. Бонифа́ций

bon mot : острота́

Bonnard, Pierre : Пьер Бонна́р

bonne chance! : жела́ю успе́ха!

bonsai : япо́нское ка́рликовое де́рево

bonum publicum : для по́льзы де́ла

bon ton : хоро́ший тон

bon viveur : люби́тель(ница) удово́льствий

bon voyage! : счастли́вого пути́!

Booker Prize : пре́мия «Бу́кер»

Boolean algebra : Бу́лева а́лгебра

Boötes (astron.) : Волопа́с

Bordeaux : Бордо́

25

bordello : бордéль (m.)

bordure (herald.) : каймá

Boreas (myth.) : Борéй

Borges, Jorje : Хóрхе Бóрхес

Borghese Gallery (Rome) : Галерéя Боргéзе

Borgia, Cesare : Чéзаре Бóрджа

Borgia, Lucrezia : Лукрéция Бóрджа

borné : ограниченный

Bosch, Hieronymus : Иерóним Босх

Bose-Einstein statistics (math.) : статистика Бóзе-
-Эйнштéйна

bosquet : рóща

bossa nova (dance) : бóсса-нóва

Bossuet, Jacques : Жак Боссюó

Boston (US) : Бостóн

Bostonians, The (James) : «Бóстонцы»

Boston Tea Party (hist.) : Бóстонское чаепитие

Boswell, James : Джеймс Бóсуэлл

Bosworth, battle of : битва при Бóсворте

Botany Bay : Бóтани-Бей

Botha, Louis : Луис Бóта

Botha, P.W. : Питер Бóта

Botticelli, Alessandro : Алессáндро Боттичéлли

Boucher, François : Франсуá Бушé

Boudicca : Будикка

bouffant : пышный

bouillabaisse (cul.) : буйабéс

bouillon (cul.) : бульóн

boule : игрá в шары

bouleversé : потрясённый/изумлённый

Boulez, Pierre : Пьер Булéз

Boulogne : Булóнь

Bourbons (hist.) : Бурбóны

bourgeois : буржуá

Bourgeois gentilhomme, Le (Molière) : «Мещанин во
дворянстве»

bourgeoisie : буржуазия

bourrée (mus.) : буррé

bourse : би́ржа
boustrophedon (vers.) : бустрофедо́н
boutique : ла́вочка
Bouvard et Pécuchet (Flaubert) : «Бува́р и Пекуше́»
Boxer Rebellion : Боксёрское восста́ние
Boyle's law (sci.) : зако́н Бо́йля
Bracebridge Hall (Irving) : «Бре́йсбридж-Холл»
Bradbury, Ray : Рей Бре́дбери
braggadocio : хвастовство́/хвасту́н
Brahe, Tycho : Ти́хо Бра́ге
Brahma : бра́хма
Brahmanism : брахмани́зм
Brahmaputra, River : Брахмапу́тра
Brahms, Johannes : Иога́ннес Брамс
Braille : систе́ма Бра́йля
Brancusi, Constantin : Константи́н Брынку́ши
Brandenburg Concertos (J.S. Bach) :
«Бранденбу́ргские конце́рты»
Brandenburg Gate (Berlin) : Бранденбу́ргские
воро́та
Brandeis University : Бранде́йский университе́т
Brandes, Georg : Гео́рг Бра́ндес
Brandt, Willi : Ви́лли Брандт
Braque, Georges : Жорж Брак
brasserie : большо́й рестора́н
bratwurst : колбаса́
Braunschweig *see* **Brunswick**
Braut von Messina, Die (Schiller) : «Месси́нская
неве́ста»
Brave New World (Huxley) : «О ди́вный но́вый мир»
bravura (mus.) : браву́ра
bread and circuses *see panem et circenses*
Breakfast at Tiffany's (Capote) : «За́втрак у
Ти́ффани»
breccia (geol.) : бре́кчия
Brecht, Bertolt : Берто́льт Брехт
Bremsstrahlung (astron.) : тормозно́е излуче́ние
Brentano, Clemens : Кле́менс Брента́но

Breton, André : Андре́ Брето́н
Bretton Woods : Бре́ттон-Ву́дс
Breughel *see* **Brueghel**
Breuil, Abbé : Абба́т Брейль
Briand—Kellogg Pact (hist.) : пакт Ке́ллога-Бриа́на
bric-à-brac : старьё
bricolage : вре́менная почи́нка; люби́тельская рабо́та
Bride of Lammermoor (Scott) : «Ламмерму́рская неве́ста»
Brideshead Revisited (Waugh) : «Сно́ва в Бра́йдсхеде»
Brigham Young : Бригха́м Янг
brillante (mus.) : блестя́ще
Brisbane : Бри́сбен
brise-soleil : солнцезащи́тный козырёк
Britain, battle of : би́тва за А́нглию
Britannicus : Брита́нник
British Columbia : Брита́нская Колу́мбия
British Commonwealth of Nations : Брита́нское содру́жество на́ций/Коммонуэ́лс
British Museum : Брита́нский музе́й
Britten, Benjamin : Бенджами́н Бри́ттен
Broadway : Бродве́й
Broadwood, John : Джон Бро́двуд
broche (cul.) : ве́ртел
broché : броше́
brochette : ве́ртел; о́рденская пла́нка
Broch, Hermann : Ге́рман Брох
Broken Hill (Australia) : Бро́кен-Хилл
Brontë, Anne : А́нна Бро́нте (А́ктон Белл)
Brontë, Charlotte : Шарло́тта Бро́нте (Ка́ррер Белл)
Brontë, Emily : Эми́лия Бро́нте (Э́ллис Белл)
Bronx : Бронкс
Bronze Age : Бро́нзовый век
Brooklyn Bridge : Бру́клинский мост
Brot der frühen Jahre, Das (Böll) : «Хлеб ра́нних лет»

brouhaha : го́мон/гул голосо́в
Brownian movement (sci.) : Бро́уновское движе́ние
brownie : бра́уни
Browning, Robert : Ро́берт Бра́унинг
Brücke, Die (art) : «Мост»
Bruckner, Anton : Анто́н Бру́кнер
Bruderbond (hist.) : «Бру́дербонд»/«Сою́з бра́тьев»
Brueghel the Elder, Pieter : Пи́тер Бре́йгель
 (Ста́рший)
Bruges : Брю́гге
Brumaire *see* **Calendar, French Revolutionary**
Brunhild (myth.) : Брю́нхильд/Брюнги́льда
Bruno, Giordano : Джорда́но Бру́но
Brunswick : Брауншве́йг
Brussels : Брюссе́ль
brut (vin.) : сухо́й
Brutus : Брут
Buchenwald : Бухенва́льд
Büchner, Georg : Гео́рг Бю́хнер
Budapest : Будапе́шт
Buddenbrooks (T. Mann) : «Будденбро́ки»
Buddha (the enlightened one) : Бу́дда
 (просветлённый)
Buddhism : Будди́зм
Buenos Aires : Буэ́нос-А́йрес
buffo (mus.) : бу́ффо
Bull Run (hist.) : Бул-Ран
Bund : сою́з
Bundesliga (sport) : бундесли́га/вы́сшая ли́га
 (футбо́л)
Bundesrat : бундесра́т (Герма́ния); Федера́льный
 сове́т (А́встрия)
Bundestag : бундеста́г
Bundeswehr : бундесве́р
Bunsen burner (sci.) : Бу́нзенская га́зовая горе́лка
Bunte Steine (Stifter) : «Пёстрые ка́мни»
Buñuel, Luis : Луи́с Бюнуэ́ль
Bunyan, John : Джон Бенья́н

BURCKHARDT, JACOB
Burckhardt, Jacob : Я́коб Буркха́рдт
burgomaster : бургоми́стр
Burgess, Malcolm : Ма́лкольм Бёрджесс
Burghers of Calais, The (Rodin) : «Гра́ждане Кале́»
Burgos : Бу́ргос
Burgundians (hist.) : бургу́нды
burgundy (vin.) : бургу́ндское вино́
Burial of Count Orgaz, The (El Greco) : «Погреб-
е́ние гра́фа Орга́са»
Buridan's ass (philos.) : бурида́нов осёл
Burke, Edmund : Э́дмунд Бёрк
*Burlador de Sevila y convivado de piedra, El (T. de
Molina)* : «Севи́льский озорни́к, и́ли Ка́менный
гость»
Burnett, Francis : Фрэ́нсис Бёрнетт
Burney, Fanny : Фэ́нни Бёрни
Burns, Robert : Ро́берт Бёрнс
Burnt-Out Case, A (Greene) : «Ценой поте́ри»
Burroughs, Edgar Rice : Эдга́р Райс Бу́ррос
Buscón, El (Quevedo) : «Исто́рия жи́зни пройдо́хи
по и́мени Дон Па́блос»
bushido (Jap.) : буши́до
Butler, Samuel : Сэ́мюэл Ба́тлер
Buys-Ballot's law (meteor.) : зако́н Бёйс-Ба́ллота
Byrd, William : Уи́льям Бёрд
Byron, Lord : Джордж Ноэ́л Го́рдон Ба́йрон
Byzantine : византи́йский
Byzantium : Византи́я

C

cabbala : каббалá
cabernet franc (wine) : кабернé фран
Cabot, John and Sebastian : Джон и Себастья́н Кáбот
cabriolet : кабриолéт
cache-sexe : плáвки/ýзкие трýсики
cachet : печáть; престúж
Cade, Jack (hist.) : Джек Кэд
cadence (mus.) : кадéнция
Cadiz : Кáдис
Cadmus (myth.) : Кадм
cadre : руководя́щий состáв
Caen : Кан
Caesar Augustus : Цéзарь Áвгуст
Caesarea Philippi (bibl.) : Кесарúя Филúппова
caesura (vers.) : цезýра
cafetière : кофéйник
Cage, John : Джон Кейдж
Caiaphas (bibl.) : Каиáфа
Cain (bibl.) : Кáин
Cain, mark of : Кáинова печáть
caique : каúк
ça ira! : «пойдёт!»
Cairo : Каúр
Cairo Conference : Каúрская конферéнция
Cakes and Ale (Maugham) : «Пирогú и пúво»
Calabria : Калáбрия
Calais : Калé
Calcutta : Калькýтта
Calderón de la Barca, Pedro : Пéдро Кальдерóн де ла Бáрка
Caldwell, Erskine : Э́рскин Кóлдуэлл
Calendar, French Revolutionary : Республикáнский календáрь

31

CALENDAR, FRENCH REVOLUTIONARY

Vendémiaire : вандемьéр
Brumaire : брюмéр
Frimaire : фримéр
Nivôse : нивóз
Ventôse : вантóз
Pluviôse : плювиóз
Germinal : жерминáль
Floréal : флореáль
Prairial : прериáль
Messidor : мессидóр
Thermidor : термидóр
Fructidor : фрюктидóр
Calendar, Gregorian : Григориáнский календáрь
Calendar, Julian : Юлиáнский календáрь
calends : калéнды
calf, the golden : золотóй телéц
California : Калифóрния
California, University of : Калифорнúйский университéт
Caligula : Гай Юлий Цéзарь Калúгула
Caliphate : Халифáт
Callaghan, James : Джеймс Кэ́ллехен
Calling of St Matthew, The (Caravaggio) : «Призвáние апóстола Матфéя»
Calliope *see* **Muses, the**
Callirrhoe (myth.) : Каллирóя
Callisto (myth.) : Каллúсто
Call of the Wild (London) : «Зов предкóв»
Calm Sea and Prosperous Voyage (Mendelssohn) : «Морскáя тишь и счастлúвое плáвание»
Caltech : Калифорнúйский институ́т техноло́гии
calvados (liqueur) : кальвадóс
Calvary (bibl.) : Лóбное мéсто
Calvinism : Кальвинúзм
Calvin, John : Жан Кальвúн
Calvino, Italo : Úтало Кальвúно
camaraderie : товáрищеские отношéния
Cambrai : Камбрé

32

Cambrian (geol.) : кембрийский период

Cambridge University : Кембриджский университет

Camembert : камамбер

camera obscura : камера-обскура

Camino Real (Tennessee Williams) : «Путь действительности»

Camões/Camoens, Luis de : Луис де Камоэнс

Campania : Кампания

campanile : колокольня

campesino : крестьянин

Camus, Albert : Альбер Камю

Canaan (bibl.) : Ханаан

Canaanites (bibl.) : ханаанеи

Canadian Shield (geol.) : Канадский щит

canaille : каналья

Canaletto, Antonio : Антонио Каналетто

Cana of Galilee (bibl.) : Кана Галилейская

canapé (cul.) : ломтик поджаренного хлеба с какой-либо закуской

canard : газетная «утка»

Canary Islands/Canarias, Las : Канарские Острова

can-can : канкан

Cancer (zod.) : Рак

Canciones (Lorca) : «Песни»

Candida (Shaw) : «Кандида»

Candide (Voltaire) : «Кандид»

Candlemas : Сретение

Canes Venatici (astron.) : Гончие Псы

Canis Major (astron.) : Большой Пёс

Canis Minor (astron.) : Малый Пёс

Cannae, battle of : битва при Каннах

Cannes : Канны

Canonical Hours (eccles.) : Уставные часы молитв

Canopus (astron.) : Канопус

Canova, Antonio : Антонио Канова

cantabile (mus.) : кантабиле

Canterbury Tales, The (Chaucer) : «Кентерберийские рассказы»

cantilena (mus.) : кантиле́на
Canute : Кнуд/Кнут
canzonetta (mus.) : пе́сенка/канцоне́тта
Cape Canaveral : мыс Кана́верал
Cape Colony : Ка́пская коло́ния
Cape Province : Ка́пская прови́нция
Capella (astron.) : Капе́лла
Capernaum : Капернау́м
Capet, Louis : Луи́ Капе́т
Capetown : Ке́йптаун
Capitol (Washington) : Капито́лий
Capitoline Hill (Rome) : Капитоли́йский холм
Capote, Truman : Тру́мэн Капо́те
cappuccino : капуччи́но
capriccio (mus.) : капри́чч(и)о
capriccioso (mus.) : капри́зно
Caprichos, Los (Goya) : «Капри́чос»
Capricorn (zod.) : Козеро́г
Captain Brassbound's Conversion (Shaw) : «Обраще́ние капита́на Брасба́унда»
Caracci family (art) : Агости́но, Анниба́ле и Людо́вико Карра́ччи
Caravaggio : Микела́нджело Карава́джо
caravanserai : карава́н-сара́й
Carbonari (hist.) : карбона́рии
Carboniferous (geol.) : каменноуго́льный пери́од
Carducci, Giosuè : Джо́зуэ Карду́ччи
Carinthia (Aust.) : Кари́нтия
Carlists (hist.) : карли́сты
Carlyle, Thomas : То́мас Карле́йль
Carmagnole, La (song) : «карманьо́ла»
Carmelites : кармели́ты
Carmel, Mount : Ка́рмель (f.)
Carmen (Bizet) : «Карме́н»
Carmina Burana (Orff) : «Ка́рмина Бура́на»
Carnap, Rudolf : Рудо́льф Ка́рнап
Carnaval des ajimaux (Saint-Saëns) : «Карнава́л живо́тных»

Carnaval romain (Berlioz) : «Ри́мский карнава́л»

Carnegie Hall : Карне́ги-холл

Carnegie Institute : Институ́т Карне́ги

Carolingians (hist.) : Кароли́нги

Carossa, Hans : Ханс Каро́сса

carpe diem : «лови́ мгнове́ние»

Carroll, Lewis : Лью́ис Кэ́рролл (Чарльз Ла́туидж До́джсон)

carte blanche : по́лная свобо́да де́йствий

Cartesian : картезиа́нский

Carthage : Карфаге́н

Carthaginians : карфаге́няне

Carthusians : картезиа́нцы

Cartier, Jacques : Жак Картье́

Casa de Bernarda Alba, La (Lorca) : «Дом Берна́рды А́льбы»

Casanova : Джова́нни Казано́ва

Cassandra (myth.) : Касса́ндра

cassata (cul.) : касса́та

Cassegrainian telescope : систе́ма рефле́ктора Кассегре́на

Cassiopeia (astron., myth.) : Кассиопе́я

cassis (liqueur) : ликёр из чёрной сморо́дины

Cassius : Гай Ка́ссий

Castellón de la Plana : Кастельо́н де ла Пла́на

Castelnuovo-Tedesco, Mario : Ма́рио Кастелнуо́во-Теде́ско

Castiglione, Baldassare : Бальдасса́ре Кастильо́не

Castilla la Nueva : Но́вая Касти́лия

Castilla la Vieja : Ста́рая Касти́лия

Castle, The (Kafka) see Schloß, Das

Castle of Otranto (Walpole) : «За́мок Отра́нто»

Castlereagh, Robert : Ро́берт Ка́слри

Castor and Pollux (astron., myth.) : Ка́стор и Поллу́кс

castrato (mus.) : певе́ц-кастра́т

Castro, Fidel : Фиде́ль Ка́стро

casus belli : «ка́зус бе́лли»

CATALOGUE RAISONNÉ

catalogue raisonné : катало́г с объясне́ниями

Catalonia/Cataluña : Катало́ния

catastrophe theory (sci.) : тео́рия катастро́фы

Catcher in the Rye (Salinger) : «Над про́пастью во ржи́»

Cathars (hist.) : ката́ры

Cathleen ni Houlihan (Yeats) : «Кэ́тлин, дочь Хулиэ́на»

Catiline conspiracy (hist.) : за́говор Катили́ны

Cato : Марк По́рций Като́н

Cat on a Hot Tin Roof (Tennessee Williams) : «Ко́шка на раскалённой кры́ше»

Cat's Cradle (Vonnegut) : «Колыбе́ль для ко́шки»

Catullus : Гай Вале́рий Кату́лл

Caucasian Chalk Circle, The (Brecht) *see* *kaukasische Kreidekreis, Der*

Caudillo (hist.): «эль кауди́льо»

cause célèbre : знамени́тое де́ло

causerie : бесе́да

Cavaliers (hist.) : кавале́ры

Cavalleria Rusticana (Mascagni, Verga) : «Се́льская честь»

ça va sans dire : са́мо собо́й разуме́ется

cave canem : береги́сь соба́ки!

Cavendish Laboratory : Ка́вендишская лаборато́рия

Caves du Vatican, Les (Gide) : «Подземе́лья Ватика́на»

Cavour, Camillo : Ками́лло Каву́р

Cawnpore : Канпу́р

Caxton, William : Уи́льям Кэ́кстон

CBC : Си-Би-Си («Кола́мбия бро́дкастинг си́стем»)

CDU (Christlich-Demokratische Union) (Germ.) : Христиа́нско-демократи́ческий сою́з

Ceausescu, Nikolae : Никола́е Чауше́ску

cedilla : седи́ль (m.)

Cela, Camilo : Ками́ло Хосе́ Се́ла

Cellini, Benvenuto : Бенвену́то Челли́ни

Celsius scale : шкала́ Це́льсия

Celtic Twilight, The (Yeats) : «Кéльтские сýмерки»

cembalo (mus.) : чéмбало

Cenci, The (Shelley) : «Чéнчи»

Cenerentola, La (Rossini) : «Зóлушка»

Cenozoic (geol.) : кайнозóйская эра

centaur : кентáвр

Centaurus (astron.) : Кентáвр

centurion : центуриóн

Cepheus (astron.) : Цефéй

Cerberus (myth.) : Кéрбер/Цéрбер

Cercyon (myth.) : Керкиóн

Cerenkov radiation (sci.) : излучéние Черенкóва

Ceres (myth.) : Церéра

CERN (*Conseil Européen de Recherches Nucléaires*) :
  Европéйский центр ядерных исслéдований

Cervantes, Miguel : Мигéль де Сервáнтес Саавéдра

cervelat (cul.) : сардéлька

c'est à dire : то есть

ceteris paribus : при прóчих рáвных услóвиях

Cetus (astron.) : Кит

Cézanne, Paul : Поль Сезáнн

CFCs : фреóны

cha-cha-cha : ча-ча-чá

chaconne (mus.) : чакóна

chacun à son goût : «у всякого свой вкус»

chaise longue : шезлóнг

Chaldean : халдéй; халдéйский

Chamberlain, Neville : Нéвилл Чемберлéн

Chamisso, Adelbert : Адельбéрт Шамиссо

chamois : зáмша; зáмшевый

champ de Mars : Мáрсово пóле

Champlain, Samuel : Сэмюэл Шамплéйн

Champollion, Jean : Жан Шампольóн

Champs-Élysées : Елисéйские поля

Chancellor, Richard : Ричард Чéнслер

Chandrasekhar limit (astron.) : предéл Чандра-
  секáра

Chan-kuo period (Chin. hist.) : периóд Чжаньгó

Channel Islands : норма́ндские острова́

Chanson de Roland : «Песнь о Рола́нде»

chansons de geste : «жёсты»

chanterelle : лиси́чка

chaos theory (sci.) : тео́рия ха́оса

charcuterie : торго́вля колба́сными изде́лиями

chardonnay (vin.) : шардоне́

chargé d'affaires : пове́ренный в дела́х

Charge of the Light Brigade, The (Tennyson) : «Ата́ка лёгкой кавалери́йской брига́ды»

Charlemagne : Карл Вели́кий

Charleroi : Шарлруа́

Charles I : Карл I

Charles V at the Battle of Mühlberg (Titian) : «Карл V в сраже́нии при Мю́льберге»

Charles Martel (hist.) : Карл Марте́лл

Charleston (US) : Ча́рлстон

charleston (dance) : ча́рлстон/чарльсто́н

charlotte (cul.) : шарло́тка

Charollais : шароле́

Charon (myth.) : Харо́н

Chartists (hist.) : чарти́сты

chartreuse (liqueur) : шартрёз

Chartreuse de Parme, La (Stendhal) : «Па́рмская оби́тель»

Chartreux : мона́х картезиа́нского о́рдена

Charybdis (myth.) *see* **Scylla**

Chateaubriand, François : Франсуа́ Рене́ Шато-бриа́н

châtelaine : кастеля́нша

Chattanooga, battle of : сраже́ние при Чаттану́ге

Chaucer, Geoffrey : Джефри Чо́сер

Chausson, Ernest : Эрне́ст Шоссо́н

chef d'équipe : бригади́р

chef-d'oeuvre : шеде́вр

chemin de fer (card game) : желе́зка

Chemins de la liberté, Les (Sartre) : «Доро́ги свобо́ды»

Chénier, André : Андре́ Шенье́

Cheops : Хео́пс

Chersonese : Херсоне́с

cherubim : херуви́м

Cherubini, Luigi : Луи́джи Керуби́ни

Cheshire Cat : чеши́рский кот

chevalier sans peur et sans reproche : ры́царь без стра́ха и упрёка

chevelure : шевелю́ра

chevron (herald.) : стропи́ло/шевро́н

Cheyenne (US) : Шайе́нн

Cheyenne (tribe) : Чейе́нны

Chiang Kai-shek : Чан-Кай-Ши́

Chianti (vin.) : кья́нти

chiaroscuro : светоте́нь (f.)

chiasmus (ling.) : хиа́зм

Chicago Tribune : «Чика́го трибю́н»

Chicago University : Чика́гский университе́т

chicane : зигзагообра́зно расста́вленное препя́т-ствие

chiffonade (cul.) : гарни́р

chiffré (mus.) : цифро́ванный

chignon : шиньо́н

Childe Harold's Pilgrimage (Byron) : «Пало́мничество Ча́йльд- Гаро́льда»

Children's Crusade (hist.) : Кресто́вый похо́д дете́й

Chimera : Химе́ра

Chimes, The (Dickens) : «Колокола́»

China, Great Wall of : Вели́кая кита́йская стена́

Ch'in Dynasty : Цинь

chinoiserie : кита́йская безделу́шка

Chippendale, Thomas : То́мас Чиппенде́йл

Chirac, Jacques : Жак Шира́к

Chirico, Giorgio de : Джо́рджио де Ки́рико

Chiron (myth.) : Хиро́н

Choctaw : Чокто́сы

Choephori (Aeschylus) : «Хоэфо́ры»

Chomsky, Noam : Нау́м Хо́мский

Chopin, Frédéric : Фридери́к Шопе́н

chopsticks : па́лочки

chop suey (cul.) : тушёные о́вощи с мя́сом

Chouans, Les (Balzac) : «Шуа́ны»

Chou, Eastern (hist.) : Восто́чная Чжо́у

Chou, Western (hist.) : За́падная Чжо́у

Chou En-lai *see* **Zhou Enlai**

Chrétien de Troyes : Кретье́н де Труа́

Christ *see* **Jesus Christ**

Christ in the Tomb (Holbein) : «Мёртвый Христо́с»

Christchurch (New Zealand) : Кра́йстчёрч

Christian Science : Христиа́нская нау́ка

Christian Science Monitor : «Кри́счен са́йенс монито́р»

Christie, Agatha : А́гата Кри́сти

Christmas Carol, A (Dickens) : «Рожде́ственская песнь в про́зе»

Christmas Oratorio (Bach) : «Рожде́ственская орато́рия»

Christopher Columbus : Христофо́р Колу́мб

Chronicles I (bibl.) : «Пе́рвая кни́га Паралипомено́н»

Chronicles II (bibl.) : «Втора́я кни́га Паралипомено́н»

Chronique des Pasquier, La (Duhamel) : «Хро́ника семьи́ Паскье́»

Chrysler : «Кра́йслер»

Chuang-tzu : «Чжуан-цзы́»

Church of Jesus Christ of Latter-day Saints *see* **Mormons**

Churchill, Winston : Уи́нстон Че́рчилль

CIA : ЦРУ (Центра́льное разве́дывательное управле́ние)

Cicero : Марк Ту́ллий Цицеро́н

Cid, El : Сид

ci-devant : бы́вший

ci-gît : здесь поко́ится

Cincinnati : Цинцинна́ти

Cinderella : Зо́лушка

cinéaste : кинóшник
cinéma-verité : реалистúческое кинó
Cinna : Лýций Корнéлий Цúнна
cinquefoil (herald.) : пятилúстник
circa : óколо
Circe (myth.) : Цирцéя/Кúрка
circumflex : облегчённое ударéние/ циркумфлéкс
cirrocumulus (meteor.) : пéристо-кучевы́е
cirrostratus (meteor.) : пéристо-слóйстые
cirrus (meteor.) : пéристые
Cistercians : Цистериáнцы
Citizen Kane : «Гражданúн Кейн»
Ciudad Real : Сьюдáд-Реáль
civil rights movement : борьбá за граждáнские правá
Civil War, American : граждáнская войнá в США
Civil War, English : [Англúйская револю́ция]
Clair de lune (Debussy) : «Лýнный свет»
Clarendon Laboratory (Oxford) : Кларендóнская
  лаборатóрия
Clarissa Harlowe (Richardson) : «Кларúсса»
Claude Lorrain(e) : Клод Лоррéн
Claudius, Emperor : Тибéрий Клáвдий Нерóн
  Гермáник
Clausewitz, Karl von : Карл фон Клáузевиц
Clayhanger (Bennett) : «Клейхéнгер»
Clemenceau, Georges : Жорж Клемансó
Clemens, Samuel Langhorne *see* **Twain, Mark**
Clementi, Muzio : Мýцио Клемéнти
Clemenza di Tito, La (Mozart) : «Милосéрдие Тúта»
Cleopatra : Клеопáтра
Clerk-Maxwell, James *see* **Maxwell, James Clerk**
Cleveland (US) : Клúвленд
cliché : избúтое выражéние/клишé
Clio *see* **Muses, the**
Clive, Robert : Рóберт Клайв
clochard : клошáр/нúщий
Clothed Maja, The (Goya) : «Мáха одéтая»
Clotho *see* **Fates, the Three**

clôture (ling.) : закры́тие

Club-footed Boy, The (Ribera) : «Хромоно́жка»

Cluniac : клюни́йский

Cluny : Клюни́

Clytemnestra (myth.) : Клитемне́стра

Cnossus : *see* **Knossus**

Cocteau, Jean : Жан Кокто́

coda (mus.) : ко́да

Code Napoléon : Ко́декс Наполео́на

cogito ergo sum (Descartes) : «Я мы́слю, сле́довательно я существу́ю»

cognoscente : знато́к

coiffure : причёска

Coimbra : Кои́мбра

Coleridge, Samuel Taylor : Сэ́мюэл Те́йлор Ко́лридж

colla parte (mus.) : [указа́ние на то, что побо́чные па́ртии (голоса́) должны́ сообразова́ться в те́мпе с гла́вной па́ртией (веду́щим го́лосом)]

Collins, William Wilkie : Уи́льям Уи́лки Ко́ллинз

Colloquia (Erasmus) : «Разгово́ры за́просто»

Cologne : Кёльн

Colorado : Колора́до

coloratura (mus.) : колорату́ра

Colosseum : Колизе́й

Colossians, Epistle to the (bibl.) : «Посла́ние к Колосся́нам»

Colossus of Rhodes *see* **Seven Wonders of the World**

Columbia University (New York) : Колумби́йский университе́т

Coma Berenices (astron.) : Во́лосы Верони́ки

Comanche : кома́нчи

Comédie-Française, La : Комеди́-Франсе́з

Comédie Humaine, La (Balzac) : «Челове́ческая коме́дия»

Comedy of Errors (Shakespeare) : «Коме́дия оши́бок»

Comenius, Jan : Ян Коме́нский

comme ci comme ça : та́к себе

commedia dell'arte : комédия мáсок/«дель áрте»

comme il faut : «комильфó»

Commodus : Лýций Элий Аврéлий Коммóд

common law : óбщее прáво

Commonwealth *see* British Commonwealth of
  Nations

Communards (hist.) : коммунáры

Commune, Paris : Парúжская коммýна

communiqué : официáльное сообщéние

Communist Manifesto, The (Marx and Engels) :
  «Манифéст Коммунистúческой пáртии»

compagnie (cie.) : óбщество

compère : церемониймéйстер

Compiègne : Компьéн

compline (eccles.) : повечéрие

compos mentis : в здрáвом умé

compote (cul.) : фруктóвое пюрé

compte rendu : отчёт

Comte, Auguste : Огюст Конт

Comus (Milton) : «Кóмус»

concertante (mus.) : концертáнте

Concert champêtre, Le (Giorgione) : «Сéльский
  концéрт»

Concertgebouw Orchestra (Amsterdam) : оркéстр
  «Концéртгебау»

concertino : концертúно

concerto : концéрто

concierge : консьéрж(ка)

Concord (US) : Кóнкорд

concordat : конкордáт

Concorde (aircraft) : Конкóрд

Place de la Concorde (Paris) : плóщадь Соглáсия

Condition humaine, La (Malraux) : «Услóвия
  человéческого существовáния»

con dolore (mus.) : печáльно

condottiere : кондотьéр

con espressione (mus.) : выразúтельно

Confederacy (hist.) : Конфедерáция/южáне

CONFÉDÉRATION GÉNÉRALE DU TRAVAIL

Confédération Générale du Travail (CGT) : Всеобщая конфедерация труда

Confessions, Les (Rousseau) : «Исповедь»

Confessions of an Opium-Eater (De Quincey) : «Исповедь англичанина-опиомана»

confrère : собрат/товарищ

Confucianism : Конфуцианство

Confucius : Конфуций

con fuoco (mus.) : с огнём

Congregationalists (relig.) : конгрегационалисты

Congress Party (India) : Индийский национальный конгресс

Congreve, William : Уильям Конгрив

Connecticut : Коннектикут

Connecticut Yankee at the Court of King Arthur, A (Twain) : «Янки из Коннектикута при дворе короля Артура»

Conquistadores (hist.) : конквистадоры

Conrad, Joseph : Джозеф Конрад (Юзеф Корженёвский)

Conservative Party : Консервативная партия

consommé (cul.) : консоме

con sordino (mus.) : засурдинить

Conspiracy of Claudius Civilis, The (Rembrandt) : «Заговор Клавдия Цивилиса»

con spirito (mus.) : живо

Constable (of France, hist.) : коннетабль

Constable, John : Джон Констебль

Constance, Lake : Боденское озеро

Constant, Benjamin : Бенжамен Констан

Constantinople : Константинополь (m.)

Constituent Assembly (hist.) : Учредительное собрание

Consuls (hist.) : консулы

contrabasso (mus.) : контрабас

contrafagotto (mus.) : контрафагот

Contrat social, Le (Rousseau) : «Об общественном договоре» *contretemps* : помéха

Convention (hist.) : Конвéнт

conversazione : собрáние; приём

Conversion of St Paul (Michelangelo) : «Обращéние Пáвла»

Cook, James : Джеймс Кук

Coolidge, Calvin : Кáлвин Кýлидж

Cooper, James Fenimore : Джеймс Фенимóр Кýпер

Copenhagen : Копенгáген

Copland, Aaron : Аарóн Коплéнд

Coppélia (Delibes) : «Коппéлия»

Copts : кóпты

Coral Sea, battle of the : бúтва за Корáлловое мóре

cor anglais : англúйский рожóк

Corbusier, Le : Шарль Ле Корбюзьé

Corday, Charlotte : Шарлóтта Кордé

Cordillera : Кордильéра

Cordoba : Кóрдова

cordon sanitaire : санитáрный кордóн

Corinth : Корúнф

Corinthian : корúнфский

Corinthians I (bibl.) : «Пéрвое послáние к Коринфя́нам»

Corinthians II (bibl.) : «Вторóе послáние к Коринфя́нам»

Coriolanus (Shakespeare) : «Кориолáн»

Coriolis force (sci.) : сúла Кориолúса

Corneille, Pierre : Пьер Корнéль

Cornelius (bibl.) : Корнúлий

Cornelius, Peter von : Пéтер фон Корнéлиус

Cornell University : Корнéлльский университéт

Cornish (ling.) : кóрнский язы́к

Corn Laws (hist.) : хлéбные закóны

Coroesus Sacrificing Himself to Save Callirhoe (Fragonard) : «Корéз и Каллирóя»

Corot, Camille : Камúль Корó

corps de ballet : кордебалéт

corps d'élite : отбóрный состáв

corps diplomatique : дипломати́ческий ко́рпус

Correggio, Antonio : Анто́нио Алле́гри Корре́джо

corrida de toros : бой быко́в/корри́да

Corridors of Power (Snow) : «Коридо́ры вла́сти»

Corsair, The (Byron) : «Корса́р»

cortège : корте́ж

Cortegiano, Il (Castiglione) : «Придво́рный»

Cortes (Spanish Parliament) : Корте́сы

Cortot, Alfred : А́льфред Корто́

Corunna : Ла-Кору́нья

corvée (hist.) : ба́рщина

coryphée (ballet) : корифе́й

Cosa Nostra : «Ко́за но́стра»

Così fan tutte (Mozart) : «Так поступа́ют все же́нщины»

Côte d'Azur : Кот д'Азю́р/Лазу́рный бе́рег

Côte Vermeille : Верме́левый бе́рег

côtes de boeuf (cul.) : говя́жья отбивна́я

Côtes-du-Nord : Кот-дю-Но́р

côtes du Rhône (vin.) : кот-дю-Ро́н

cotillon (dance) : котильо́н

couchant (herald.) : лега́вый

couleur locale : ме́стный колори́т

Coulomb's law (sci.) : зако́н Куло́на

Council of Nicaea (eccles. hist.) : Нике́йский собо́р

Counter-Reformation : Контрреформа́ция

Count of Monte Cristo, The (Dumas) : «Граф Мо́нте-Кри́сто»

coup de grâce : после́дний уда́р

coup d'état : госуда́рственный переворо́т

coup de théâtre : неожи́данная завя́зка

courante (mus.) : кура́нта

Courbet, Gustave : Гюста́в Курбе́

Courier-Sud (Saint-Exupéry) : «Ю́жный почто́вый»

Cours de philosophie positive (Comte) : «Курс позити́вной филосо́фии»

couscous (cul.) : куску́с

Cousine Bette, La (Balzac) : «Кузе́н Бет»

Cousin Pons, Le (Balzac) : «Кузéн Понс»

couturier : модельéр

Covent Garden (London) : Кóвент-Гáрден

Coward, Noel : Нóэл Кóуард

Cowper, William : Уи́льям Кáупер

Crab Nebula (astron.) : Крабови́дная тумáнность

cracovienne (dance) : краковя́к

Crane, Stephen : Сти́вен Крейн

Cranford (Gaskell) : «Крéнфорд»

Crapp's Last Tape (Beckett) : «Послéдняя лéнта Крэ́ппа»

Crassus : Марк Лици́ний Красс

Creation, The (Haydn) : «Сотворéние ми́ра»

Creationism : креациони́зм

crèche : я́сли

Crécy, battle of : би́тва при Креси́

Credo : Крéдо

crème Chantilly : взби́тые сли́вки

crème de la crème : сáмый лу́чший

creole (ling.) : креóльский язы́к

crêpe de Chine : крепдеши́н

crescendo (mus.) : крещéндо/с возрастáющей си́лой

Cretaceous (geol.) : меловóй перио́д

Crete : Крит

Cricket on the Hearth, The (Dickens) : «Сверчóк на ками́не»

cri de coeur : крик души́

Crimean War : Кры́мская войнá

Crime de Sylvestre Bonnard, Le (France) : «Преступлéние Сильвéстра Боннáра»

crime passionel : уби́йство из рéвности

Critique of Pure Reason (Kant) see Kritik der reinen Vernunft

Croce, Benedetto : Бенедéтто Крóче

crochet : вязáльный крючóк

Croesus (myth.) : Крез

croissant (cul.) : подкóвка

Croix de Guerre : крест «За боевы́е заслу́ги»

Cro-Magnon Man (prehist.) : кроманьόнец

Crome Yellow (Huxley) : «Жёлтый Кром»

Cromwell, Oliver : Όливер Крόмвель

croquette (cul.) : крокέт/битόк

crotchet (mus.) : четвертнάя нόта

croustade (cul.) : пирόг с хрустя́щей кόрочкой

croûton (cul.) : гренόк

crown of thorns (bibl.) : тернόвый венέц

Crucifixion (Tintoretto) : «Распя́тие»

Crucifixion of St Peter (Michelangelo) : «Распя́тие апόстола Петрά»

crudités (cul.) : сыры́е όвощи

crusaders : крестонόсцы

Crusades : Крестόвые похόды

Crusoe, Robinson (Defoe) see Robinson Crusoe

Crystal Palace : Хрустάльный дворέц

Cuba : Кýба

Cuban Crisis (hist.) : Карибский кризис

Cubism : кубизм

Cuenca : Куэ́нка

cuestión palpitante, La (Pardo Bazán) : «Животрепέщущий вопрόс»

cui bono? (leg.) : в чьих интерέсах?

cuisine : кýхня

cul-de-sac : тупик

Cultural Revolution (hist.) : Культýрная револю́ция

Cummings, E.E. : Э.Э. Кάммингс

cumulonimbus (meteor.) : кýчево-дождевы́е

cumulus (meteor.) : кучевы́е

Cunning Little Vixen, The (Janáček) : «Лисичка--плутόвка»

Cupid : Купидόн

curaçao : кюрасό

curé : кюрέ

Curia : Кýрия

Curie's law (sci.) : закόн Кюри

curriculum vitae : крάткое жизнеописάние

Curzon Line (hist.) : линия Кέрзона

cuvée (vin.) : кювé
Cuyp, Albert : Альбéрт Кёйп
Cybele (myth.) : Кибéла
Cyclops (myth.) : Киклóпы/циклóпы
Cygnus (astron.) : Лéбедь (m.)
Cymbeline (Shakespeare) : «Цимбелúн»
Cynics (philos.) : Кúники
Cyprus : Кипр
Cyrano de Bergerac (Rostand) : «Сирáно де
  Бержерáк»
Cyrenaics (philos.) : Кирéнская шкóла
Cyrene : Кирéна
Cyropaedia : Киропéдия
Cyrus : Кир
Cytherean (myth.) : кифéрский/относя́щийся к
  Афродúте
Czerny, Karl : Карл Чéрни

D

da capo (mus.) : с нача́ла
Dachau : Даха́у
dacoit : банди́т
dactyl (vers.) : да́ктиль (m.)
Dadaism : дадаи́зм
Daedalus (myth.) : Деда́л
daguerrotype : дагерроти́п
Dáil Eireann (Irish Parliament) : Пала́та представ-
и́телей ирла́ндского парла́мента
Daily Telegraph : «Де́йли телегра́ф»
Daimler-Benz : Да́ймлер-Бенц
Daladier, Édouard : Эдуа́рд Даладье́
Dalai Lama : Дала́й-Ла́ма
Dali, Salvador : Сальвадо́р Дали́
Dalila *see* **Delilah**
Dallapiccola, Luigi : Луи́джи Даллапи́ккола
Dallas (US) : Да́ллас
dal segno (mus.) : от зна́ка
Damascus : Дама́ск
Dame aux Camélias, La (Dumas) : «Да́ма с каме́л-
иями»
Damnation de Faust, La (Berlioz) : «Осужде́ние
Фа́уста»
Damocles : Дамо́кл
Damocles, sword of : Дамо́клов меч
Dan (bibl.) : Дан
Danaë (myth.) : Дана́я
Dance of Death (Holbein) : «Пля́ска сме́рти»
Dance to the Music of Time, A (Powell) : «Та́нец под
му́зыку вре́мени»
Danegeld (hist.) : да́тская по́шлина
Danelaw (hist.) : О́бласть да́тского пра́ва
Dangling Man, The (Bellow) : «Праздношат-
а́ющийся»

Daniel (bibl.) : «Кни́га Проро́ка Дании́ла»

Daniel Deronda (George Eliot) : «Даниэ́ль Деро́нда»

d'Annunzio, Gabriele : Габриэ́ле Д'Анну́нцио

danse macabre : пля́ска сме́рти

Dante Alighieri : Да́нте Алигьэ́ри

Dantean/Dantesque : да́нтовский

Dantons Tod (Büchner) : «СмертьДанто́на»

Danube, River : Дуна́й

Daphne (myth.) : Да́фна

Daphnis et Chloë (Ravel) : «Да́фнис и Хло́я»

Darius : Да́рий

Darwin, Charles : Чарльз Да́рвин

Darwinism : дарвини́зм

Dasein *(philos.)* : прису́тствие/существова́ние

Daubigny, Charles : Шарль Франсуа́ Добиньи́

Daudet, Alphonse : Альфо́нс Доде́

Daumier, Honoré : Оноре́ Домье́

dauphin *(hist.)* : дофи́н/насле́дник престо́ла

Dauphin, le Grand *(hist.)* : сын Людо́вика XIV

David *(bibl.)* : Дави́д

David, Jacques Louis : Жак Луи́ Дави́д

David Copperfield (Dickens) : «Дэ́вид Ко́пперфильд»

Davidsbündler-Tänze (Schumann) : «Давидс-
бю́ндлери»

Davis Cup : Ку́бок Дэ́виса

Davy Lamp : ла́мпа Де́ви

Day-Lewis, Cecil : Се́сил Дей-Лью́ис

D-Day *(hist.)* : Норма́ндская деса́нтная опера́ция

Dead Sea : Мёртвое мо́ре

Dead Sea Scrolls : кумра́нские ру́кописи

De Anima (Aristotle) : «О душе́»

Death and the Maiden (Schubert) : «Де́вушка и
смерть»

Death in the Afternoon (Hemingway) : «Смерть по́сле
полу́дня»

Death in Venice (T. Mann) see *Tod in Venedig, Der*

Death of a Salesman (Miller) : «Смерть комми-
вояжёра»

DEATH OF OENONE

Death of Oenone (Tennyson) : «Смерть Эно́ны»

Death of Procris (Piero di Cosimo) : «Смерть Прокри́ды»

Death of Socrates (David) : «Смерть Сокра́та»

Death of Virgil, The (Broch) *see Tod des Vergil, Der*

De Augmentis Scientiarum (Bacon) : «Вели́кое восстановле́ние нау́к»

Débâcle, La (Zola) : «Разгро́м»

Deborah (bibl.) : Дево́ра/Дебо́ра

de Broglie wavelength (sci.) : Во́лны де Бро́йля

Debussy, Claude : Клод Дебюсси́

debut : дебю́т

débutante : де́вушка, впервы́е появля́ющаяся в вы́сшем о́бществе

Decameron (Boccaccio) : «Декамеро́н»

Deccan (India) : Декан́

De Civitate Dei (Augustine) : «О гра́де Бо́жием»

Declaration of Independence (hist.) : Деклара́ция незави́симости

déclassé : декласси́рованный

Decline and Fall (Waugh) : «Упа́док и крах»

Decline and Fall of the Roman Empire, The (Gibbon) : «Исто́рия упа́дка и разруше́ния Ри́мской импе́рии»

Decline of the West, The (Spengler) *see Untergang des Abendlandes, Der*

décolletage : декольте́

De Consolatione Philosophiae (Boethius) : «Утеше́ние филосо́фское»

decoupage : вырезывание

decrescendo (mus.) : декреще́ндо

de facto : де-фа́кто

De Finibus (Cicero) : «О преде́лах добра́ и зла́»

Defoe, Daniel : Даниэ́ль Дефо́

Degas, Edgar : Эдга́р Дега́

de Gaulle, Charles : Шарль де Го́лль

dégustation : дегуста́ция

de gustibus non est disputandum : «о вку́сах не спо́рят»

Dei gratia : Бо́жьей ми́лостью

De Institutione Oratoria (Quintilian) : «Об образова́нии ора́тора»

déjà entendu : иллю́зия уже́ слы́шанного

déjà vu : дежа-вю́/иллю́зия уже́ ви́денного

Déjeuner sur l'herbe (Manet) : «За́втрак на траве́»

de jure : де-ю́ре

Delacroix, Eugène : Эже́н Делакруа́

Delaware, River : Де́лавэр

Delhi : Де́ли

Delibes, Léo : Ле́о Дели́б

Delilah (bibl.) : Дали́да

delirium tremens : бе́лая горя́чка

Delius, Frederick : Фре́дерик Ди́лиус

Delphi : Де́льфы

de luxe : люкс

Delvaux, Paul : Поль Дельво́

démarche : дема́рш/реши́тельный шаг

Demeter (myth.) : Деме́тра

Demian (Hesse) : «Демиа́н»

demimondaine : же́нщина лёгкого поведе́ния

demimonde : демимо́нд/полусве́т

demi-pension : полупансио́н

demi-sec (vin.) : полусухо́е

demisemiquaver (mus.) : шестна́дцатая но́та

demiurge : демиу́рг

Democratic Party (US) : Демократи́ческая па́ртия

Democritus : Демокри́т

Demoiselles d'Avignon, Les (Picasso) : «Авиньо́нские де́вушки»

de Moivre formula (sci.) : фо́рмула Муа́вра

Demosthenes : Демосфе́н

denarius : дена́рий

Deneb (astron.) : Де́неб

Deng Xiaoping : Дэн Сяопи́н

dénouement : развя́зка

de novo : с нача́ла

De Officiis (Cicero) : «Об обя́занностях»

DEO GRATIAS

Deo gratias : слáва Бóгу!

Deo volente : даст Бог

de profundis : из глубины́

De Profundis (Wilde) : «De Profundis»

De Quincey, Thomas : Томас де Куи́нси

déraciné : человéк в чужóй странé/непривы́чной средé; потеря́вший пóчву

derailleur : переключáтель скоростéй на велосипéде

Derby at Epsom, The (Géricault) : «Дéрби в Э́псоме»

De Rerum Natura (Lucretius) : «О прирóде вещéй»

de rigueur : обязáтельный

Derrida, Jacques : Жак Дерридá

Der Zug war pünktlich (Böll) : «Пóезд прихóдит вóвремя»

Desastres de la Guerra, Los (Goya) : «Бéдствия войны́»

Descartes, René : Ренé Декáрт

Descent from the Cross (Rubens) : «Сня́тие с крестá»

Deserted Village, The (Goldsmith) : «Пок#инутая дерéвня»

déshabillé : дезабильé

Desire Under the Elms (O'Neill) : «Любóвь под вя́зами»

Des Knaben Wunderhorn (Brentano) : «Волшéбный рог мáльчика»

Des Meeres und der Liebe Wellen (Grillparzer) : «Вóлны мóря и любви́»

Des Moines (US) : Де-Мойн

Des Teufels General (Zuckmayer) : «Генерáл дья́вола»

détente : разря́дка

Detroit : Детрóйт

de trop : ли́шний

deus ex machina : «бог из маши́ны» [развя́зка вслéдствие вмешáтельства непредви́денного обстоя́тельства]

Deuteronomy (bibl.) : «Пя́тая кни́га Моисéева. Второзакóние»

Deutschland über alles : «Герма́ния превы́ше всего́»

deutschmark : неме́цкая ма́рка

Deuxième sexe, Le (de Beauvoir) : «Второ́й пол»

De Valera, Éamon : И́мон Де Вале́ра

Devil's Disciple, The (Shaw) : «Учени́к дья́вола»

de visu : воо́чию

Devonian (geol.) : дево́нский перио́д

Dewar flask (sci.) : сосу́д Дью́ара

Dewey, John : Джон Дью́и

Diabelli Variations (Beethoven) : «Вариа́ции на те́му ва́льса Диабе́лли»

Diable bôiteux, Le (Le Sage) : «Хромо́й бес»

diablerie : колдовство́

diacritic (ling.) : диакрити́ческий знак

Diaghilev, Sergei Pavlovich : Серге́й Па́влович Дя́гилев

Dialogus de Oratoribus (Tacitus) : «Диало́г об ора́торах»

diamanté : укра́шенный алма́зами

Diana (myth.) : Диа́на

diaspora : диа́спора/расселе́ние

Diaz, Bartholomew : Бартоломе́у Ди́аш/Ди́ас

Dichterliebe (Schumann) : «Любо́вь поэ́та»

Dichtung und Wahrheit (Goethe) : «Поэ́зия и пра́вда»

Dickens, Charles : Чарльз Ди́ккенс

Diderot, Denis : Дени́с Дидро́

Dido (myth.) : Дидо́на

Dien Bien Phu, battle of : би́тва за Дьенбьенфу́

diesel engine : ди́зель (m.)

Dies Irae : День гне́ва/День стра́шного суда́

differential equation : дифференциа́льное уравне́ние

digestif : ликёр

diminuendo (mus.) : диминуэ́ндо

Dimos (astron.) : Де́ймос

Ding an sich (philos.) : вещь в себе́

Diocletian, Emperor : Гай Авре́лий Вале́рий Диоклетиа́н

Diogenes : Диоге́н Сино́пский

DIOMEDES

Diomedes : Диоме́д

Dionysian : диониси́йский

Dionysus : Дио́ни́с

Diophantine equations (math.) : диофа́нтовы уравне́ния

Dioscuri (myth.) : Диоску́ры

Directoire/Directory (hist.) : Директо́рия

dirigiste : управле́нческий

dirndl : неме́цкий национа́льный же́нский костю́м

Disciples, the Twelve : Двена́дцать Апо́столов

  Simon, who is called Peter : Симо́н, называ́емый Петро́м

  Andrew, his brother : Андре́й, брат его́

  James the son of Zebedee : Иа́ков Зеведе́ев

  John, his brother : Иоа́нн, брат его́

  Philip and Bartholomew : Фили́пп и Варфоломе́й

  Thomas and Matthew the publican : Фома́ и Матфе́й мы́тарь

  James the son of Alphaeus : Иа́ков Алфе́ев

  Lebbaeus, whose surname was Thaddaeus : Левве́й, про́званный Фадде́ем

  Judas the brother of James : Иу́да Иа́ковлев

  Simon the Canaanite/Zelotes : Симо́н Канани́т/Зило́т

  Judas Iscariot, who also betrayed Him : Иу́да Искарио́т, кото́рый и пре́дал его́

Discours de la méthode (Descartes) : «Рассужде́ние о ме́тоде»

Discours sur l'inégalité (Rousseau) : «Рассужде́ние о нача́ле и основа́нии нера́венства ме́жду людьми́»

disjecta membra : разбро́санные оста́нки

Disney, Walt : Уо́лт Ди́сней

Disraeli, Benjamin : Бе́нджамин Дизра́эли

Dissolution of the Monasteries (hist.) : секуляр-иза́ция

District Attorney : окружно́й прокуро́р

District of Columbia (US) : Федера́льный о́круг Колу́мбия

dithyramb : дифира́мб/похвала́

diva : звезда́

divertimento (mus.) : дивертисме́нт

divertissement : дивертисме́нт

divide et impera! : «разделя́й и вла́ствуй!»

Divina Commedia, La (Dante) : «Боже́ственная
  коме́дия»

divorceé : разведённая

Dix, Otto : О́тто Дикс

dixieland : диксиле́нд

DNA (deoxyribonucleic acid) : ДНК (дезоксирибо-
  нуклеи́новая кислота́)

Doctor's Dilemma, The (Shaw) : «Диле́мма врача́»

Doctor Strangelove : «До́ктор Стре́нджлав»

Dodsworth (Sinclair Lewis) : «До́дсворт»

Dodgson, Charles Lutwidge *see* **Carroll, Lewis**

doge : дож

Doktor Faustus (T. Mann) : «До́ктор Фа́устус»

Dolce vita, La : «Сла́дкая жизнь»

Dollfuss, Engelbert : Э́нгельберт До́льфус

Doll's House, A (Ibsen) : «Ку́кольный дом»

doloroso (mus.) : печа́льно

domaine (vin.) : име́ние

Dombey and Son (Dickens) : «До́мби и сын»

Domesday Book (hist.) : Кни́га Стра́шного Суда́

dominant (mus.) : домина́нта

Dominic, St : св. Домини́к

Dominicans : доминика́нцы

Domitian, Emperor : Тит Фла́вий Домициа́н

Don Carlos (Verdi) : «Дон Ка́рлос»

Don Giovanni (Mozart) : «Дон Жуа́н»

Donizetti, Gaetano : Гаета́но Донице́тти

donnée : исхо́дный факт

Donne, John : Джон Донн

Don Pasquale (Donizetti) : «Дон Паскуа́ле»

Don Quixote de La Mancha (Cervantes) : «Дон
  Кихо́т»/«Хитроу́мныйида́льго Дон Кихо́т
  Лама́нческий»

DOPPELGÄNGER

doppelgänger : двойни́к

Doppler effect (sci.) : эффе́кт До́плера

Dordogne : Дордо́нь (f.)

Dorian mode (mus.) : дори́йский лад

Doric (archit.) : дори́йский

dormeuse : раскладно́е кре́сло (settee); дорме́з (carriage)

Dornier : Дорнье́

Dorsey, Tommy : То́мми До́рси

dos-à-dos (do-si-do) : спино́й к спине́

Dos Passos, John : Джон Дос Па́ссос

double entendre : двусмы́сленная фра́за

Down and Out in Paris and London (Orwell) : «Соба́чья жизнь в Пари́же и Ло́ндоне»

Dow Jones Index : И́ндекс До́у Джо́нса

doyen : старшина́/дуайе́н

Doyle, Arthur Conan : Атру́р Ко́нан Дойл(ь)

Drake, Francis : Фрэ́нсис Дрейк

dramatis personae : де́йствующие ли́ца

Drang nach Osten (hist.) : «дранг нах о́стен»/на́тиск на Восто́к

Dream of Gerontius, The (Elgar) : «Сновиде́ние Геро́нтиуса»

Dreigroschenoper, Die (Weill) : «Трёхгрошо́вая о́пера»

Dreiser, Theodore : Теодо́р Дра́йзер

Dresden : Дре́зден

dressage : вы́ездка (ло́шади)

Dreyfus affair (hist.) : де́ло Дре́йфуса

dreyfusard (hist.) : дрейфуса́р

Dr Faustus, The Tragical History of (Marlowe) : «Траги́ческая исто́рия до́ктора Фа́уста»

Dr Jekyll and Mr Hyde (Stevenson) : «Стра́нная исто́рия д-ра Дже́киля и м-ра Ха́йда»

droit de seigneur : пра́во синьо́ра

Droste-Hülshoff, Annette : Анне́тта Дро́сте-Хю́льсхофф

Druids : дру́иды

Drury Lane (London) : «Дру́ри-лейн»
Drusus, Marcus Livius : Марк Ли́вий Друз
Dryads (myth.) : Дриа́ды
Dryden, John : Джон Дра́йден
Dublin : Ду́блин
Dubliners (Joyce) : «Ду́блинцы»
ducat : дука́т
Duce (hist.) : «ду́че»
Dudevant *see* **Sand, George**
Duelo en el paraíso (Goytisolo) : «Печа́ль в раю́»
duenna : дуэ́нья/компаньо́нка
Dufy, Raoul : Рау́ль Дюфи́
du Gard *see* **Martin du Gard**
Duhamel, Georges : Жорж Дюаме́ль
Duineser Elegien (Rilke) : «Дуи́нские эле́гии»
Dukas, Paul : Поль Дюка́
Duke Ellington : Дюк Э́ллингтон
Dulles, John Foster : Джон Фо́стер Да́ллес
Duluth (US) : Дулу́т
Dumbarton Oaks Conference (hist.) : Да́мбартон-
 -Окс конфере́нция
dum spiro, spero : «пока́ дышу́, наде́юсь»
Dumas, Alexandre (père) : Алекса́ндр Дюма́-оте́ц
d'un certain âge : определённого во́зраста
Dunciad, The (Pope) : «Дунсиа́да»
Dunkirk (hist.) : Дюнке́ркская опера́ция
Duns Scotus : Дунс Скот
Dupin, Amandie *see* **Sand, George**
Durban : Ду́рбан
durbar : дурба́р
Dürer, Albrecht : Альбре́хт Дю́рер
Dürkheim, Émile : Эми́ль Дюркге́йм
Durrell, Lawrence : Ло́уренс Да́ррелл
Dürrenmatt, Friedrich : Фри́дрих Дюрренма́тт
Düsseldorf : Дю́ссельдо́рф
Dutch Reformed Church : Голла́ндская Реформ-
 а́тская Це́рковь
duumvir (Rom. hist.) : дуумви́р/член колле́гии двух

DVÄRGEN
Dvärgen (Lagerkvist) : «Ка́рлик»
Dvořák, Anton : Анто́н Дво́ржак
Dynasts, The (Hardy) : «Дина́сты»
dystopia : дисто́пия
D-Zug : ско́рый по́езд

E

East India Company (hist.) : Óст-Индская компáния

East London (South Africa) : Ист-Лóндон

East of Eden (Steinbeck) : «К востóку от рáя»

East of Suez (hist.) : райóны к востóку от Суэ́ца

Easter Sunday : Пáсха

Eastman School of Music (Rochester, US) : Ѝстменская музыкáльная шкóла

eau-de-cologne : одеколóн

eau-de-vie : настóйка/ликёр

Ecce Homo! : вот человéк!

Ecclesiastes (bibl.) : «Книга Екклезиáста или Проповéдника»

ECG (electrocardiograph) : ЭКГ (электрокардиогрáфия)

Eckhart, Meister : Мéйстер Экхарт

éclat : блеск

Eclogues (Vergil) : «Букóлики»

École des Beaux-Arts (Paris) : Шкóла изя́щных искýсств

École des femmes, L' (Molière) : «Шкóла жён»

écossaise (dance) : экосéз

Eco, Umberto : Умбéрто Эко

Ecstasy of St Teresa (Bernini) : «Экстáз св. Терéзы»

Edda *see Elder Edda, The* and *Younger Edda, The*

Eden, garden of : Эдéм

Edict of Nantes (hist.) : Нáнтский эди́кт

Edinburgh : Эдинбýрг

Edison, Thomas : Тóмас Эдисóн

editio princeps : пéрвое издáние

Éducation sentimentale, L' (Flaubert) : «Воспитáние чувств»

Edward the Confessor : Эдуáрд Исповéдник

EEC (European Economic Community) : ЕЭС (Европéйское экономи́ческое соóбщество)

EFFI BRIEST

Effi Briest (Fontane) : «Э́ффи Брист

EFTA : ЕАСТ (Европе́йская ассоциа́ция свобо́дной торго́вли)

e.g. : наприме́р

Egmont (Beethoven, Goethe) : «Эгмо́нт»

eheu, fugaces! : «увы́, прохо́дят быстроте́чные го́ды!»

Eichendorff, Joseph von : Йо́зеф фон Эйхендо́рф

Eichendorff songs (Wolf) : цикл на стихи́ Эйхендо́рфа

Eiffel Tower : Э́йфелева ба́шня

Eikonoklastes (Milton) : «Иконобо́рец»

Eisenhower, Dwight : Дуа́йт Эйзенха́уэр

Eisenhower Doctrine (hist.) : доктри́на Эйзенха́уэра

Eisteddfod : эйсте́дфод

El Alamein : Эль-Аламе́йн

élan vital (psych.) : «жи́зненный поры́в»

Elba : Э́льба

Elbe, River : Э́льба

Elder Edda, The : «Ста́ршая Э́дда»

elders (eccles.) : пресви́теры

Eleanor of Aquitaine : Алиено́ра Аквита́нская

Eleanor of Castile : Алиено́ра Касти́льская

Elegy in a Country Churchyard (Gray) : «Эле́гия, напи́санная на се́льском кла́дбище»

Elektra (Euripides, R. Strauss) : «Эле́ктра»

Elevation of the Cross (Rubens) : «Воздви́жение креста́»

Elgar, Edward : Эдуа́рд Э́лгар

El Greco : Эль Гре́ко

Eli ((bibl.) : И́лий

Eli, Eli, lama sabachthani? (bibl.) : «Или́, Или́! Ла́ма савахфа́ни?»

Elijah the Tishbite (bibl.) : Илия́ Тесвитя́нин

Eliot, George : Джордж Элио́т (Мэ́ри Анн Э́ванс)

Eliot, T.S. : То́мас Стернс Элио́т

Elisha (bibl.) : Елисе́й

Elisir d'Amore, L' (Donizetti) : «Любо́вный напи́ток»

Elixiere des Teufels, Die (Hoffmann) : «Эликси́р дья́вола»

elixir vitae : эликси́р жи́зни

el niño (geog., meteor.) : «эль ни́ньо»

Elohim : Элохи́м

Elsinore : Хельсингёр/Эльсино́р

Elysée (Paris) : Елисе́йский дворе́ц

Elysian Fields (myth.) : Елисе́йские поля́

Elysium (myth.) : Эли́зиум

Embarquement pour Cythère (Watteau) : «Пало́мничество на о́стров Киферу́»

embarras de richesses : затрудне́ние от избы́тка

Ember Days (relig.) : по́стные дни

embonpoint : полнота́

embouchure (mus.) : амбушю́р

emeritus (professor) : заслу́женный профе́ссор в отста́вке

Emerson, Ralph Waldo : Ральф Ва́льдо Э́мерсон

Émile (Rousseau) : «Эми́ль»

Emilia Galotti (Lessing) : «Эми́лия Гало́тти»

éminence grise : та́йный сове́тник

emir : эми́р

Emmaus (bibl.) : Эмма́ус

'Emperor' Concerto (Beethoven) : [пя́тый конце́рт для фортепья́но Бетхо́вена]

Emperor's New Clothes, The (Andersen) : «Но́вое пла́тье короля́»

Empire State Building (New York) : Эмпа́йр стейт би́лдинг

en bloc : целико́м

en brosse : ёжиком

enceinte : по́яс укрепле́ний

en clair : откры́тым те́кстом

encore! : бис!

encyclopédiste : энциклопеди́ст

End Game (Beckett) : «Коне́ц игры́»

Endlösung (hist.) : коне́чное реше́ние

Endore, woman of (bibl.) : же́нщина в Аендо́ре

Endymion (myth.) : Эндимио́н

en effet : в са́мом де́ле

Enemy of the People, An (Ibsen) : «Враг наро́да»

en famille : до́ма/ме́жду свои́ми; неформа́льно

Enfant et les sortilèges, L' (Ravel) : «Дитя́ и волшебство́»

enfant terrible : [челове́к, смуща́ющий окружа́ющих свои́м поведе́нием]

en fête : пра́здничный

enfilade : продо́льный ого́нь

engagé(e) (polit.) : занима́ющий/заня́вший каку́ю-нибудь определённую пози́цию

Engels, Friedrich : Фри́дрих Э́нгельс

England Made Me (Greene) : «Меня́ создала́ А́нглия»

English Stage Company : «И́нглиш стейдж ко́мпани»

Enigma Variations (Elgar) : «Эни́гма-вариа́ции»

enjambement (vers.) : перено́с/анжамбеме́н

en masse : все вме́сте

Enneads (Plotinus) : «Эннеа́ды»

ennui : тоска́

en pension : на пансио́не

en plein air : на све́жем во́здухе

en rapport : в соотве́тствии с

Enrico IV (Pirandello) : «Ге́нрих IV»

en route : по доро́ге

Enschede : Э́нсхеде

Enseigne de Gersaint, L' (Watteau) : «Вы́веска Жерсе́на»

ensemble (mus.) : анса́мбль (m.)

entartete Kunst **(degenerate art) (hist.)** : упа́дочное иску́сство

Entebbe : Энте́ббе

Entente cordiale (hist.) : Анта́нта

Entertainer, The (Osborne) : «Комедиа́нт»

Entführung aus dem Serail, Die (Mozart) : «Похище́ние из сера́ля»

Entombment, The (Raphael) : «Погребе́ние»

entourage : окружа́ющие

en-tout-cas : зо́нтик

entr'acte : антра́кт

en train : в хо́де (+ gen.)

entrechat (ballet) : антраша́

entrecôte (cul.) : антреко́т

entrée : пе́рвое блю́до (cul.); пра́во на вход (right of entry)

entremets (cul.) : лёгкое блю́до, подава́емое пе́ред десе́ртом

entre nous : ме́жду на́ми

entrepreneur : предпринима́тель (owner of business enterprise); антрепренёр (impresario)

Entscheidungsproblem (math.) : пробле́ма реше́ния

Enver Pasha : Э́нвер-Паша́

envoi (lit.) : посы́лка

Eocene (geol.) : эоце́новый пери́од

Ephesians, Epistle to the (bibl.) : «Посла́ние к Эфеся́нам»

Ephesus : Эфе́с

Ephraim (bibl.) : Ефре́м

Epicureanism : эпикуреи́зм

Epicurus : Эпику́р

epiphany : (по)явле́ние

Epiphany (eccles.) : Богоявле́ние

Epistolae ex Ponto (Ovid) : «Понти́йские посла́ния»/ «Пи́сьма с По́нта»

Epitaph for George Dillon (Osborne) : «Дья́вол, сидя́щий в нём»

epithalamium (lit.) : эпитала́ма

Epstein, Jacob : Дже́коб Эпште́йн

équipe : брига́да

Erasmus : Эра́зм Роттерда́мский

Erato *see* **Muses, the**

Eratosthenes (hist.) : Эратосфе́н

Erdbeben in Chili, Das (Kleist) : «Землетрясе́ние в Чи́ли»

EREWHON

Erewhon (Butler) : «Едгин»

ergo : следовательно

Erie, Lake : óзеро Эри

Erinyes : Эринии *see also* **Furies**

Erlkönig : лесной царь

ermine (herald.) : горностаевый

Ernst, Max : Макс Эрнст

'Eroica' Symphony (Beethoven) : «Героическая» симфония

Eros : Эрос

errare humanum est : «человеку свойственно ошибáться»

ersatz : запасной

Esau (bibl.) : Исáв

escargot (cul.) : улитка

Escher, Martin : Мáртин Эшер

escritoire : письменный стол

Eskimos : эскимóсы

ESP (extra-sensory perception) : сверхчувствительное восприятие

Esperanto : эсперáнто

espresso : (чёрный) кофе «эспрéссо»

esprit de corps : корпоративный дух

esprit de l'escalier   il a l'esprit de l'escalier : «он зáдним умóм крéпок»

Esprit des lois, L' (Montesquieu) : «О дýхе закóнов»

ESR (electron-spin resonance) : электрóнный резонáнс

Essais (Montaigne) : «Óпыты»

Essay on Criticism (Pope) : «Óпыт о критике»

esse est percipi (Berkeley) : «бытиé — спосóбность быть воспринятым»

Essenes : кумрáниты

estancia : эстáнсия

Esther (Bibl.) : «Книга Есфирь»

état-major (milit.) : штаб

États-Généraux (hist.) : генерáльные штáты

et cetera : и прóчее

Eteocles : Этео́кл

Ethelred the Unready (hist.) : Э́тльред «него́товый»

Étranger, L' (Camus) : «Посторо́нний»

Être et le néant, L' (Sartre) : «Бытие́ и небытие́»

Etruria : Этру́рия

Etruscans : этру́ски

étude (mus.) : этю́д

Euboea : Эвбе́я

Eucharist : евхари́стия

Euclid : Евкли́д

Euclidean geometry : Евкли́дова геоме́трия

Eudemian ethics (philos.) : Евде́мова э́тика

Eugène, Prince, of Savoy : принц Евге́ний Саво́йский

Eugénie Grandet (Balzac) : «Евге́ния Гранде́»

Euler number (math.) : число́ Э́йлера

Eumenides : Эвмени́ды

Euphrates, River : Евфра́т

eureka! : э́врика

Euripides : Еврипи́д

Europa (myth.) : Евро́па

European Economic Community *see* **EEC**

European Free Trade Association *see* **EFTA**

Euryanthe (myth.) : Эвриа́нта

Eurydice (myth.) : Эвриди́ка

Euterpe *see* **Muses, the**

Euthydemus (Plato) : «Эвтиде́м»

Euthyphro (Plato) : «Эвтифро́н»

Euxine Sea : Эвкси́нский Понт

Evan Harrington (Meredith) : «И́вен Ха́ррингтон»

Evans, Mary Ann *see* **Eliot, George**

Eve (bibl.) : Е́ва

Eve of St Agnes, The (Keats) : «Кану́н св. Агне́ссы»

Every Man in his Humour (Jonson) : «Всяк в своём нра́ве»

Every Man out of his Humour (Jonson) : «Всяк не в своём нра́ве»

Ewig-weibliche, das (Goethe) : «ве́чно же́нственное

ex cathedra : авторите́тный; авторите́тно

Exclusion principle (sci.) (Pauli) : при́нцип Па́ули

Execution of Falero, The (Delacroix) : «Казнь до́жа Мари́но Фалье́ро»

Execution of the Insurgents during the night of 3 May 1808 (Goya) : «Расстре́л повста́нцев в ночь на 3 ма́я 1808 го́да»

exeunt : ухо́дят

exeunt omnes : все ухо́дят

ex gratia : из любе́зности

Existenz (philos.) : «экзисте́нция»

exit : ухо́дит

ex-libris : из книг

Exodus (bibl.) : «Втора́я кни́га Моисе́ева. Исхо́д»

ex officio : по до́лжности

explication de texte : коммῆнта́рий

exposé : экспозе́/изложе́ние

ex post facto : ретроспекти́вно

expressionism : экспрессиони́зм

extempore : экстемпора́ле

extra-sensory perception *see* **ESP**

Extremadura : Эстремаду́ра

Ezekiel (bibl.) : «Кни́га Проро́ка Иезеки́иля»

Ezra (bibl.) : «Кни́га Е́здры»

F

Fabian Society : Фабиа́нское о́бщество
Fabius Maximus Cunctator : Фа́бий Ма́ксим
  Кункта́тор
fabliau (lit.) : фа́блио/фабльо́
fabula (lit.) : фа́була
façade : фаса́д (front of a building); показно́е
  (deceptive appearance)
façon de parler : мане́ра выража́ться
Faerie Queene, The (Spenser) : «Короле́ва фей»
Fahrenheit 451 (Bradbury) : «451 по Фаренге́йту»
Fahrenheit scale : шкала́ Фаренге́йта
faïence : фая́нс
*Fair Maid of Perth, The (Bizet) see jolie fille de Perth,
  La»*
Fair Maid of Perth, The (Scott) : «Пе́ртская
  краса́вица»
fait accompli : сверши́вшийся факт
Falange (hist.) : фала́нга
Falconet, Etienne : Этье́нн Мо́рис Фальконе́
Falklands Campaign : вооружённый конфли́кт из-за
  Фолкле́ндских острово́в
Falla, Manuel de : Мануэ́ль де Фа́лья
Fall (bibl.) : грехопаде́ние
Fall of the House of Usher, The (Poe) : «Паде́ние
  до́ма Э́шеров»
Fallen Angel : па́дший а́нгел
Falstaff (Verdi) : «Фальста́ф»
familia de Pascual Duarte, La (Cela) : «Семья́
  Паскуа́ля Дуа́рте»
Family of Charles IV (Goya) : «Семья́ короля́ Ка́рла
  IV»
fandango (dance) : фанда́нго
fanfaron : фанфаро́н/хвасту́н
Faraday, Michael : Майкл Фараде́й

Faraday effect (sci.) : эффе́кт Фараде́я

farandole (dance) : фарандо́ла

farce (cul.) : фарш

Farewell to Arms, A (Hemingway) : «Проща́й, ору́жие!»

Far from the Madding Crowd (Hardy) : «Далеко́ от обезу́мевшей толпы́»

Faro (card game) : Фа́ру

Faroe Islands : Фаре́рские острова́

farouche : ди́кий/нелюди́мый

Fasching : ма́сленица

Fastnachtspiel : ма́сленичные и́гры/Фа́стнахтшпиль

fata Morgana (meteor., myth.) : фа́та-морга́на

Fates, the Three : Мо́йры (Greek); Па́рки (Roman)

  Clotho : Кло́то, пе́рвая мо́йра

  Lachesis : Лахе́сис, втора́я мо́йра

  Atropos : А́тропос, тре́тья мо́йра

Father, The (Strindberg) : «Оте́ц»

fatted calf (bibl.) : упи́танный теле́ц

Faulkner, William : Уи́льям Фо́лкнер

Faust (Gounod) : «Фа́уст»

faute de mieux : за неиме́нием лу́чшего

Fauves, Les (art) : фови́сты/«ди́кие»

fauvism (art) : фови́зм

Faux-monnayeurs, Les (Gide) : «Фальшивомоне́тчики»

faux pas : опло́шность

FBI : Федера́льное бюро́ рассле́дований

Fear and Trembling (Kierkegaard) : «Страх и тре́пет»

Feast in the House of Levi, The (Veronese) : «Пир в до́ме Ле́вия»

Feast of Tabernacles (relig.) : Пра́здник ку́щей

Feast of the Gods, The (Bellini) : «Пи́ршество бого́в»

Federal Bureau of Investigation *see* **FBI**

Federal Republic of Germany : Федерати́вная Респу́блика Герма́нии (ФРГ)

feeding of the 5000 : насище́ние 5000

Feen, Die (Wagner) : «Фе́и»

Fehmgericht (hist.) *see Femgericht*

feierlich (mus.) : торжéственно

feldgrau (milit.) : защи́тного цвéта

Feldwebel (milit.) : стáрший сержáнт/фельдфéбель

Felix Holt (George Eliot) : «Фéликс Хольт, радикáл»

Fellowship of the Ring, The (Tolkien) : «Брáтство кольцá»

Femgericht (hist.) : фéме/тáйное суди́лище

femme fatale : обольсти́тельница

fermata (mus.) : фермáта

Fermat's principle (math.) : принцип Фермá

Fermi-Dirac statistics (sci.) : стати́стика Фéрми-Дирáка

fesse (herald.) : пóяс

Festschrift : юбилéйный сбóрник

Festspielhaus : концéртный зал (в Байрёйте)

fête-champêtre : зáгородное гуля́нье

Fêtes galantes (Watteau) : «Галáнтные прáзднества»

fettucine (cul.) : тальятéлле

Feuchtwanger, Lion : Лиóн Фейхтвáнгер

Feuerbach, Ludwig : Лю́двиг Фейербáх

feuilleton : фельетóн

fez : фéска

fiacre : фиáкр

fiancé : жени́х

fiancée : невéста

Fianna Fail (polit.) : Фиáнна файл

fiat lux! : да бýдет свет!

Fibonacci numbers/sequence (math.) : чи́сла Фибонáччи

Fichte, Johann : Иогáнн Фи́хте

Fidelio (Beethoven) : «Фидéлио»

Fielding, Henry : Гéнри Фи́лдинг

Fiestas (Goytisolo) : «Прáздники»

Figaro, Le : «Фи́гаро»

Fighting Téméraire, The (Turner) : «Послéдний рейс корабля́ «Отвáжный»

filet (cul.) : филé

71

FILIPINO
Filipino : филиппи́но
film noir : фильм у́жасов
Filostrato : Филостра́то
fin-de-siècle : относя́щийся к концу́
    (девятна́дцатого) ве́ка; декаде́нтский
Fine Gael (polit.) : Фи́не гэл
finesse : изя́щество (elegance); то́нкость (tact)
Fingal's Cave/Hebrides Overture (Mendelssohn) :
    «Финга́лова пеще́ра»/«Гебри́ды»
Finistère : Финисте́р
Finnegan's Wake (Joyce) : «Поми́нки по Финнега́ну»
Firdausi, Abú-'l Kasim : Абулькаси́м Фирдоуси́
Firebird, The (Stravinsky) : «Жар-пти́ца»
Firenze *see* **Florence**
Fitzgerald, F. Scott : Фре́нсис Скотт Фицджера́льд
Fitzwilliam Museum (Cambridge) : музе́й
    Фицуи́льяма
flagellants (relig.) : флагелла́нты
Flagellation (Piero della Francesca) : «Бичева́ние
    Христа́»
flag of convenience : «удо́бный флаг»
flamenco : фламе́нко
Flamsteed, John : Джон Фле́мстид
Flanders : Фла́ндрия
flâneur : праздношата́ющийся
Flaubert, Gustave : Гюста́в Флобе́р
Fledermaus, Die (J. Strauss) : «Лету́чая мышь»
Fleming, Alexander : Алекса́ндер Фле́минг
fleur-de-lis : геральди́ческая ли́лия
Fleurs du mal, Les (Baudelaire) : «Цветы́ зла»
fliegende Holländer, Der (Wagner) : «Лету́чий
    голла́ндец»
Flight into Egypt, The (Tintoretto) : «Бе́гство в
    Еги́пет»
Floréal *see* **Calendar, French Revolutionary**
Florence : Флоре́нция
Florentine School (art) : флоренти́нская шко́ла
Florida : Флори́да

flügelhorn (mus.) : флюгельгóрн

Flying Dutchman, The (Wagner) *see fliegende Holländer, Der*

FM (frequency modulation) : частóтная модуляция

föhn (meteor.) : фён

folie de grandeur : мáния велѝчия

folio verso : на слéдующей странѝце

Fomalhaut (astron.) : Фомальгáут

fondue (cul.) : фондю́

fons et origo : первоначáльный истóчник

Fontainebleau : Фонтенблó

Fontainebleau, School of (art) : Шкóла Фонтенблó

Fontane, Theodor : Теодóр Фонтáне

Fonteyn, Margot : Маргóт Фóнтейн

Forbidden City (Lhasa) : Запрéтный гóрод (Лхáса)

force de frappe : удáрная сѝла

force majeure (leg.) : форс-мажóр

Force of Destiny, The (Verdi) *see Forza del destino, La*

Foreign Legion *see* **French Foreign Legion**

Forge of Vulcan, The (Velázquez) : «Кýзница Вулкáна»

Forster, E.M. : Эдуáрд Мóрган Фóрстер

Forsyte Sage, The (Galsworthy) : «Сáга о Форсáйтах»

forte : сѝльная сторонá; фóрте (mus.)

fortepiano : фортепья́но

Forth, Firth of : Ферт-оф-Фóрт

fortissimo (mus.) : фортѝссимо

For Whom the Bell Tolls (Hemingway) : «По ком звонѝт кóлокол»

Forza del destino, La (Verdi) : «Сѝла судьбы́»

Foucault pendulum (sci.) : мáятник Фукó

Fountain of the Four Rivers (Bernini) : «Фонтáн «четырёх рек»

Four Horsemen of the Apocalypse, The (Ibáñez) : «Четы́ре всáдника апокáлипсиса»

Fourier analysis (math.) : мéтод Фурьé

Four Quartets (T.S. Eliot) : «Четы́ре квартéта»

FOWLES, JOHN

Fowles, John : Джон Фа́улз
fox-trot : фокстро́т
Fra Filippo *see* **Lippi**
Fragonard, Jean : Жан Оноре́ Фрагона́р
France-Presse : «Франс-Пресс»
France-Soir : «Франс-суа́р»
Franciscans : францискáнцы
Francis of Assisi, St : св. Франци́ск Асси́зский
Franco, General : генера́л Фра́нко *see also*
　Caudillo
Franco-Prussian War : фра́нко-пру́сская война́
francs juges, Les (Berlioz) : «Та́йные су́дьи»
franc-tireur (hist.) : франтирёр/во́льный стрело́к
franglais : франгли́йский язы́к
Frankenstein (Mary Shelley) : «Франкенште́йн, и́ли
　совреме́нный Промете́й»
Frankfurt-am-Main : Фра́нкфурт-на-Ма́йне
Frankfurt-an-der-Oder : Фра́нкфурт-на-О́дере
frankfurter : соси́ска
Frankfurter Allgemeine : «Фра́нкфуртер альгема́йне»
Franklin, Benjamin : Бенджами́н Фра́нклин
Franks (hist.) : фра́нки
Franny and Zooey (Salinger) : «Фрэ́нни и Зу́и»
frappé : охлаждённый напи́ток; охлаждённый
Frascati (vin.) : фраска́ти
Frau Jenny Treibel (Fontane) : «Госпожа́ Же́нни
　Тра́йбель»
Frauenliebe und Leben (Schumann) : «Любо́вь и
　жизнь же́нщины»
Fräulein : ба́рышня
Fraunhofer diffraction/lines (astron.) : Фрауенгоф-
　е́ровы ли́нии
Frau ohne Schatten, Die (Hofmannsthal, R. Strauss) :
　«Же́нщина без те́ни»
Frazer, James : Джеймс Фре́зер (Фрэ́зер)
Frederick I Barbarossa : Фри́дрих I Барбаро́сса
Free Fall (Golding) : «Паде́ние»
Freemason : франкмасо́н

Free Trade (hist.) : фритре́дерство

Freia/Freyja (myth.) : Фре́йя

Freiherr (hist.) : баро́н

Freischütz, Der (Weber) : «Во́льный стрело́к»

French Foreign Legion : францу́зский иностра́нный легио́н

French Lieutenant's Woman, The (Fowles) : «Подру́га францу́зского лейтена́нта»

fresco buono (art) : «чи́стая» фре́ска/буо́н фре́ска

fresco secco (art) : фре́ска по-сухо́му

Fresnel diffraction (sci.) : дифра́кция Френе́ля

Freud, Sigmund : Зи́гмунд Фрейд

Freudian slip : огово́рка по Фре́йду

Freyr (myth.) : Фрейр

Friends, Society of *see* **Quakers**

Friesian : фрисла́ндец; фри́зский/фрисла́ндский

Friesland : Фрисла́ндия

Frimaire *see* **Calendar, French Revolutionary**

Frisch, Max : Макс Фриш

frisson : содрога́ние

Frogs, The (Aristophanes) : «Лягу́шки»

fromage frais : творо́г

Fronde (hist.) : фро́нда

Frost, Robert : Ро́берт Ли Фрост

Fructidor *see* **Calendar, French Revolutionary**

fruits de mer (cul.) : дары́ мо́ря

Fuente Ovejuna (Lope de Vega) : «Фуэ́нте Овеху́на»

fugue (mus.) : фу́га

Führer (hist.) : фю́рер

Fuhrmann Henschel (Hauptmann) : «Во́зчик Ге́ншель»

Fujiyama, Mount : Фудзия́ма

Fuller, Buckminster : Бакми́нстер Фу́ллер

Funchal : Фунша́л

Funeral March (Chopin) : «Тра́урный/Похоро́нный марш»

Furies : Фу́рии *see also* **Erinyes**

furs (herald.) : меха́

FURTWÄNGLER, WILHELM
Furtwängler, Wilhelm : Вильге́льм Фуртве́нглер
futurism : футури́зм

G

Gabriel, Archangel : архáнгел Гаврии́л
Gad (bibl.) : Гад
Gadarenes (bibl.) : Гададри́ны
Gaddafi, Muamar : Муáмар Каддáфи
Gaelic (ling.) : гэ́льский/гаэ́льский язы́к
Gaia (myth.) : Гéя
Gainsborough, Thomas : Тóмас Гéйнсборо
Galahad (Arthur.) : сэр Гáлахад
Galatea (myth.) *see* **Acis and Galatea**
Galatians, Epistle to the (bibl.) : «Послáние к Галáтам»
Galbraith, J.K. : Джон Кéннет Голбрéйт
Galicia : Гали́сия
Galilean transformation (sci.) : преобразовáние Галилéя
Galileo Galilei (Brecht) : «Жизнь Галилéя»
Gallego : «гальéго»; галиси́йский (язык)
Gallipoli campaign (hist.) : Дарданéлльская операция
Gallup Poll : опрóс по мéтоду Гэ́ллопа
Galsworthy, John : Джон Голсуóрси
Galway : Голуэ́й
Gama, Vasco da *see* **Vasco da Gama**
gamin : мальчи́шка
gamine : девчóнка
Gandhi, Mahatma : Махáтма Гáнди
Ganges, River : Ганг/Гáнга
Ganymede (myth.) : Ганимéд
Garden of Earthly Delights, The (Bosch) : «Сад наслаждéний»
Garden of Eden *see* **Eden, garden of**
Gargantua et Pantagruel (Rabelais) : «Гаргантюá и Пантагрюэ́ль»
Garibaldi, Giuseppe : Джузéппе Гарибáльди

GARNI

garni (cul.) : с гарни́ром

Garonne, River : Гаро́нна

Gascon : гаско́нец; гаско́нский

Gaskell, Mrs Elizabeth : Элизабе́т Га́скелл

Gastarbeiter : рабо́чий-иммигра́нт

gâteau : сла́дкий пиро́г

Gate of Heavenly Peace (Beijing) : Воро́та небе́сного споко́йствия

Gates of Hell, The (Rodin) : «Врата́ а́да»

GATT (General Agreement on Tariffs and Trade) : ГАТТ/Генера́льное соглаше́ние о тари́фах и торго́вле

Gatwick Airport (London) : аэропо́рт Га́туик/ Га́твик

gaucherie : нело́вкость

gaucho : га́учо

gaudeamus igitur : «сле́довательно весели́мся»

Gauguin, Paul : Поль Гоге́н

Gaul, Cisalpine : Цизальпи́нская Га́ллия

Gaul, Transalpine : Трансальпи́нская Га́ллия

Gauleiter (nat. soc.) : гауле́йтер

Gaullist : сторо́нник де Го́лля/деголлевец; голли́стский/деголлевский

Gauloise : «голуа́з»

Gauss's law (math.) : при́нцип Га́усса

gavotte : гаво́т

Gawain (Arthur.) : сэр Гаве́йн

Gazza Ladra, La (Rossini) : «Соро́ка-воро́вка»

Geburt der Tragödie, Die (Nietzsche) : «Рожде́ние траге́дии из ду́ха му́зыки»

Gegenschein (astron.) : противосия́ние

Gehenna : Гее́нна

Geiger counter : счётчик Ге́йгера

geisha : ге́йша

gelée (cul.) : заморо́женный

Gemini (zod.) : Близнецы́

gemütlich : ую́тный

gendarme : жанда́рм

gendarmerie : жандармéрия

General Agreement on Tariffs and Trade *see* **GATT**

General Assembly (UN) : Генерáльная ассамблéя

General Electric : «Джéнерал элéктрик»

General Motors : «Джéнерал мóторс корпорéйшен»

Generative Grammar, Theory of : теóрия порож-
дáющей граммáтики

Genesis, Book of (bibl.) : «Пéрвая кнíга Моисéева.
Бытиé»

Geneva : Женéва

Geneva Convention : Женéвская конвéнция

Genghis Khan : Чингíз-Хан

genius loci : гéний мéста/дух мéста

Gennesaret, Land of (bibl.) : земля́ Геннисарéтская

Genoa : Гéнуя

gentil : лáсковый

Gentiles : язы́чники

Geoffroy Saint-Hilaire, Étienne : Этьéнн Жоффруá
Сент-Илéр

George I : Геóрг I

George, Henry : Гéнри Джордж

Georgia (Caucasian Republic) : Грýзия

Georgia (US) : Джóрджия

georgic (lit.) : геóргика

Georgics (Vergil) : «Геóргики»

Géricault, Theodore : Теодóр Жерикó

German Democratic Republic : Гермáнская
Демократи́ческая Респýблика (ГДР)

Germania (hist.) : Гермáния

German Requiem, A (Brahms) : «Немéцкий рéквием»

Germinal *see* **Calendar, French Revolutionary**

Germinie Lacerteux (Goncourt brothers) : «Жерминí
Ласертé»

Gerona : Жерóна

Gershwin, George : Джордж Гéршвин

Gerusalemme liberata, La (Tasso) : «Освобождённый Иерусали́м»

Gesamtkunstwerk : óбщее произведéние искýсства

GESCHICHTE VOM BRAVEN KASPERL
Geschichte vom braven Kasperl und dem schönen
  Annerl (Brentano) : «Исто́рия о хра́бром Каспе́рле
  и прекра́сной Анне́рль»
Gestalt psychology : гештальтпсихоло́гия
Gestapo (nat. soc.) : геста́по/та́йная
  госуда́рственная поли́ция
Gesundheit! : «ва́ше здоро́вье!»
Gethsemane (bibl.) : Гефсима́ния
Gettysberg, battle of : сраже́ние при Геттисбе́рге
Gewandhaus (Leipzig) : Гева́ндхауз
Gewürztraminer (vin.) : гевурцтрамине́р
Ghent : Гент
Ghibellines (hist.) *see* **Guelphs and Ghibellines**
Ghiberti, Lorenzo : Лоре́нцо Гибе́рти
Ghosts (Ibsen) : «Привиде́ния»
Giacometti, Alberto : Альбе́рто Джакоме́тти
Giant's Causeway : «Мостова́я гига́нтов»
Giaour, The (Byron) : «Гяу́р»
Gibbon, Edward : Эдуа́рд Гиббо́н
Gibeonites (bibl.) : гаваонитя́не
Gibraltar : Гибралта́р
Gibraltar, Straits of : Гибралта́рский проли́в
Gide, André : Андре́ Жид
Gideon (bibl.) : Гедео́н
Gigli, Beniamino : Беньами́но Джи́льи
gigot (cul.) : за́дняя но́жка
gigue (mus.) : (д)жи́га
Gilbert and Sullivan : Ги́льберт и Са́лливен
Gil Blas de Santillane (Le Sage) : «Исто́рия Жиль
  Бла́за из Сантилья́ны»
Gilboa, Mount (bib.) : гора́ Гелву́а
Gilgamesh Epic (myth.) : Гильга́меш
Gin Lane (Hogarth) : «Переу́лок джи́на»
Ginsburg, Alan : А́лан Ги́нзбург
ginseng : женьше́нь (m.)
giocoso (mus.) : шутли́во
Giorgione : Джорджо́не
Giotto di Bondone : Джо́тто ди Бондо́не

Giovanni Arnolfini and his Wife (Van Eyck) : «Супру́ги Арнольфи́ни»

Gipsy Baron, The (J. Strauss) see Zigeunerbaron, Der

Giraudoux, Jean : Жан Жироду́

Gironde (hist.) : жиронди́сты

Giscard d'Estaing, Valéry : Вале́ри Жиска́р д'Эсте́н

Giselle (ballet) : «Жизе́ль»

Gissing, George : Джордж Ги́ссинг

gîte : приста́нище для тури́стов

Give me a firm place to stand and I will move the earth (Archimedes) : «Да́йте мне то́чку опо́ры, и я сдви́ну зе́млю»

glace (cul.) : моро́женое

glacé (cul.) : глясе́

Gladiators (hist.) : гладиа́торы

Gladstone, William : Уи́льям Гла́дстон

Glasgow : Гла́зго

Glasperlenspiel, Das (Hesse) : «Игра́ в би́сер»

Glass Menagerie, The (Tennessee Williams) : «Стекля́нный звери́нец»

Glaucus (myth.) : Главк

Gleichschaltung (nat. soc.) : наси́льственое приобще́ние к госпо́дствующей идеоло́гии

glissando (mus.) : глисса́ндо

global village (the) : «глоба́льная дере́вня»

Glockenspiel : гло́кеншпиль (m.)

Gloriana (Britten) : «Глориа́на»

Glorious Revolution (hist.) : Сла́вная револю́ция

Gluck, Christoph : Кри́стоф Глюк

glühwein : глинтве́йн

Glyndebourne : Гла́йндборн

GMT (Greenwich Mean Time) : Ме́стное сре́днее со́лнечное вре́мя на Гри́нвичском меридиане/ Вре́мя по Гри́нвичу

gnocchi (cul.) : нью́окки

gnomic verse : стихотво́рные афори́змы

Gnosticism : гностици́зм

Gobelin tapestry : шпале́ра Гобеле́на

GÖDEL, KURT

Gödel, Kurt : Курт Гёдель

Gödel's theorem : теоре́ма Гёделя

God's Little Acre (Caldwell) : «Акр го́спода бо́га»

Goebbels, Joseph : Ио́зеф Ге́ббельс

Goering, Hermann : Ге́рманн Ге́ринг

Goethe, Johann Wolfgang von : Иога́нн Во́льфганг фон Гёте

Goethe songs (Wolf) : цикл на стихи́ Гёте

Goidelic (ling.) : гойде́льские языки́

Golan Heights : гола́нские высо́ты

Golda Meir : Го́льда Мейр

Goldberg Variations (J.S. Bach) : «Гольдбе́ргские вариа́ции»

Gold Bug, The (Poe) : «Золото́й жук»

Golden Ass, The (Apuleius) : «Золото́й осёл»

Golden Bough, The (Frazer) : «Золота́я ветвь»

Golden Bowl, The (James) : «Золота́я ча́ша»

Golden calf (bibl.) : златой теле́ц

Golden fleece : золото́е руно́

Golden Gate (San Francisco) : Золоты́е воро́та

Golding, William : Уи́льям Го́лдинг

goldne Topf, Der (Hoffmann) : «Золото́й горшо́к»

Goldoni, Carlo : Ка́рло Гольдо́ни

Gold Rush (hist.) : «золота́я лихора́дка»

Goldsmith, Oliver : О́ливер Го́лдсмит

Golgi body (bio.) : ко́мплекс Го́льджи

Golgotha (bibl.) : Голго́фа

Goliath (bibl.) : Голиа́ф

Gomorrah (bibl.) *see* **Sodom and Gomorrah**

Goncourt brothers : Гонку́р, бра́тья Эдмо́н и Жюль

gondola : гондо́ла

gondolier : гондолье́р

Gondwanaland (prehist.) : Гондва́на

Gongora, Luis : Луи́с де Гонго́ра-и-Арго́те

gongorismo : гонгори́зм

Good Friday : Вели́кая/Страстна́я пя́тница

Good Hope, Cape of : мыс До́брой Наде́жды

Goodman, Benny : Бе́нни Гу́дман

Good Samaritan (bibl.) : милосе́рдный самаря́нин

Good Shepherd : До́брый Па́стырь

Gordian knot (myth.) : го́рдиев у́зел

Gorgias (Plato) : «Го́ргий»

Gorgons (myth.) : Горго́ны

Göring, Hermann *see* **Goering, Hermann**

Gothic : го́тика; готи́ческий

Goths (hist.) : го́ты

Götterdämmerung (Wagner) : «Зака́т бого́в»/«Ги́бель бого́в»

Gottfried von Strassburg : Го́тфрид Страсбу́ргский

Gotthelf, Jeremias : Иереми́я Го́тхельф

Göttingen University : Гёттингенский университе́т

Gottsched, Johann : Иога́нн Го́тшед

Götz von Berlichingen (Goethe) : «Гётз фон Берли́хинген»

gouache (art) : гуа́шь (f.)

goujon (cul.) : песка́рь (m.)

Gounod, Charles : Шарль Гуно́

gourmand : гурма́н

gourmet : гастроно́м

Goya, Francisco : Franси́ско Го́йя

Goytisolo, Juan : Хуа́н Гойтисо́ло

Grabbe, Christian : Кристиа́н Гра́ббе

Gracchi (brothers) : Гра́кхи, Тибе́рий и Гай

Graces, The : Хари́ты

Graeco-Persian wars : гре́ко-перси́дские во́йны

Grahame, Kenneth : Ке́ннет Грэ́хем (Грэм)

Grail, Holy : свято́й Граа́ль (m.)

Grainger, Percy : Пе́рси Гре́йнджер

Gramsci, Antonio : Анто́нио Грамши́

Granada : Грана́да

grand cru (vin.) : вино́ из лу́чших сорто́в виногра́да

Grande Jatte, La (Seurat) : «Воскре́сная прогу́лка на о́строве Гранд Жатт»

Grande Odalisque, La (Ingres) : «Больша́я одали́ска»

Grand Guignol : Гран-Гинье́оль (m.); «стра́сти--морда́сти» *grandioso (mus.)* : грандио́зно

grand mal : си́льный припа́док эпиле́псии

Grand Meaulnes, Le (Alain-Fournier) : «Большо́й Мольн»

Grand Prix : гла́вный приз

Grand Vizier : вели́кий визи́рь

Grapes of Wrath, The (Steinbeck) : «Гро́здья гне́ва»

graph theory (math.) : тео́рия гра́фиков

Grass, Günter : Гю́нтер Грасс

Grass Harp, The (Capote) : «Лесна́я а́рфа»

grave (mus.) : гра́ве

grave accent (ling.) : тяжёлое ударе́ние/гра́вис

Graves (vin.) : бе́лое бордо́ское вино́

gravitas : досто́инство/соли́дность

Gray, Thomas : То́мас Грей

grazioso (mus.) : грацио́зно

Great Bear (astron.) *see* **Ursa Major**

Great Expectations (Dickens) : «Больши́е наде́жды»

Great Gatsby, The (Scott Fitzgerald) : «Вели́кий Гэ́тсби»

Great Lakes : Вели́кие озёра

Great Leap Forward (hist.) : большо́й скачо́к

Great Plains : Вели́кие равни́ны

Great Strike (hist.) : Всео́бщая ста́чка 1926

Great Trek (hist.) : Вели́кий трек

Greek Orthodox Church : Гре́ческая правосла́вная це́рковь

Greenbackers : гри́нбекеры

Greene, Graham : Грэм Грин

Greenland : Гренла́ндия

Greenpeace : «Гринпис»

Greenwich : Гри́нвич

Greenwich Mean Time *see* **GMT**

Gregor vom Steine (Hartmann von Aue) : «Сто́лпник Григо́рий»

Gregorian Chant : григориа́нское пе́ние

Gregory (Pope) : Григо́рий

grenadine : гренади́н (silk); грана́товый сиро́п

Grenoble : Гренобль

Gresham's Law : закон Грешема

Grieg, Edvard : Эдуард Григ

griffin (myth.) : гриф

Griffith, D.W : Дейвид Уорк Гриффит

grigri : амулет (у африканцев)

Grillparzer, Franz : Франц Грильпарцер

Grimm, Brothers : Гримм, братья Якоб и
Вильгельм

Grimmelshausen, Hans : Ханс Якоб Кристоф фон
Гриммельсхаузен

grisaille (art) : гризайль (m.); живопись в серых
тонах

grisette : гризетка

gris-gris *see* **grigri**

Gropius, Walter : Вальтер Гропиус

groschen (Aust.) : грош

grosgrain : шёлк/грогрен

grosso (mus.) : гроссо

Grosz, George : Жорж Грос

Grove, Charles : Чарльз Гров

Growth of the Soil, The (Hamsun) : «Соки земли»

grüne Heinrich, Der (Keller) : «Зелёный Генрих»

Grünewald, Matthias : Матис Грюневальд

Gruyère : швейцарский сыр/грюйер

Guadalajara : Гвадалахара

Guadalcanal : Гуадалканал

Guelphs and Ghibellines (hist.) : гвельфы и
гибеллины

Guernica (Picasso) : «Герника»

guerra carlista, La (Valle-Inclán) : «Карлистская
война»

guerre à outrance : война до победного конца

Guevara, Ernesto (Che) : Эрнесто (Че) Гевара

Guggenheim Museum (New York) : Музей
Соломона Р. Гуггенхейма

Guide for the Perplexed (Maimonides) : Путевод-
итель колеблющихся»

GUIGNOL

guignol (theatr.) : гиньо́ль (m.)

Guillaume Tell (Rossini) : «Ви́льгельм Телль»

guillotine : гильоти́на

Guinevere (Arthur.) : Гине́вра

Guizot, François : Франсуа́ Гизо́

gules (herald.) : червле́нь (f.)

Gulf Stream : Гольфстри́м

Gulf War : Война́ в Перси́дском Зали́ве

Gulliver's Travels (Swift) : «Путеше́ствия Гулливе́ра»

Gunpowder Plot : «Порохово́й За́говор»

Gürrelieder (Schönberg) : «Пе́сни Гу́рре»

guru : гу́ру

gute Mensch von Sezuan, Der (Brecht) : «До́брый челове́к из Сезуа́на»

Gutenberg, Johann : Иога́нн Гу́тенберг

gutta-percha : гуттапе́рча

Guy Fawkes (hist.) : Гай Фокс

Guy Mannering (Scott) : «Гай Мэ́ннеринг»

Gyges und sein Ring (Hebbel) : «Гиг и его́ кольцо́»

H

Haakon, King : король Хо́кон

Habakkuk (bibl.) : «Кни́га Проро́ка Авваку́ма»

habeas corpus : «ха́бэас ко́рпус»

habitué : завсегда́тай

Habsburgs (hist.) : Га́бсбурги

hacienda : асье́нда/гасие́нда

Hades : Ад/Га́дес/Аи́д

Hadith (Arab.) : Хади́с

hadj/haj (Islam) : хадж

hadji/haji (Islam) : хаджи́

Hadrian, Emperor : Пу́блий Э́лий Адриа́н

Hadrian's Wall : Ри́мский вал

Hafiz : Хафи́з Ибрахи́м

'Haffner' serenade (Mozart) : «Ха́фнер»-серена́да

'Haffner' symphony (Mozart) : «Ха́фнер»-симфо́ния

Hagar (bibl.) : Ага́рь

Hagerup, Inge : И́нге Ха́геруп

Haggadah (relig.) : Аггада́

Haggai (bibl.) : «Кни́га Проро́ка Агге́я»

Hague, The : Гаа́га

Hague Conventions : Гаа́гские конве́нции

Hahn, Otto : О́тто Ган

haiku : ха́йку/хо́кку

Haile Selassie : Ха́йле Села́ссие

Haiti : Гаи́ти

hakenkreuz : сва́стика

Halevi, Judah : Иеху́да Гале́ви

Halévy, Élie : Э́ли Галеви́

Halévy, Jacques : Жак Галеви́

Halifax : Галифа́кс

Hallé Orchestra (Manchester) : орке́стр Га́лле

Halley's comet : коме́та Галле́я

Hallstatt cultures (prehist.) : гальшта́тские
  культу́ры

HALS, FRANS

Hals, Frans : Франс Халс

Ham (bibl.) : Хам

hamadryad (myth.) : гамадриáда

hamartia : погрéшность

Hamburg : Гáмбург

hamburger : гáмбургер/бýлочка с рýбленым бифштéксом

Hamilcar : Гамилькáр

Hamlet (Shakespeare) : «Гáмлет»

Hammarskjöld, Dag : Даг Хаммершéльд

'Hammerklavier' sonata (Beethoven) : «сонáта для молотóчкового фортепья́но»

Hammerstein, Oscar : Óскар Хáммерштейн

Hammurabi : Хаммурáпи

Hamsun, Knut : Кнут Гáмсун

Handel, George Frederick : Геóрг Фри́дрих Гéндель

Han, Eastern (hist.) : Востóчная Хань

Han, Western (hist.) : Зáпадная Хань

Hanging Gardens of Babylon *see* **Seven Wonders of the World**

Hannah (bibl.) : Áнна

Hannibal : Ганнибáл

Hanoi : Ханóй

Han(n)over : Ганнóвер

Hanover, House of (hist.) : Ганнóверская дина́стия

Hanseatic League (hist.) : Гáнза

Hänsel und Gretel (Humperdinck) : «Гéнсель и Грéтель»

hara-kiri : хараки́ри

Hard Times (Dickens) : «Тяжёлые времена́»

Hardy, Thomas : Тóмас Хáрди

Hare Krishna : Хáри Кри́шна

Hargreaves, James : Джеймс Хáргривс

haricots verts (cul.) : зелёные бобы́

Harlem : Гáрлем

Harlequin (theatr.) : Арлеки́н

Harlowe (Richardson) *see* **Clarissa**

Haroun-al-Raschid *see* **Harun-al-Rashid**

Harpies (myth.) : Га́рпии

Harriman, William Averell : Уи́льям А́верелл Га́рриман

Harrisburg (US) : Ха́ррисбург

Harry Richmond (Meredith) : «Приключе́ния Га́рри Ри́чмонда»

Hartmann von Aue : Га́ртман фон А́уе

Harun-al-Rashid : Гару́н ар-Раши́д

Harvard School : Га́рвардская шко́ла

Harvard University : Га́рвардский университе́т

Harvest Festival (eccles.) : Пра́здник жа́твы

Harvey, William : Уи́льям Гарве́й

Harwell (UK) : Ха́руэлл

Háry János (Kodaly) : «Ха́ри Я́нош»

Harz Mountains : Гарц

Hasdrubal : Га́сдрубал

Hashemite : хашими́т; хашими́тский

hashish : гаши́ш

Hastings, battle of : би́тва при Га́стингсе

Hastings, Warren : Уо́ррен Хе́йстингс

Hauptmann, Gerhart : Ге́рхарт Га́уптман

Hauptmann von Köpenick, Der (Zuckmayer) : «Капита́н из Кёпеника»

haute couture, maison de : дом моде́лей

haute cuisine : хоро́шая ку́хня

Haute-Savoie : Саво́йя Ве́рхняя

Hautes-Alpes : А́льпы Ве́рхние

Hauts-de-Seine : О-де-Се́н

Hautes-Pyrénées : Пирене́и Ве́рхние

hauteur : надме́нность

Havana : Гава́на

Havel, Vaclav : Ва́цлав Га́вел

Havre, Le *see* **Le Havre**

Hawaii : Гава́йи

Hawkins, John : Джон Га́укинс

Hawthorne, Nathaniel : Ната́ниел Хо́торн (Го́торн)

Haydn, Franz Joseph : Франц Йо́зеф Га́йдн

Haymakers, The (Bastien-Lepage) : «Сеноко́с»

HAYWAIN, THE

Haywain, The (Bosch) : «Воз сéна»

Hay-Wain, The (Constable) : «Телéга для сéна»

Hayward Gallery (London) : Хéйуордская галерéя

Hazlitt, William : Уи́льям Хэ́злитт

Heartbreak House (Shaw) : «Дом, где разбивáются сердцá»

Heart of Darkness (Conrad) : «Сéрдце тьмы»

Heart of Midlothian (Scott) : «Эдинбýргская темни́ца»

Heart of the Matter, The (Greene) : «Суть дéла»

Heath, Edward : Эдуáрд Хит

Heathrow Airport (London) : аэропóрт Хитрóу

Heaviside layer (sci.) : слой Хевисáйда

Hebbel, Christian Friedrich : Кристиáн Фри́дрих Хéббель

Hebe (myth.) : Гéба

Hebrew : еврéй; еврéйский (язы́к)

Hebrew (modern) : иври́т

Hebrides Overture (Mendelssohn) see *Fingal's Cave*

Hebron (bibl.) : Хеврóн

Hecate (myth.) : Гекáта

heckelphone (mus.) : геккельфóн

Hector (myth.) : Гéктор

Hecuba (myth.) : Гекýба

Hedda Gabler (Ibsen) : «Гéдда Гáблер»

hedgrah see *hegira*

Heep, Uriah : Ури́я Хип

Hegel, G.W.F. : Гéорг Вильгéльм Фри́дрих Гéгель

Hegelian : гéгелевский

Hegelianism : гегелья́нство

hegira (hist.) : хи́джра

Heidegger, Martin : Мáртин Хáйдéггер

Heidelberg : Гéйдельберг

Heifetz, Jascha : Я́ша Хéйфец

Heilbronn : Хéйльбронн

Heimskringla (Sturluson) : «Хеймскри́нгла»

Heimweh : тоскá по рóдине

Heine, Heinrich : Гéнрих Гéйне

Heinrich der Löwe : Ге́нрих Лев

Heinrich von Ofterdingen (Novalis) : «Ге́нрих фон О́фтердинген»

Heisenberg's uncertainty principle (phys.) : при́нцип неопределённости Ге́йзенберга

Heldenleben, Ein (R. Strauss) : «Жизнь геро́я»

Heldentenor (mus.) : драмати́ческий те́нор

Helen of Troy : Еле́на Прекра́сная

Helicon, Mount : Гелико́н

Helios (myth.) : Ге́лиос

Hella (myth.) : Ге́лла

Heller, Joseph : Джо́зеф Хе́ллер

Hellespont : Геллеспо́нт

Hellman, Lilian : Лилиа́н Хе́льман

Héloïse : Элои́за

Helot (hist.) : ило́т

Helsinki : Хе́льсинки

Helvetia : Гельве́ция

hemidemisemiquaver (mus.) : три́дцать втора́я но́та

Hemingway, Ernest : Эрне́ст Хемингуэ́й

Henry IV (Shakespeare) : «Ге́нрих IV»

Henry V (Shakespeare) : «Ге́нрих V»

Henry VI (Shakespeare) : «Ге́нрих VI»

Henry VIII (Shakespeare) : «Ге́нрих VIII»

Henry, O. : О'Ге́нри (Уи́льям Си́дни По́ртер)

Henry Esmond (Thackeray) : «Исто́рия Ге́нри Э́смонда»

Henry the Navigator : Ге́нрих Морепла́ватель

Hephaestus (myth.) : Гефе́ст

Hepworth, Barbara : Ба́рбара Хе́пуорт

Hera (myth.) : Ге́ра

Heracles/Hercules : Гера́кл/Геркуле́с

Heracles, the labours of : По́двиги Гера́кла

  The Nemean Lion : Неме́йский лев

  The Lernean Hydra : Лерне́йская ги́дра

  The Ceryneian hind : Кери́не́йская лань

  The Erymanthian Boar : Эрима́нфский каба́н

  The stables of Augeias : А́вгиевы коню́шни

HERACLES, THE LABOURS OF (cont.)

The Stymphalian birds : Стимфали́йские пти́цы

The Cretan bull : Кри́тский бык

The mares of Diomedes : Ко́ни Диоме́да

Hippolyte's girdle : По́яс Ипполи́ты

The cattle of Geryon : Коро́вы/Быки́ Герио́на

The apples of the Hesperides : Я́блоки Геспери́д

The capture of Cerberus : Ке́рбер/Це́рбер

Heraclitus : Геракли́т Эфе́сский

Herbert, George : Джордж Хе́рберт

Herculaneum : Геркула́нум

Hercules *see* **Heracles**

Herder, Johann : Иога́нн Го́тфрид Ге́рдер

Hereward the Wake (Kingsley) : «Эреуо́рд»

Hermannschlacht, Die (Grabbe) : «Би́тва Ге́рмана»

Hermann und Dorothea (Goethe) : «Ге́рман и Дороте́я»

Hermaphroditus (myth.) : Гермафроди́т

Hermes (myth.) : Герме́с

Hermione (myth.) : Гермио́на

Hermitage (St Petersburg) : Эрмита́ж

Hernani (Hugo) : «Эрна́ни»

Hero and Leander (myth.) : Геро́ и Леа́ндр

Herod the tetrarch (bibl.) : И́род четвертовла́стник

Herodes und Mariamne (Hebbel) : «И́род и Мариа́мне»

Herodias (bibl.) : Иродиа́да

Herodotus : Геродо́т

Herrenvolk (nat. soc.) : «хе́рренфольк»/на́ция госпо́д

hertz (sci.) : герц

Hertzsprung—Russell diagram (astron.) : диагра́мма Герцшпру́нга-Ра́сселла

Herschel, William : Ви́ллем Ге́ршель

Herzog (Bellow) : «Ге́рцог»

Hesiod : Гесио́д

Hesperides (myth.) : Геспери́ды

Hess, Rudolf : Рудо́льф Гесс

Hesse, Hermann : Ге́рман Хе́ссе

Hessen : Ге́ссен

Hestia (myth.) : Гéстия

Hesychasm (relig.) : исихáзм

heu! : увы́!

Heuss, Theodor : Теодóр Хейс

hexameter : гекзáметр

Heyerdahl, Thor : Тур Хейердáл

Heyse, Paul : Пáуль Хéйзе

Hezekiah (bibl.) : Езекия

Hiawatha, Song of (Longfellow) : «Песнь о Гайавáте»

hic jacet : здесь покóится

hidalgo : идáльго

High Priests (bibl.) : первосвящéнники

Hilbert space (math.) : Ги́льбертово прострáнство

Hildebrandslied : «Песнь о Хильдебрáнте»

Hildegard von Bingen : Хильдегáрда би́нгенская

Himalayas : Гималáи

Himmler, Heinrich : Гéнрих Ги́ммлер

Hindemith, Paul : Пáуль Хиндеми́т

Hindenburg, Paul von : Пáуль фон Гинденбýрг

Hinduism : Индуи́зм

Hindu Kush : Гиндукýш

Hippocrates : Гиппокрáт

Hippocratic oath : Кля́тва Гиппокрáта

Hippocrene (fountain of the Muses) : Гиппокрéна

Hippolyta (myth.) : Ипполи́та

Hippolyte's girdle *see* **Heracles, the labours of**

Hippolytus (myth.) : Ипполи́т

Hirohito, Emperor : Хирохи́то

Hiroshima : Хироси́ма

Histoire de Port-Royal : «Истóрия Пор-Роя́ля»

Historia calamitatum mearum (Abelard) : «Истóрия мои́х бéдствий»

Historiae (Tacitus) : «Истóрия»

Hitchcock, Alfred : Альфрéд Хи́чкок

Hitler, Adolf : Адóльф Ги́тлер *see also* **Führer**

Hitlerjugend (nat. soc.) : гитлерю́генд/Ги́тлеровская молодёжь

Hittites (hist.) : Хéтты

93

Hobbes, Thomas : Тóмас Гоббс

Hobbit, The (Tolkien) : «Хóббит»

Ho Chi Minh : Хо Ши Мúн

Ho Chi Minh Trail : Хо Ши Мúн тропá

Hoffmann, E.T.A. : Эрнст Феодóр Амадéй Гóфман

Hofmannsthal, Hugo von : Гýго фон Гóфмансталь

Hofmeister, Der (Brecht, Lenz) : «Домáшний учúтель»

Hogarth, William : Уúльям Хóгарт

Hohenstaufens (hist.) : Гогенштáуфены

Hohenzollerns (hist.) : Гогенцóллерны

hoi polloi : простóй нарóд

Holbein, Hans : Ханс Гольбéйн Млáдший

Holberg, Ludvig : Лю́двиг Хóльберг (Гóльберг)

Hölderlin, Johann : Иогáнн Кристúан Фрúдрих Гёльдерлин

hollandaise (cul.) : соýс из яúчных желткóв и мáсла с лимóнным сóком

Hollow Men, The (T.S. Eliot) : «Пустýе лю́ди»

Holmes, Sherlock *see Adventures of Sherlock Holmes, The*

Holocaust (hist.) : мáссовое уничтожéние еврéев

Holocene (geol.) : голоцéновый перúод

Holst, Gustav : Гýстав Холст

Holy Alliance (hist.) : Свящéнный сою́з

Holy of Holies : святáя святы́х

Holy Roman Empire : Свящéнная Рúмская импéрия

Holy Scripture : Писáния

Home Guard (hist.) : отря́ды граждáнской самооборóны

Homer : Гомéр

Homer, Winslow : Уúнсло Хóмер

Home Rule (hist.) : «гомрýль» (m.)

Homestead Act (hist.) : Гóмстед-акт

Hommes de bon volonté, Les (Romains) : «Лю́ди дóброй вóли»

Homo erectus : человéк прямоходя́щий

Homo faber : человéк, производя́щий орýдия трудá

Homo Faber (Frisch) : «Homo Faber»

Homo habilis : челове́к уме́лый

Homo ludens : челове́к игра́ющий

Homo sapiens : го́мо-са́пиенс/челове́к разу́мный

homo sum, humani nihil a me alienum puto
  (Terence) : «я челове́к, ничто́ челове́ческое мне не
  чу́ждо»

Honegger, Arthur : Артю́р Онегге́р

Hong Kong : Сянга́н/Гонко́нг

Honolulu : Гонолу́лу

honoris causa : за заслу́ги

Hooch or Hoogh, Pieter de : Пи́тер де Хох

Hoover, Herbert : Ге́рберт Гу́вер

Hopkins, Gerard Manley : Дже́рард Мэ́нли
  Го́пкинс

hoplites (hist.) : гопли́ты

Horace : Квинт Гора́ций Флакк

Horeb, Mount (bibl.) : Хо́рив

Horn, Cape : мыс Горн

Horowitz, Vladimir : Влади́мир Го́ровиц

horribile dictu : стра́шно сказа́ть

hors de combat : побеждённый/вы́шедший из стро́я

hors de la loi : вне зако́на

hortus siccus : герба́рий

Hosea (bibl.) : «Кни́га Проро́ка Оси́и»

hôtel de ville : ра́туша

Hottentots : готтенто́ты

Hound of the Baskervilles, The (Conan Doyle) :
  «Соба́ка Баскерви́лей»

houri : краса́вица

House of Commons : пала́та о́бщин

House of Lords : пала́та ло́рдов

House of Representatives : пала́та представи́телей

House of the Seven Gables, The (Hawthorne) : «Дом
  о семи́ шпи́лях»

Housman, A.E. : Алфре́д Эдуа́рд Ха́усман

Houston (US) : Хью́стон

Howard, Ebenezer : Эбини́зер Хо́уард

Howards End (Forster) : «Хо́уардс-Энд»

Hubbard, L. Ron : Л. Рон Ха́ббард

Hubble constant (astron.) : постоя́нная Ха́ббла

Hubble Space Telescope : косми́ческий телеско́п Хаббл/спу́тник-телеско́п Хаббл

hubris : надме́нность/гордыня

Hudibras (Butler) : «Гу́дибрас»

Hudson's Bay Company : Компа́ния Гудзо́нова зали́ва

Huelva : Уэ́льва

Huesca : Уэ́ска

Hughes, Thomas : То́мас Хьюз

Hugo, Victor : Викто́р Гюго́

Huguenots : гугено́ты

Huis Clos (Sartre) : «За за́пертой две́рью»

Huizinga, Johan : Йо́хан Хёйзинга

Humboldt, Alexander : Алекса́ндр Гу́мбольдт

Hume, David : Де́вид Юм

humoresque (mus.) : юморе́ска

Humperdinck, Engelbert : Энгельбе́рт Гу́мпердинк

Humphry Clinker (Smollett) : «Путеше́ствие Ха́мфри Кли́нкера»

Hundejahre (Grass) : «Соба́чьи го́ды»

Hundred Years War : Столе́тняя война́

Hunger (Hamsun) : «Го́лод»

Hungerpastor, Der (Raabe) : «Голо́дный па́стор»

Huns (hist.) : гу́нны

Hunters in the Snow (Brueghel) : «Охо́тники на снегу́»

Huron, Lake : о́зеро Гуро́н

Hurons : гуро́ны

Hurstmonceaux : Хёрстмонсо

Hussein, King : коро́ль Хусе́йн

Husserl, Edmund : Э́дмунд Гу́ссерль

Hussites (hist.) : гуси́ты

Huttens letzte Tage (Meyer) : «После́дние дни Гу́ттена»

Huxley, Aldous : О́лдос Ха́ксли

Huygen's principle (math.) : при́нцип Гю́йгенса

Huysmans, Joris Karl : Жори́с Карл Гюйсманс

Hyacinthus (myth.) : Гиаки́нф/Гиаци́нт

Hyades (astron., myth.) : Гиа́ды

Hyde Park (London) : Гайд-Парк

Hyderabad : Хайдараба́д

hydra (myth.) : ги́дра

Hygeia (myth.) : Гигие́я

Hylas (myth.) : Ги́лас/Гил

Hymen (myth.) : Гимене́й

Hymnen an die Nacht (Novalis) : «Ги́мны к но́чи»

Hypatia (Kingsley) : «Ипа́тия»

Hyperboreans (myth.) : гипербо́реи

Hyperion (myth.) : Гиперио́н

I

IAEA (International Atomic Energy Authority) : МАГАТЭ (Междунаро́дное аге́нство по а́томной эне́ргии)

iamb (vers.) : ямб

iambic (vers.) : ямби́ческий

Ibáñez, Vicente Blasco : Висе́нте Бла́ско Иба́ньес

ibidem : там же

Ibn Rushd *see* **Averroes**

Ibn Sina *see* **Avicenna**

Ibsen, Henrik : Ге́нрик И́бсен

Icarus (myth.) : Ика́р

Ice Age (geol.) : леднико́вый пери́од

Iceman Cometh, The (O'Neill) : «Разно́счик льда́ грядёт»

ichor : су́кровица; ихо́р (geol.)

ICI (Imperial Chemical Industries) : «Импи́риал Ке́микал Инда́стрис»

id (psych.) : ид

Idaho : Айда́хо

idée fixe : навя́зчивая мысль

idée reçue : изби́тая мысль

Ideen zur Philosophie der Geschichte der Menschheit (Herder) : «Иде́и к филосо́фии исто́рии челове́чества»

ides : и́ды

idiot savant : слабоу́мный учёный

Idler, The : «Досу́жий»

Idomeneo (Mozart) : «Идомене́о»

Idylls of the King (Tennyson) : «Короле́вские иди́ллии»

i.e. : то есть

Ignatius Loyola : Игна́тий Лойо́ла

Île de France : Иль-де-Фра́нс

Iliad (Homer) : «Илиа́да»

Ilium *see* **Troy**

Illinois : Иллино́йс

Illuminations, Les (Rimbaud) : «Озаре́ния»

Illusions perdues, Les (Balzac) : «Утра́ченные иллю́зии»

Illyrians (hist.) : иллири́йцы

Il Penseroso (Milton) : «Il penseroso»/«Заду́мчивый»

Imam : има́м

IMF (International Monetary Fund) : МВФ (Междунаро́дный валю́тный фонд)

Immaculate Conception (relig.) : непоро́чное зача́тие

Immensee (Storm) : «И́ммензее»

impasse : тупи́к

imperfect cadence (mus.) : полови́нная/несоверше́нная каде́нция

Imperial Chemical Industries *see* **ICI**

Imperial City (Beijing) : Импера́торский го́род

Imperial War Museum (London) : Импе́рский вое́нный музе́й

impetuoso (mus.) : поры́висто

Importance of Being Earnest, The (Wilde) : «Как ва́жно быть серьёзным»

Impressionism : импрессиони́зм

imprimatur : разреше́ние на вы́пуск в свет

improvvisatore : импровиза́тор

Im Schlaraffenland (H. Mann) : «Земля́ обетова́нная»

Im Westen nichts Neues (Remarque) : «На за́падном фро́нте без переме́н»

Inadmissible Evidence (Osborne) : «Неподсу́дное де́ло»

in camera : при закры́тых дверя́х

Incas : и́нки

In Chancery (Galsworthy) : «В петле́»

Incoherence of the Incoherence, The (Averroës) : «Опроверже́ние опроверже́ния»

In Cold Blood (Capote) : «Обыкнове́нное уби́йство»

incommunicado : в изоляции

Incoronazione di Poppea, L' (Monteverdi) : Коронация Поппеи»

Independence Day (US) : День независимости

In der Strafkolonie (Kafka) : «В исправительной колонии»

Indiana : Индиана

Indian Mutiny (hist.) : Индийское народное восстание

Indus, River : Инд

Industrial Revolution (hist.) : Промышленный переворот

Indy, Vincent d' : Венсан д'Энди

in extenso : полностью/дословно

in extremis : в крайнем случае

in flagrante delicto : на месте преступления

infra dig : унизительный

ingénue : наивная женщина

Ingres, Jean : Жан Огюст Энгр

in loco parentis : временно замещая родителей

in medias res : в самую суть дела

in memoriam : в память (+ gen.)

Innocents Abroad (Twain) : «Простаки за границей»

in nomine : во имя (+ gen.)

Innsbruck : Инсбрук

Inquiry into the Nature and Causes of the Wealth of Nations (Adam Smith) : «Исследование о природе и причинах богатства народов»

Inquisition (Spanish) : Инквизиция

in re : на деле

in saecula saeculorum : во веки веков

in situ : в месте нахождения

insouciance : беззаботность

in statu pupillari : студентом

intaglio (art) : инталия

inter alia : среди прочих

Interglacial Period (geol.) : Межледниковый период/межледниковье

International Brigade (hist.) : Интернациона́льная
  брига́да

International Date Line : Междунаро́дная ли́ния
  сме́ны дат

Internet : И́нтернет

Interpol : «Интерпо́л»/Междунаро́дная организа́ция
  уголо́вной поли́ции

International Monetary Fund *see* **IMF**

interrupted cadence (mus.) : пре́рванная каде́нция

**In the name of the Father, the Son, and the Holy
  Ghost** : «Во и́мя Отца́, Сы́на и Свято́го Ду́ха»

In the Shadow of the Glen (Synge) : «В су́мраке
  доли́ны»

Invalides (Paris) : Дом Инвали́дов

Invisible Man, The (Wells) : «Челове́к-невиди́мка»

Invitation au château, L' (Anouilh) : «Приглаше́ние
  в за́мок»

Invitée, L' (Beauvoir) : «Го́стья»

in vitro : в лаборато́рии/в проби́рке

Io (astr., myth.) : Ио́

Ionian : иони́ский

Ionic (archit.) : иони́ческий

Iowa : А́йова

Iphigenia in Aulis (Euripides) : «Ифиге́ния в Авли́де»

Iphigenia in Tauris (Euripides) : «Ифиге́ния в
  Таври́де»

Iphigenie auf Tauris (Goethe) : «Ифиге́ния в
  Таври́де»

Iphigénie en Aulide (Gluck) : «Ифиге́ния в Авли́де»

Iphigénie en Tauride (Gluck) : «Ифиге́ния в Таври́де»

ipso facto : в си́лу самого́ фа́кта

IQ : коэффицие́нт интеллектуа́льности

IRA : Ирла́ндская республика́нская а́рмия

Iris (myth.) : Ири́да

Irish Republican Army *see* **IRA**

Iron Age (prehist.) : Желе́зный век

Iron Cross (hist.) : Желе́зный крест

Iron Curtain (hist.) : желе́зный за́навес

IROQUOIS

Iroquois : ирокéзы

Irredentism (hist.) : ирредентизм

Irrungen, Wirrungen (Fontane) : «Путú-перепýтья»

Irving, Washington : Вашингтóн Йрвинг

Isaac (bibl.) : Исаáк

Isaiah (bibl.) : «Кнúга Прорóка Исáии»

Ishmael (bibl.) : Измаúл

Isis (myth.) : Исúда/Изúда

Islam : Ислáм

Island of Dr Moreau, The (Wells) : «Óстров дóктора Морó»

Islands in the Stream (Hemingway) : «Островá в океáне»

Islands Klukkan (Laxness) : «Ислáндский кóлокол»

Isle of Man : Óстров Мэн

Isle of Wight : Óстров Уáйт

Israel : Изрáиль (m.)

Israelis : израильтя́не

Israelites (bibl.) : израильтя́не

Issachar (bibl.) : Иссахáр

Istanbul : Стамбýл

Isthmian games : Истмúйские úгры

Italiana in Algeri, L' (Rossini) : «Италья́нка в Алжúре»

Ithaca : Итáка

Ivanhoe (Scott) : «Айвéнго»

Ives, Charles : Чарльз Айвс

Iwein (Arthur.) : Ивéйн

J

Jackson (US) : Джéксон
Jacob (bibl.) : Иáков
Jacobin (hist.) : якобúнец; якобúнский
Jacob's well (bibl.) : колóдезь Иáковлев
Jacquerie (hist.) : Жакерúя
Jadis et naguère (Verlaine) : «Далёкое и блúзкое»
j'adoube (chess) : я ещё не хожý
Jaén : Хаэ́н
Jäger : éгерь (m.)
Jagganath (relig.) : Яганáт *see also* **Juggernaut**
Jainism (relig.) : Джайнúзм
Jairus (bibl.) : Иаúр
Jakarta : Джакáрта
James I : Яков I
James the son of Alphaeus *see* Disciples, The Twelve
James the son of Zebedee *see* Disciples, The Twelve
James, Epistle of (bibl.) : «Послáние Иáкова»
James, Henry : Гéнри Джеймс
Janáček, Leos : Лéош Янáчек
Jane Eyre (Charlotte Brontë) : «Джейн Эйр»
Janissary (hist.) : янычáр
Jansenists (relig.) : янсенúсты
Janus (myth.) : Янус
Japheth (bibl.) : Иафéт
japonaiserie : япóнское худóжественное издéлие
Jason (myth.) : Ясóн/Язóн
Jaspers, Karl : Карл Ясперс
Jaurès, Jean : Жан Жорéс
jazz : джаз
Jeanne d'Arc : Жáнна д'Арк
Jean Paul : Жан Поль
Jedermann (Hofmannsthal) : «Всякий человéк»
Jefferson, Thomas : Тóмас Джéфферсон
Jefferson City (US) : Джéфферсон-Сúти

jehad *see* **jihad**

Jehoshaphat (bibl.) : Иосафа́т

Jehovah : Иего́ва

Jehovah's Witnesses : Свиде́тели Иего́вы

Jehu (bibl.) : Иу́й

Jena : Йе́на

Jennie Gerhardt (Dreiser) : «Дже́нни Герха́рдт»

Jenseits von Gut und Böse (Nietzsche) : «По ту сто́рону добра́ и зла»

Jephtha (Handel) : «Иевфа́й»

Jeremiad : иеремиа́да/го́рькая жа́лоба

Jeremiah (bibl.) : «Кни́га Проро́ка Иереми́и»

Jericho : Иерихо́н

Jeroboam : Иеровоа́м

Jerome, Jerome K. : Джеро́м К. Джеро́м

Jerusalem : Иерусали́м

Jesse (bibl.) : Ие́ссе

Jesuits : иезуи́ты/Общество Иису́са

Jesus Christ : Иису́с Христо́с

Jesus of Galilee : Иису́с Галиле́янин

Jesus of Nazareth : Иису́с Назоре́й

jeu de paume : зал для игры́ в мяч/жёдёпо́м

jeu d'esprit : остроу́мная шу́тка

Jeune Parque, La (Valéry) : «Ю́ная па́рка»

jeune premier/première (theatr.) : пе́рвый любо́вник/ пе́рвая геро́иня

jeunesse dorée : золота́я молодёжь

Jew of Malta, The (Marlowe) : «Мальти́йский евре́й»

Jezebel (bibl.) : Иезаве́ль

Jiang Zemin : Цзян Цзэми́нь

jihad : джиха́д

Joab (bibl.) : Ио́ав

Joachim, Joseph : Йо́зеф Ио́ахим

Joan of Arc *see* **Jeanne d'Arc**

Job (bibl.) : «Кни́га Ио́ва»

Jocasta : Иока́ста

Jodrell Bank Observatory : Джо́дрелл-Бе́нкская радиоастрономи́ческая обсервато́рия

Joel (bibl.) : «Кни́га проро́ка Иои́ля»

Johannesburg : Йоха́ннесбург

John I (bibl.) : «Пе́рвое посла́ние Иоа́нна»

John II (bibl.) : «Второ́е посла́ние Иоа́нна»

John III (bibl.) : «Тре́тье посла́ние Иоа́нна»

John, Gospel according to St : «От Иоа́нна свято́е благовествова́ние»

John Birch Society (US) : О́бщество Джо́на Бёрча

John Bull's Other Island (Shaw) : «Друго́й о́стров Джо́на Бу́лля»

John Chrysostom : Иоа́нн Златоу́ст

John Gabriel Borkman (Ibsen) : «Йу́н Габриэ́ль Бо́ркман»

John Lackland (hist.) : Иоа́нн Безземе́льный

John of Gaunt : Джон Го́нта

Johnson, Lyndon Baines : Ли́ндон Бейнс Джо́нсон

Johnson, Samuel : Сэ́мюэль Джо́нсон

John the Baptist : Иоа́нн Крести́тель

John the Evangelist : Иоа́нн Богосло́в

joie de vivre : жизнера́достность

jolie fille de Perth, La (Bizet) : «Пе́ртская краса́вица»

Jonah (bibl.) : «Кни́га Проро́ка Ио́ны»

Jonathan (bibl.) : Ионафа́н

Jonathan Wild the Great (Fielding) : «Исто́рия жи́зни поко́йного Джо́натана Уа́йльда Вели́кого»

jongleur : жонглёр

Jonson, Ben : Бен Джо́нсон

Joplin, Scott : Скотт Джо́плин

Joppa (bibl.) : Ио́ппия

Jordan, River : Иорда́н

Joseph (bibl.) : Ио́сиф

Joseph Andrews (Fielding) : «Исто́рия приключе́ний Джо́зефа Э́ндрюса»

Joseph of Arimathea (bibl.) : Ио́сиф из Аримафе́и

Josephson effect (sci.) : эффе́кт Джо́зефсона

Joshua (bibl.) : «Кни́га Иису́са Нави́на»

Joshua, son of Nun (bibl.) : Иису́с Нави́н

Josquin des Prés : Жоске́н Депре́

105

joule (sci.) : джóуль (m.)

Joule's law (sci.) : закон Джóуля

jour de fête : прáздник

Joyce, James : Джеймс Джойс

Juan Carlos : Хуáн Кáрлос

Judah (bibl.) : Иýда

Judaism : иудаúзм

Judas Iscariot *see* **Disciples, the Twelve**

Judas, kiss of : Иýдин поцелýй/Поцелýй Иýды

Judas the brother of James (bibl.) : Иýда Иáковлев

Jude (bibl.) : «Послáние Иýды»

Judenbuche, Die (Droste-Hülshoff) : «Еврéйский бук»

Jude the Obscure (Hardy) : «Джуд незамéтный»

Judges (bibl.) : «Кнúга Судéй Изрáилевых»

Judith (Apocrypha) : «Юдифь»

Judith und Holofernes (Nestroy) : «Юдифь и Холофéрн»

judo : дзю-дó

Juegos de manos (Goytisolo) : «Лóвкость рук»

Jugendstil (art) : «югендштиль» (m.)

Juggernaut (relig.) : Джагернáут *see also* **Jagganath**

Jugurthine War : Югуртúнская войнá

julienne (cul.) : суп «жюльéн»

Julius Caesar : Гай Юлий Цéзарь

Julliard School (New York) (mus.) : Джульярдская шкóла

Juneau (US) : Джýно

Jung, C.G. : Карл Гюстав Юнг

'Junges Deutschland' (hist.) : «Молодáя Гермáния»

Jungfrau (mountain) : Юнгфрау

Jungfrau von Orleans, Die (Schiller) : «Орлеáнская дéва»

Jungian : (поня́тие) по Юнгу

Jungle Book, The (Kipling) : «Кнúга джýнглей»

Junker : юнкер

Juno (myth.) : Юнóна

junta : хýнта

Jupiter (astron., myth.) : Юпи́тер
Jura : Ю́ра
Jurassic (geol.) : ю́рский пери́од
Jürg Jenatsch (Meyer) : «Юрг Ена́ч»
Justinian, Emperor : Юстиниа́н
Just So Stories (Kipling) : «Ска́зки про́сто так»
Jutes (hist.) : ю́ты
Jutland : Ютла́ндия
Jutland, battle of : ютла́ндское сраже́ние
Juvenal : Де́цим Ю́ний Ювена́л

K

Kabale und Liebe (Schiller) : «Ков́арство и люб́овь»
kabbala *see* **cabbala**
kaffir : кафр
Kaffir Wars : ќафрские в́ойны
Kafka, Franz : Франц Ќафка
Kaiser (hist.) : ќайзер (m.)
kalendae : кал́енды
Kalevala (myth.) : Калев́ала
Kamerad : тов́арищ
kamikaze : камиќадзе
Kampf ums Dasein : «борьб́а за существов́ание»
Kansas : Канз́ас
Kansas City : Канз́ас-С́ити
Kansas—Nebraska Bill (hist.) : Канз́ас-Небр́аска
  билль
Kant, Immanuel : Иммуну́ил Кант
Kapellmeister (mus.) : капельм́ейстер
Kapital, Das (Marx) : «Капит́ал»
kaput : разб́итый/исп́орченный; поѓибший
Karajan, Herbert von : Ќараян, Ѓерберт фон
karate : карат́е
Karlsruhe : Ќарлсруэ
Kärnten (Aust.) *see* **Carinthia**
Kashmir : Кашм́ир
Káta Kabanová (Janácek) : «Ќатя Каб́анова»
Käthchen von Heilbronn, Das (Kleist) : «Ќетхен из
  Гейльбр́онна»
Katz und Maus (Grass) : «Ќошка и мышь»
katzenjammer : похм́елье
kaukasische Kreidekreis, Der (Brecht) : «Кавќазский
  медов́ой круг»
Keats, John : Джон Китс
Keller, Gottfried : Ѓотфрид Ќеллер
Kells, Book of : Ев́ангелие из Ќелса

Kelvin, Lord : лорд Ке́львин
Kelvin temperature scale (sci.) : шкала́ Ке́львина
Kenilworth (Scott) : «Ке́нилворт»
Kennedy, John : Джон Ке́ннеди
Kent, Rockwell : Рокуэ́лл Кент
Kentucky : Кенту́кки
Kenya : Ке́ния
Kenyatta, Jomo : Джо́мо Кениа́та/Кенья́тта
kepi : ке́пи
Kepler, Johann : Иога́нн Ке́плер
Kerouac, Jack : Джек Керуа́к
Keynes, John Maynard : Джон Ме́йнард Кейнс
Keynesianism : кейнсиа́нство
khaki : защи́тный цвет
khamsin (meteor.) : хамси́н
Khartoum : Харту́м
Khedive : хеди́в
Khmer Rouge : Кра́сный кхмер/Кхмер руж
kibbutzim : кибу́цы
Kidnapped (Stevenson) : «Похи́щенный»
Kiel : Киль
Kierkegaard, Søren : Сёрен Кье́ркегор
Kim (Kipling) : «Ким»
kimono : кимоно́
Kinderszenen (Schumann) : «Де́тские сце́ны»
Kindertotenlieder (Mahler) : «Пе́сни об уме́рших
   де́тях»
Kinder- und Hausmärchen (Brothers Grimm) :
   «Де́тские и семе́йные ска́зки»
King John (Shakespeare) : «Коро́ль Джон»
King, Martin Luther *see* **Martin Luther King**
King Lear (Shakespeare) : «Коро́ль Лир»
King Oedipus (Sophocles) see Oedipus Rex
King of the Jews, The (bibl.) : «Царь Иуде́йский»
Kings I (bibl.) : «Тре́тья кни́га Царств»
Kings II (bibl.) : «Четвёртая кни́га Царств»
Kingsley, Charles : Чарльз Ки́нгсли
Kipling, Rudyard : Ре́дьярд Ки́плинг

KIRCHNER, ERNST

Kirchner, Ernst : Эрнст Лю́двиг Ки́рхнер
Kismet : судьба́
Kiss me, Kate : «Поцелу́й меня, Кэт»
'kitchen sink' drama : социа́льно-бытова́я дра́ма
kitsch : кич/безвку́сица
Kjeldahl method (sci.) : ме́тод Кье́лдаля
Klee, Paul : Па́уль Кле́е
Klein bottle (math.) : буты́лка Кле́йна
Kleist, Heinrich von : Ге́нрих фон Клейст
Klimt, Gustav : Густа́в Климт
Klondike : Клонда́йк
Klopstock, Friedrich : Фри́дрих Клопшто́к
Knesset (Israeli Parliament) : Кне́ссет
Knight's Cross (hist.) : Ры́царский крест
Knights of St John/Hospitallers : О́рден
  иоанни́тов/госпитальеров
Knights of the Round Table : Ры́цари Кру́глого
  стола́
Knights Templar : О́рден тамплие́ров
Knittelvers (ling.) : «кни́ттельферс»; ви́рши
knödel (cul.) : кне́дли
Knossos : Кнос(с)
Knox, John : Джон Нокс
København *see* **Copenhagen**
Köchel index (of Mozart's works) : указа́тель
  Кёхеля
Kodály, Zoltán : Золта́н Ко́дай
Koestler, Arthur : Арту́р Кёстлер
Kohl, Helmut : Ге́льмут Коль
koine (ling.) : койне́/о́бщий язы́к
Kollwitz, Käthe : Ке́те Ко́львиц
Köln *see* **Cologne**
König Ottokars Glück und Ende (Grillparzer) :
  «Вели́чие и паде́ние короля́ Оттока́ра»
Königsberg : Кёнигсберг
Kon-Tiki Expedition : Экспеди́ция Кон-Ти́ки
Konzertmeister : концертме́йстер
Konzertstück (mus.) : концертштю́к

110

Koran : Кора́н

Korean War : коре́йская война́

Korzeniowski, Josef Konrad *see* **Conrad, Joseph**

kosher : коше́рный

Kotzebue, August : А́вгуст Коцебу́

Krafft-Ebing, Richard : Ри́хард Краффт-Э́бинг

Kraft durch Freude (nat. soc.) : «си́ла че́рез ра́дость»

Krakatoa : Кракату́а

Kreisler, Fritz : Фриц Кре́йслер

Kreisleriana (Schumann) : «Крейслериа́на»

'Kreutzer' Sonata (Beethoven) : Кре́йцерова сона́та

Krishna : Кри́шна

Kristallnacht (hist.) : «хруста́льная ночь»

Kritik der praktischen Vernunft (Kant) : «Кри́тика практи́ческого ра́зума»

Kritik der reinen Erfahrung (Avenarius) : «Кри́тика чи́стого о́пыта»

Kritik der reinen Vernunft (Kant) : «Кри́тика чи́стого ра́зума»

Kritik der Urteilskraft (Kant) : «Кри́тика спосо́бности сужде́ния»

Kronos (myth.) : Крон/Кро́нос

Kublai Khan : Хубила́й

kudos : сла́ва

Ku-Klux-Klan : Ку-Клукс-Кла́н

Kulturkampf (hist.) : культу́ркампф

kung fu : кунг-фу́

Kunstmärchen (lit.) : литерату́рная ска́зка

Kuomintang (hist.) : Гоминьда́н

kursaal : курза́л

Kwangtung Army (hist.) : Кванту́нская а́рмия

Kyrie eleison : «Ки́рие элеисо́н»

L

Laban (bibl.) : Ла́ван
La Belle Dame Sans Merci (Keats) : «Безжа́лостная краса́вица»
Labour Monthly : «Ле́йбор ма́нсли»
Labour Party : Лейбори́стская па́ртия
Lacedaemon (Sparta) : Лакедемо́н
Lachesis *see* Fates, the Three
Laches (Plato) : «Ла́зет»
Laclos, Pierre : Пьер Шодерло́ де Лакло́
La Coruña *see* Corunna
Lady Chatterley's Lover (D.H. Lawrence) : «Любо́вник ле́ди Ча́ттерли»
Lady of the Lake, The (Scott) : «Де́ва о́зера»
Lady Day *see* Annunciation
Lady Windermere's Fan (Wilde) : «Ве́ер ле́ди Уи́ндермир»
Laertes : Лаэ́рт
La Fayette, Marie, Comtesse de : Мари Лафайе́т, графи́ня
Lafayette, Marie Joseph, marquis de : Мари́ Жозе́ф Лафайе́т, марки́з де
La Fontaine, Jean : Жан Лафонте́н
Lagerkvist, Per : Пер Ла́герквист
Lagrange's equations (math.) : уравне́ния Лагра́нжа
LaGuardia Airport (New York) : аэропо́рт Ла--Гуа́рдия
La Guerre de Troie n'aura pas lieu (Giradoux) : «Троя́нской войны́ не бу́дет»
Lais, Les (Villon) : «Лэ»
laissez-faire : невмеша́тельство
Lake Poets : «озёрная шко́ла»
L'Allegro (Milton) : «L'allegro»/«Жизнера́достный»
Lalo, Édouard : Эду́ар Лало́
lama (relig.) : ла́ма

112

lamaism (relig.) : ламаи́зм

Lamb, Charles : Чарльз Лэм

La Manche : Ла-Ма́нш

Lamarck, Jean Baptist : Жан Бати́ст Ламáрк

Lamarckism (sci.) : ламарки́зм

Lamentations, Book of (bibl.) : «Кни́га Плач Иереми́и»

lamentoso (mus.) : жа́лобно

Lamia (Keats) : «Лáмия»

Lampedusa : Тома́зи ди Лампеду́за

Lancastrians (hist.) : ланка́стеры

Lancelot (Arthur.) : сэр Ланселóт

Land (Germ./Aust. province) : земля́

land flowing with milk and honey (bibl.) : «земля́, кипя́щая млéком и мёдом»

landau : ландó

Landes, les : Лáнды

Landgrave (hist.) : ландгрáф

ländler (mus.) : лéндлер

Landsknecht (hist.) : ландскнéхт/наёмный солдáт

Landsmål (ling.) : лáнсмол

Landswehr (hist.) : ландсвéр

Landtag : лáндтаг/парлáмент земли́

Langland, William : Уи́льям Лéнгленд

langlauf : лы́жная гóнка

Langley (US) : Лэ́нгли

Langobards (hist.) : лангобáрды

langue (ling.) : язы́к

langue d'oc (ling.) : провансáльский/окситáнский язы́к

langue d'oïl (ling.) : «лангдóйль»

Laocoön (myth.) : Лаокоóн

Laodiceans (bibl.) : лаодикéйцы

Lao-tzu : Лáо-цзы́

lapis lazuli : лазури́т/ля́пис-лазу́рь

Laplace, Pierre : Пьер Лаплáс

Laplace equation (math.) : уравнéние Лаплáса

Lares and Penates (myth.) : Лáры и Пенáты

LARGAMENTE

largamente (mus.) : протя́жно

larghetto (mus.) : ларге́тто

largo (mus.) : ла́рго

La Rochefoucauld, François de : Франсуа́ де Ларошфуко́

La Rochelle : Ла-Роше́ль

Larousse Encyclopedia : энциклопе́дия Ла́русса

La Scala (Milan) : Теа́тр «Ла Ска́ла»

Lascaux : Ласко́

Las Palmas : Лас-Па́льмас

Lassalle, Ferdinand : Фердина́нд Ласса́ль

Last Judgement, The (Michelangelo, Rubens) : «Стра́шный суд»

Last of the Mohicans, The (Cooper) : «После́дний из могика́н»

Last Supper, The (Leonardo, Tintoretto) : «Та́йная ве́черя»

Last Tycoon, The (Fitzgerald) : «После́дний магна́т»

Latium (hist.) : Ла́ций

La Tour, Georges de : Жорж де Лату́р

Latter-Day Saints, Church of The *see* **Mormons**

Laurentian Heights (Canada) : Лавренти́йская возвы́шенность

Laval, Pierre (hist.) : Пьер Лава́ль

Lawrence, D.H. : Де́йвид Ге́рберт Ло́ренс/Лоуренс

Lawrence St, River : св. Лавре́нция

Lawrence, T.E./Lawrence of Arabia : То́мас Эдуа́рд Ло́уренс/Ло́уренс Арави́йский

Laxness, Haldór : Ха́льдоур Ла́кснесс

Lazarus (bibl.) : Ла́зарь

League of Nations : Ли́га На́ций

Leah (bibl.) : Ли́я

Leaves of Grass (Whitman) : «Ли́стья травы́»

Lebanon : Лива́н

Lebbaeus *see* **Disciples, the Twelve**

Lebensansichten des Katers Murr (Hoffmann) : «Жите́йские воззре́ния кота́ Му́рра»

lebensraum (hist.) : «жи́зненное простра́нство»

114

Lebrun, Albert : Альбе́р Лебре́н
Lecocq, Charles : Шарль Леко́к
Leconte de Lisle, Charles : Шарль Леко́нт де Лиль
Le Corbusier : Ле Корбюзье́
LED (light-emitting diode) : светоизлуча́ющий дио́д
Leda (myth.) : Ле́да
lederhosen : ко́жаные брю́ки
Leeuwenhoek, Anton van : А́нтон ван Ле́венгук
legato (mus.) : лега́то
Léger, Fernand : Ферна́н Леже́
legerdemain : ло́вкость рук
Leghorn *see* **Livorno**
Légion d'honneur : о́рден Почётного легио́на
legionnaire : легионе́р
Lehár, Franz : Франц Лега́р
Le Havre : Гавр
Leibniz, Gottfried von : Го́тфрид Ле́йбниц
Leiden des jungen Werthers, Die (Goethe) :
  «Страда́ния ю́ного Ве́ртера»
Leif Ericsson : Лейф Э́йриксон
Leipzig : Ле́йпциг
leitmotif (mus.) : лейтмоти́в
Le Mans : Ле-Ма́н
Lemminkäinen (Sibelius) : «Лямминкя́йнен»
Le Monde : «Монд»
le mot juste : то́чное сло́во
Lend-Lease (hist.) : ленд-ли́з
Lent (relig.) : Вели́кий Пост
lento (mus.) : ле́нто
Lenz, Jakob : Я́коб Ленц
Leo (zod.) : Лев
León : Лео́н
Leonardo da Vinci : Леона́рдо да Ви́нчи
Leoncavallo, Ruggiero : Руджо́ро Леонкава́лло
Leopardi, Giacomo : Джако́мо Леопа́рди
Lepidus : Марк Эми́лий Ле́пид
leprechaun : лепреху́н
Lérida : Ле́рида

LE SAGE, ALAIN

Le Sage, Alain René : Алéн Ренé Лесáж

lèse-majesté : оскорблéние велúчества

les jeux sont faits : «стáвок бóльше нет»

Lessing, Gotthold : Гóтхольд Эфрáйм Лéссинг

l'état, c'est moi : «госудáрство — э́то я»

Lethe (myth.) : Лéта

Let's Make an Opera (Britten) : «Давáйте создадúм óперу»

Letters and Social Aims (Emerson) : «Литератýра и общéственные задáчи»

lettre de cachet (hist.) : [королéвский укáз об изгнáнии, о заточéнии без судá и слéдствия]

Lettres provinciales (Pascal) : «Пúсьма к провинциáлу»

Letzeburgesch (ling.) : лю́ксембургский язы́к

Leucippus : Левкúпп

Leute von Seldwyla, Die (Keller) : «Лю́ди из Зельдвúлы»

levée en masse : нарóдное ополчéние

Levellers (hist.) : левéллеры

Levi (bibl.) : Лéвий

Levi, Primo : Прúмо Лéви

Leviathan (Hobbes) : «Левиафáн»

Lévi-Bruhl, Lucien : Люсьéн Лéви-Брю́ль

Lévi-Strauss, Claude : Клод Лéви-Стрóс

Leviticus (bibl.) : «Трéтья кнúга Моисéева. Левúт»

Lewis, C.S. : Клайв Стэ́плс Льюис

Lewis, Sinclair : Сúнклер Льюис

lexis : лéксика

lex talionis (leg.) : закóн возмéздия

Liaisons dangereuses, Les (Laclos) : «Опáсные свя́зи»

Liberal Democrats : Пáртия социáл-либерáльных демокрáтов

liberté, égalité, fraternité : «свобóда, рáвенство, брáтство»

libido (psych.) : либúдо

Libra (zod.) : Весы́

Library of Congress (US) : Библиотéка кóнгресса

Libro de buen amor (Ruiz) : «Кни́га благо́й любви́»
Lick Observatory (California) : Ли́кская
  астрономи́ческая обсервато́рия
Liebfrau(en)milch (vin.) : Либфра́уэнмильх
Liebknecht, Karl : Карл Ли́бкнехт
Lied von der Erde, Das (Mahler) : «Пе́сня о земле́»
Lieder eines fahrenden Gesellen (Mahler) : «Пе́сни
  стра́нствующего подмасте́рья»
Liederkreis : «Круг пе́сен»
Lieder ohne Worte (Mendelssohn) : «Пе́сни без слов»
Liège : Льеж
Life of Samuel Johnson (Boswell) : «Жизнь Сэмюэ́ля
  Джо́нсона»
Light in August (Faulkner) : «Свет в а́вгусте»
Light that Failed, The (Kipling) : «Свет пога́с»
Ligurian Republic (hist.) : Лигури́йская респу́блика
Lilith (myth.) : Лили́т
Lille : Лилль (m.)
limbo : лимб
limerick : ли́мерик/шу́точное стихотворе́ние
Limoges : Лимо́ж
Lincoln, Abraham : Авраа́м Ли́нкольн
Linear A script (ling.) : лине́йное письмо́ А
Linear B script (ling.) : лине́йное письмо́ Б
Lines Written in the Euganean Hills (Shelley) :
  «Стро́ки, напи́санные среди́ Энгане́йских холмо́в»
Lin Pao : Линь Бяо
lingua franca : о́бщий язы́к
Linnaean system (sci.) : систе́ма Линне́я
Linnaeus, Carolus : Карл Линне́й
Lippi (Fra Filippo) : Ли́ппи/Фра Фили́ппо
Lisboa/Lisbon : Лиссабо́н
Liszt, Franz : Фе́ренц (Франц) Лист
literati : литера́торы
litotes : лито́та
littérateur : литера́тор
Little Dorrit (Dickens) : «Кро́шка До́ррит»
Little Rock : Литл-Ро́к

LIU SHAO-CH'I

Liu Shao-ch'i : Лю Шао-цѝ

Lives of the English Poets (Johnson) : «Жизне-
описа́ния важне́йших англи́йских поэ́тов»

Livingstone, David : Де́йвид Ли́вингстон

Livius Andronicus : Ли́вий Андро́ник

Livorno : Ливо́рно

Livy : Тит Ли́вий

Llanto por Ignacio Sánchez Mejías (Lorca) : «Плач по
Игна́сио Са́нчесу Мехиа́са»

Lloyd George, David : Де́йвид Ллойд Джордж

Locarno, Treaties of : лока́рнские догово́ры

loc. cit. : в упомя́нутом ме́сте

Locke, John : Джон Локк

Lockheed : «Ло́кхид»

Locksley Hall Sixty Years After (Tennyson) : «Ло́ксли
Холл шестьдеся́т лет спустя́»

locum tenens : челове́к, замеща́я друго́го

locus classicus : подходя́щая цита́та

Logical positivism (philosoph.) : логи́ческий
позитиви́зм

Logroño : Логро́ньо

Lohengrin (Wagner) : «Лоэнгри́н»

Loire, River : Луа́ра

Loki (myth.) : Ло́ки

Lombardy League (hist.) : Ломба́рдская ли́га

London, Jack : Джек Ло́ндон

Long Day's Journey into Night (O'Neill) : «До́лгий
день ухо́дит в по́лночь»

Longest Journey, The (Forster) : «Са́мое до́лгое
путеше́ствие»

Longfellow, Henry Wadsworth : Ге́нри Уо́дсворт
Лонгфе́лло

Longinus (hist.) : Лонги́н

Long Island : о́стров Лонг А́йленд

Long Knives, Night of the (hist.) : «ночь дли́нных
ноже́й»

Long March (hist.) : перебази́рование Кра́сной
а́рмии Кита́я

Long Parliament (hist.) : До́лгий парла́мент

longueur : тоска́; тоскли́вое вре́мя

Look Back in Anger (Osborne) : «Огляни́сь во гневе́»

Lope de Vega : Фе́ликс Ло́пе де Ве́га Ка́рпьо

Lorca, Federigo Garcia : Федери́ко Гарси́а Ло́рка

Lord Jim (Conrad) : «Лорд Джим»

Lord of the Flies (Golding) : «Повели́тель мух»

Lord of the Rings (Tolkien) : «Властели́н коле́ц»

Lord Protector (hist.) : лорд-проте́ктор

Lord's Prayer, The *see* **Paternoster**

Lorelei : Лореле́я

Lorentz transformation (sci.) : преобразова́ние Ло́ренца

lorgnette : бино́кль (m.)

Lorraine *see* **Alsace-Lorraine**

Los Angeles : Лос-А́нджелес

Lost World, The (Conan Doyle) : «Зате́рянный мир»

Lot (bibl.) : Лот

Lotte in Weimar (T. Mann) : «Ло́тта в Вейма́ре»

Louis XIV : Людо́вик XIV

Louis Bonaparte : Луи́ Бонапа́рт

Louisiana : Луизиа́на

Louis-Philippe : Луи́ Фили́пп

Lourdes : Лурд

Louvre : Лувр

Love and Mr Lewisham (Wells) : «Любо́вь и ми́стер Люишем»

Love for Love (Congreve) : «Любо́вь за любо́вь»

Love's Labour's Lost (Shakespeare) : «Беспло́дные уси́лия любви́»

Lucan : Марк А́нней Лука́н

Lucerne : Люце́рн

lucha por la vida, La (Baroja y Nessi) : «Борьба́ за существова́ние»

Lucia di Lammermoor (Donizetti) : «Лучи́я ди Ла́ммермур»

Lucifer : Люцифе́р

Lucknow (hist.) : Лакхна́у

Luck of Barry Lindon, The (Thackeray) : «Сча́стье Ба́рри Ли́ндона»

Lucky Jim (Kingsley Amis) : «Счастли́вчик Джим»

Lucretius : Тит Лукре́ций Кар

Lucullus : Лу́ций Лици́нний Луку́лл

Luddites (hist.) : лудди́ты

Ludendorff, Erich von : Э́рих фон Лю́дендорф

Ludlow Massacre (hist.) : Лудло́ская бо́йня

Ludwig of Bavaria : Людо́вик Бава́рский

Luftwaffe (hist.) : люфтва́ффе

Luisa Miller (Verdi) : «Луи́за Ми́ллер»

Luke, Gospel according to St : «Ева́нгелие от Луки́»/ «От Луки́ свято́е благовествова́ние»

Lulu (Berg) : «Лу́лу»

lumpenproletariat : лю́мпен-пролетариа́т

Lusiads, The (Camoens) : «Лузиа́ды»

lustigen Weiber von Windsor, Die (Nicolai) : «Виндзо́рские прока́зницы»

lustige Witwe, Die (Lehár) : «Весёлая вдова́»

lustrum : пятиле́тие; искупи́тельная же́ртва

Lutheranism : лютера́нство

Luther, Martin : Ма́ртин Лю́тер

Luxembourg : Люксембу́рг

Luxor : Луксо́р

lycée : лице́й

Lycidas (Milton) : «Лю́сидас»

Lycurgus : Лику́рг

Lydian mode (mus.) : лиди́йский лад

Lyon(s) : Лио́н

Lyonnais(e) : лио́нец/лио́нка; лио́нский

Lyra (astron.) : Ли́ра

Lysistrata (Aristophanes) : «Лисистра́та»

M

MA : маги́стр гуманита́рных нау́к
Maas, River : Ма́ас
Maastricht : Ма́астрихт
macaroni (cul.) : макаро́ны
macaronic verse : макарони́ческая поэ́зия
MacArthur, Douglas : Ду́глас Мака́ртур
McCarthy, Joseph : Джо́зеф Макка́рти
McCarthyism (hist.) : маккарти́зм
Macaulay, David Babington : Де́йвид Ба́бингтон
  Мако́лей
Macbeth (Shakespeare) : «Макбе́т»
Maccabaeus (Apocrypha) : «Маккабе́й Иу́да»
MacDiarmid, Hugh : Хью Макди́армид
Macdonald, John : Джон Макдо́нальд
McDonnell—Douglas : «Мак-До́ннелл-Ду́глас»
McGill University (Canada) : университе́т Мак-
  -Ги́лла
McLuhan, Marshall : Ма́ршалл Маклю́эн
macédoine (cul.) : маседуа́н
Mach, Ernst : Эрнст Мах
Mach number (sci.) : число́ Ма́ха
Machiavelli, Niccolo : Никко́ло Макиаве́лли
Machtpolitik : поли́тика си́лы
Maclaurin series (math.) : ряд Макло́рена
Mâcon (vin.) : мако́н
Madam Butterfly (Puccini) : «Мада́м
  Баттерфля́й»/«Чио-Чио-са́н»
Madame : госпожа́
Madame Bovary (Flaubert) : «Госпожа́ Бовари́»
Madame Gervaisais (brothers Goncourt) : «Мада́м
  Жервезе́»
Madeira (wine) : маде́ра
Madeira, Island of : Маде́йра
madeleine (cul.) : мадле́н

Mademoiselle : мадемуазéль

Madonna of Burgomaster Meyer (Holbein) :
«Мадóнна бургомúстра Мéйера»

Madonna of the Long Neck (Parmigianino) :
«Мадóнна с длúнной шéей»

madrasah (Indian school) : медресé

Madrid : Мадрúд

maelstrom : водоворóт

maenad (myth.) : менáда

maestoso (mus.) : маэстóзо

maestro : маэ́стро

Mafeking : Мáфекинг

mafia : мáфия

mafioso : член мáфии/мафиóзи

Magellan, Straits of : Магеллáнов пролúв

Magellanic Cloud, Large (astron.) : Большóе
Магеллáново Óблако

Magellanic Cloud, Small (astron.) : Мáлое
Магеллáново Óблако

Magi : волхвьí

Magic Flute, The (Mozart) see Zauberflöte, Die

Magic Mountain, The (T. Mann) see Zauberberg, Der

Maginot line (hist.) : лúния Мажинó

Magna Carta : Велúкая хáртия вóльностей

Magnificat (relig.) : величáние/магнификáт

magnum opus : шедéвр

Magritte, René : Ренé Магрúт

Magyars : вéнгры

Mahabharata : Махабхáрата

maharajah : Махарáджа

maharani : Махарáни

Maharishi : Махарúши Мáхеш Йóги

mahatma : махáтма

Mahdi (hist.) : Махдú Судáнский

mah-jong : маджóнг/мачжáн/китáйское доминó

Mahler, Gustav : Густáв Мáлер

Mahomet : Магомéт *see also* Mohammed

Maia (myth.) : Мáйя

Maid of Orleans, The (Schiller) *see Jungfrau von Orleans, Die*

Mailer, Norman : Норман Мейлер

maillot jaune (sport) : жёлтая майка лидера

Maimonides : Маймонид

Maine : Мэн

Main Street (Sinclair Lewis) : «Главная улица»

Mainz : Майнц

Maistre, Joseph de : Жозеф де Местр

maître d'hotel : метрдотель (m.)

Major Barbara (Shaw) : «Майор Барбара»

majority system (polit.) : мажоритарная система

majuscule : прописная буква

Malachi (bibl.) : «Книга Пророка Малахии»

Malade imaginaire, Le (Molière) : «Мнимый больной»

Málaga : Малага

Malagasy : Малагасийская республика

malaise : недомогание

Malavoglia, I (Verga) : «Семья Малаволья»

mal de mer : морская болезнь

Malebranche, Nicola : Никола Мальбранш

malentendu : недоразумение

malgré soi : против воли

Mallarmé, Stéphane : СтҢфан Малларме

Mallorca : Майорка/Мальорка

Malone meurt (Beckett) : «Мэлон умирает»

Malory, Thomas : Томас Мэлори

Malraux, André : Андре Мальро

Malta : Мальта

Malthus, Thomas : Томас Мальтус

Malthusianism (hist.) : мальтузианство

Mamelukes (hist.) : мамлюки/мамелюки

mammon : маммона

Man and Superman (Shaw) : «Человек и сверхчеловек»

Manasseh (bibl.) : Манассия

Manche, La : Ламанш

MANCHU

Manchu : Маньчжу́

Manchurian : маньчжу́рский

Mandela, Nelson : Не́льсон Манде́ла

manège : вы́ездка (ло́шади); мане́ж

Manet, Édouard : Эдуа́р Мане́

mange-tout (cul.) : бобы́/горо́х

Manhattan : Манха́ттан

Manicheanism (relig.) : манихе́йство

Manifesti del Futurismo : «Манифе́сты футури́зма»

Manifesto of Surrealism : «Манифе́ст сюрреали́зма»

Manitoba : Манито́ба

manna (bibl.) : ма́нна

mannequin : манеке́н

Mannheim : Манге́йм

Mann, Heinrich : Ге́нрих Манн

Mann, Thomas : То́мас Манн

Man of Property, A (Galsworthy) : «Со́бственник»

Manon (Massenet) : «Мано́н»

Manon Lescaut (Prévost, Puccini) : «Мано́н Леско́»

manqué : несостоя́вшийся

Mansfield Park (Austen) : «Ме́нсфилд-парк»

Mantegna, Andrea : Андре́а Манте́нья

many are called, but few are chosen : «мно́го зва́ных, но ма́ло и́збранных»

mantling (herald.) : ма́нтия

Manx (ling.) : мэ́нский язы́к

Manzoni, Alessandro : Алесса́ндро Мандзо́ни

Maori : ма́ори; маори́йский

Mao Tse-tung/Mao Zedong : Ма́о Цзэ-ду́н

maquillage : гримирова́ние

Maquis (hist.) : партиза́нское движе́ние

maquisard (hist.) : партиза́н

maraschino : мараски́н

Marathi (hist.) : Мара́тхские кня́жества

Marathon : Марафо́н

Marat, Jean-Paul : Жан Пол Мара́т

marcato (mus.) : подчёркнуто

Marcus Aurelius : Марк Авре́лий

Marcuse, Herbert : Ге́рберт Марку́зе

Mardi Gras : после́дний день карнава́ла

Margaux (vin.) : марго́

mariage de convenance : брак по расчёту

Maria Magdalena (Hebbel) : «Мари́я Магдали́на»

Maria Medici (Rubens) : «Мари́я Ме́дичи»

Maria Stuart (Schiller) : «Мари́я Стю́арт»

Maria Theresa : Мари́я Тере́зия

Marie-Antoinette : Мари́я Антуане́тта

Marinetti, Filippo : Фили́ппо Марине́тти

marivaudage (lit.) : вы́чурность

Mark Antony : Марк Анто́ний

Mark, Gospel according to St : «Ева́нгелие от Ма́рка»/«От Марка свято́е благовествова́ние»

Marlborough (Duke of) : Ма́льборо (Джон Чёрчилль)

Marlborough s'en va-t-en guerre : «Мальбру́к в похо́д поёхал»

Marlowe, Christopher : Кри́стофер Ма́рло

Marmorbild, Das (Eichendorff) : «Мра́морная карти́на»

Marne, battle of the : Ма́рнское сраже́ние

Marne, River : Ма́рна

Marriage à la mode (Hogarth) : «Мо́дный брак»

Marriage of Figaro, The (Mozart) : «Сва́дьба Фи́гаро»

marrons glacés : глазиро́ванные кашта́ны

Mars (astron., myth.) : Марс

Marsala (vin.) : марсала́

Marseillaise : Марселье́за

Marseille : Марсе́ль (m.)

Marshall Plan (hist.) : план Ма́ршалла

Marston Moor, battle of : би́тва при Ма́рстон-Мур

Martial : Марк Вале́рий Марциа́л

Martin Arrowsmith (Sinclair Lewis) : «Ма́ртин Э́роусмит»

Martin Chuzzlewit (Dickens) : «Ма́ртин Че́злвит»

Martin du Gard, Roger : Роже́ Марте́н дю Га́р

Martinez de la Rosa : Марти́нес де ла Ро́са

125

Martin Luther King : Ма́ртин Лю́тер Кинг

Martyrdom of St Matthew (Caravaggio) : «Муче́ние апо́стола Матфе́я»

Marx, Karl : Карл Маркс

Marxist : маркси́ст; маркси́стский

Mary Barton (Mrs Gaskell) : «Ме́ри Ба́ртон»

Mary Magdalene : Мари́я Магдали́на

Mary Queen of Scots : Мари́я Стю́арт

Mary Tudor : Мари́я Тю́дор

Maryland : Мэ́риленд

Mascagni, Pietro : Пье́тро Маска́ньи

Masefield, John : Джон Ме́йсфилд

Masked Ball, A (Verdi) see Ballo in Maschera, Un

masque : ма́ска

Massachusetts : Массачу́сетс

Massachusetts Institute of Technology *see* **MIT**

Massacre at Chios, The (Delacroix) : «Резня́ на Хи́осе»

Massacre of the Innocents, The (Brueghel) : «Избие́ние младе́нцев»

Massenet, Jules : Жюль Массне́

mässig (mus.) : умеренно

Masson, André : Андре́ Массо́н

Master-Builder, The (Ibsen) : «Строи́тель Со́льнес»

Master of Ballantrae, The (Stevenson) : «Владе́лец Балланре́»

Mäster Olof (Strindberg) : Ме́стер У́луф

matador : матадо́р

materfamilias : мать семе́йства

matériel : те́хника/обору́дование

Mathis der Maler (Hindemith) : «Мати́с-живопи́сец»

matineé : дневно́й спекта́кль

matins (eccles.) : у́треня

Matisse, Henri : Анри́ Мати́сс

Matterhorn (mountain) : Ма́ттерхорн

Matthew *see* **Disciples, the Twelve**

Matthew, Gospel according to St : «Ева́нгелие от Матфе́я»/«От Матфе́я свято́е благове́ствование»

Matthias (bibl.) : Ма́тфий

Maugham, Somerset : Со́мерсет Мо́эм

Mau Mau (hist.) : Ма́у-Ма́у

Maupassant, Guy de : Ги де Мопасса́н

Mauriac, François : Франсуа́ Мориа́к

Mauritshuis Museum (The Hague) : Маурицхёйс

Maurois, André : Андре́ Моруа́

mauvais ton : дурно́й тон

Má Vlast (Smetana) : «Моя́ Ро́дина»

Maxwell, James Clerk : Джеймс Клерк Ма́ксвелл

Maxwell—Boltzmann distributions (sci.) : распред-еле́ния Ма́ксвелла-Бо́льцмана

Maxwell's equations (sci.) : уравне́ния Ма́ксвелла

Mayor of Casterbridge, The (Hardy) : «Мэр Ке́стер-бриджа»

Mazeppa (Byron) : «Мазе́па»

mazurka : мазу́рка

Mazzini, Giuseppe : Джузе́ппе Мадзи́ни

mea culpa : моя́ вина́

Mead, Margaret : Ма́ргарет Мид

Measure for Measure (Shakespeare) : «Ме́ра за ме́ру»

Medea (Euripides) : «Меде́я»

Médée (Corneille) : «Меде́я»

Medes and Persians, law of the : зако́н Мидя́н и Пе́рсов

mediant (mus.) : медиа́нта

Medici, Lorenzo the Magnificent : Лоре́нцо Ме́дичи, Великоле́пный

Meditationes de Prima Philosophia (Descartes) : «Раз-мышле́ния о пе́рвой филосо́фии»

Medusa (myth.) : Меду́за

Mefistofele (Boito) : «Мефисто́фель»

Mein Kampf (Hitler) : «Моя́ борьба́»

Mein Name sei Gantenbein (Frisch) : «Допу́стим, меня́ зову́т Га́нтенбайн»

Meissen (pottery) : Ме́йсенский фарфо́р

Meistersänger von Nürnberg, Die (Wagner) : «Ню́рн-бергские мейстерзи́нгеры»

Melbourne : Мéльбурн

Meleager (myth.) : Мелеáгр

mêlée : рукопáшная свáтка

Melpomene *see* **Muses, the**

Melville, Herman : Гéрман Мéлвилл

memento mori : пóмни о смéрти

Mémoires d'outre-tombe (Chateaubriand) : «Замогíльные запíски»

Mémoires écrits par lui-même (Casanova) : «Воспоминáния»

Memoirs of Socrates (Xenophon) : «Воспоминáния о Сокрáте»

ménage à trois : любóвь втроём

Menander : Менáндр

Men at Arms (Waugh) : «Вооружённые лю́ди»

Mendelssohn, Felix : Фéликс Мендельсóн

mendicant orders (relig.) : ни́щенствующие орденá

Menelaus (myth.) : Менелáй

mene, mene, tekel, upharsin (bibl.) : «мéне, мéне, тéкел, упáрсин»

menhirs (prehist.) : менги́ры

Meninas, Las (Velázquez) : «Лас Мени́нас/ «Фрéйлины»

Menippean satire (lit.) : Мени́ппова сати́ра

Mennonites (relig.) : меннони́ты

Meno (Plato) : Менóн

meno mosso (mus.) : мéдленнее

Menotti, Gian-Carlo : Джан Кáрло Менóтти

mens sana in corpore sano : в здорóвом тéле здорóвый дух

Mercator's projection : проéкция Меркáтора

Merchant of Venice, The (Shakespeare) : «Венециáнский купéц»

Mercia (hist.) : Мéрсия

Mercury (astron., myth.) : Меркýрий

Meredith, George : Джордж Мéредит

Mérimée, Prosper : Проспéр Меримé

Merlin (Arthur.) : Мерли́н

Mermaid Theatre (London) : «Мéрмейд тíэтр»
Merovingians (hist.) : меровíнги
Merry Widow, The (Lehar) *see lustige Witwe, Die*
Merry Wives of Windsor, The (Shakespeare, Nicolai) :
 «Виндзóрские прокáзницы»
mésalliance : мезальянс/нерáвный брак
Mesolithic (prehist.) : мезолíт
Mesopotamia : Двурéчье
Mesozoic (geol.) : мезозóйская éра
Messerschmitt : Мéссершмитт
Messiaen, Olivier : Оливьé Мессиáн
Messiah, The (Handel) : «Мессíя»
Messidor *see* **Calendar, French Revolutionary**
mestizo : метíс/метíска
Metamorphosen (R. Strauss) : «Метаморфóзы»
Metamorphosis (Kafka) see Verwandlung, Die
Metaphysics (Aristotle) : «Метафíзика»
Methodists : методíсты
Methuselah (bibl.) : Мафусáл
métier : ремеслó; специáльность
Metro Goldwyn Meyer : Мéтро-Гóлдвин-Мáйер
Metropolitan Museum (New York) : музéй
 Метрополитен
Metropolitan Opera (New York) : «Метрополитен-
 -óпера»
Metternich, Prince Clemens : Клéменс Меттернíх
Meuse, River : Мёз
Meyerbeer, Giacomo : Джакомо Мейербéр
Meyer, Konrad : Кóнрад Мéйер
mezza voce (mus.) : вполгóлоса
mezzo-soprano : мéццо-сопрáно
mezzotint (art) : мéццо-тíнто
M.I.5 : пя́тое отделéние Британской развéдки
Miami : Майáми
Micah (bibl.) : «Кни́га Пророка Михéя»
Micawber : Микóбер
Michael, archangel : Михаил
Michael Kohlhaas (Kleist) : «Михаэ́ль Кольхáас»

MICHAELMAS

Michaelmas : Миха́йлов день
Michelangelo Buonarotti : Микела́нджело
  Буонарро́ти
Michelson—Morley experiment (sci.) : о́пыт
  Ма́йкельсона
Michigan : Ми́чига́н
Michigan, Lake : о́зеро Ми́чига́н
Mickiewicz, Adam : Ада́м Мицке́вич
Microsoft : «Ма́йкрософт»
Midas (myth.) : Мида́с
Middle High German (ling.) : средневерх-
  ненеме́цкий
Middlemarch (George Eliot) : «Миддлма́рч»
Midianites (bibl.) : мадианитя́не
Midnight's Children (Rushdie) : «Де́ти полу́ночи»
Midsummer Night's Dream, A (Shakespeare) : «Сон в
  ле́тнюю ночь»
Midway, battle of : сраже́ние за Ми́дуэй
Midwest (US) : Мидве́ст
Mighty Five/Handful (mus.) : «Могу́чая ку́чка»
mikado : мика́до
Milan(o) : Мила́н
Milesian School (philos.) : Миле́тская шко́ла
Milhaud, Darius : Да́риюс Мийо́
milieu : среда́
Milky Way (astron.) : Мле́чный Путь
Mill, John Stuart : Джон Стю́арт Милль
Millais, John : Джон Ми́ллес
millefeuille (cul.) : наполео́н
millefleurs : орна́мент из ра́зных цвето́в
Miller, Arthur : Арту́р Ми́ллер
Mill on the Floss, The (George Eliot) : «Ме́льница на
  Фло́ссе»
Milne, A.A. : А.А. Милн
Milo of Crotona : Мило́н Крото́нский
Milton, John : Джон Ми́льтон
Milwaukee : Милуо́ки
Minerva (myth.) : Мине́рва

minestrone (cul.) : суп по-итальянски (с рисом и
овощами)

Ming Dynasty : Мин

minim (mus.) : половинная нота

Minkowskian space (sci.) : пространство
Минковского

Minna von Barnhelm (Lessing) : «Минна фон
Барнхельм»

Minneapolis : Миннеаполис

minnesinger : миннезингер

Minnesota : Миннесота

Minnesota University : Миннесотский университет

Minoan : минойский

Minos : Минос

Minotaur (myth.) : Минотавр

Minutemen (US hist.) : минитмены

Miocene (geol.) : миоценовая эпоха

mirabelle (cul.) : мирабель (f.); мирабелевая
настойка

mirabile dictu : как это ни удивительно

Miriam (bibl.) : Мариамь

Miro, Joan : Хоан Миро

Misanthrope, Le (Molière) : «Мизантроп»

mise-en-scène : мизансцена/постановка

Misérables, Les (Hugo) : «Отверженные»

misère : мизер

missa brevis (mus.) : короткая месса

Missa Solemnis (Beethoven) : «Торжественная месса»

Mississippi : Миссисипи

Miss Julie (Strindberg) : «Фрёкен Юлия»

Missouri : Миссури

Missouri Compromise (hist.) : Миссурийский
компромисс

misterioso (mus.) : мистериозо

mistral (meteor.) : мистраль (m.)

MIT : Массачусетский технологический институт

Mitbestimmung : участие в управлении
предприятием

Mithraism (relig.) : митраи́зм

Mithridates : Митрида́т

mit Nachdruck (mus.) : осо́бенно подчеркну́ть

Mittelstand : сре́дний слой (о́бщества)

Mitterand, François : Франсуа́ Миттера́н

Mixolydian mode (mus.) : миксолиди́йский лад

Mizar (astron.) : Мица́р

Mnemosyne *see* **Muses, the**

Moabites (bibl.) : моавитя́не

Moby Dick (Melville) : «Мо́би Дик»

moderato (mus.) : модера́то

Modes (mus.) : лады́

Modigliani, Adameo : Адаме́о Модилья́ни

modus operandi : спо́соб де́йствия

modus vivendi : мо́дус виве́нди

Möbius strip (math.) : лист Мёбиуса

Mohammed : Муха́ммед *see also* Mahomet

Mohawks : мохо́ки

Moho (Mohorovicic discontinuity) (geol.) :
Мохоро́вичича пове́рхность

mojahedin *see* **mujaheddin**

Molière : Молье́р (Жан Бати́ст Покле́н)

Moll Flanders (Defoe) : «Молль Фле́ндерс»

Molloy (Beckett) : «Молло́й»

Molotov—Ribbentrop Pact : Сове́тско-герма́нский
догово́р о ненападе́нии

molto : мно́го/о́чень

Mona Lisa : Джоко́нда

Mondrian, Piet : Пит Мондриа́н

Monégasque : жи́тель/жи́тельница Мона́ко;
мона́кский

Monet, Claude : Клод Моне́

Monroe Doctrine (hist.) : доктри́на Монро́

Mons : Монс

Monseigneur : монсенье́р

Monsieur : месье́/мосье́

monstre sacré : свяще́нный и́дол

montage : монта́ж

Montagnards (hist.) : Монтанья́ры/Гора́

Montaigne, Michel de : Мише́ль де Монте́нь

Montana : Монта́на

Mont Blanc : Монбла́н

Montesquieu, Charles de : Шарль де Монтескье́

Monteverdi, Giovanni : Джова́нни Монтеве́рди

Montfort, Simon de : Симо́н де Монфо́р

Montgomery, Field-Marshal : Монтго́мери
  Аламе́йнский

Montherlant, Henri de : А́нри де Монтерла́н

Montpel(l)ier : Монпелье́

Montreal : Монреа́ль (m.)

Moon and Sixpence, The (Maugham) : «Луна́ и
  грош»

Moonies (relig.) : Муни́зм/Це́рковь едине́ния

'Moonlight' Sonata (Beethoven) : «Лу́нная» сона́та

Moonstone, The (Collins) : «Лу́нный ка́мень»

Moore, Henry : Ге́нри Мур

Moravia, Alberto : Альбе́рто Мора́виа

Moravians (relig.) : мора́вские бра́тья

mordent (mus.) : морде́нт

morendo (mus.) : замира́я

mores : нра́вы

More, Thomas : То́мас Мор

Moriae encomium (Erasmus) : «Похвала́ глу́пости»

Mörike, Eduard : Эдуа́рд Мёрике

Mörike songs (Wolf) : цикл пе́сен на стихи́ Мёрике

Morisco : маврита́нец; маврита́нский

**Mormons/Church of Jesus Christ of Latter-day
  Saints** : Мормо́ны/Це́рковь Иису́са Христа́ святы́х
  после́дних дней

Morpheus (myth.) : Морфе́й

Morris, William : Уи́льям Мо́ррис

Morse Code : А́збука Мо́рзе

Morte d'Arthur (Malory) : «Смерть Арту́ра»

Mosel, River : Мо́зель (m.)

Mosel (vin.) : мозельве́йн

Moses (bibl.) : Моисе́й

133

Moses, Life of (Botticelli) : «Сце́ны из жи́зни Моисе́я»

Moses und Aron (Schoenberg) : «Моисе́й и Ааро́н»

Moslem *see* **Muslim**

Mosley, Oswald : О́свальд Мо́сли

mosque : мече́ть (f.)

Mössbauer effect (sci.) : эффе́кт Мёссбауера

mosso (mus.) : «оживлённо

Mother and Child (Picasso) : «Мать и дитя́»

Mother of Jesus : Ма́терь Иису́са

Mother Teresa : Мать Тере́за

moto perpetuo see perpetuum mobile

moue : недово́льная грима́са

mouillé (cul.) : промо́кший

Moulin de la Galette (Renoir) : «Муле́н де ля Гале́т»

Moulin Rouge (Toulouse-Lautrec) : «В Муле́н-Ру́ж»

Mountain, The (hist.) *see* **Montagnards**

Mounties *see* **Royal Canadian Mounted Police**

Mount Palomar Observatory : Ма́унт-Палома́рская астрономи́ческая обсервато́рия

Mount Wilson Observatory : Ма́унт-Ви́лсоновская астрономи́ческая обсервато́рия

Mourning Becomes Electra (O'Neill) : «Тра́ур к лицу́ Эле́ктре»

moussaka : муса́ка

mouvementé : оживлённый

Mozarabic verse : мосара́бская поэ́зия

Mozart, Wolfgang Amadeus : Во́льфганг Амаде́й Мо́царт

Mozart auf der Reise nach Prag (Mörike) : «Мо́царт на пути́ в Пра́гу»

mozzarella : моццаре́лла/италья́нский свѐжий сыр

Mrs Dalloway (Woolf) : «Ми́ссис Де́ллоуей»

Mrs Warren's Profession (Shaw) : «Профе́ссия госпожи́ Уо́ррен»

MS : манускри́пт/ру́копись

Much Ado About Nothing (Shakespeare) : «Мно́го шу́ма из ничего́»

mufti (Arab.) : му́фтий
mujaheddin : моджахе́ды
mulatto : мула́т
Mullah : мулла́
Munch, Edvard : Э́двард Мунк
Munich : Мю́нхен
Munich Agreement (hist.) : Мю́нхенское соглаше́ние
Murcia : Му́рсия
Murder in the Cathedral (T.S. Eliot) : «Уби́йство в
  собо́ре»
Murders in the Rue Morgue, The (Poe) : «Уби́йства
  на у́лице Морг»
Murdoch, Iris : А́йрис Мёрдок (Ме́рдок)
Murillo, Bartolomé : Бартоломе́ Мури́льо
Murphy (Beckett) : «Мёрфи»
Muscadet (vin.) : мюскаде́
muscat : муска́т
Muses, the : Му́зы
  Calliope : Каллио́па, му́за эпи́ческой поэ́зии
  Clio : Кли́о, му́за исто́рии
  Erato : Эра́то, му́за любо́вных пе́сен
  Euterpe : Эвте́рпа, му́за ли́рики
  Melpomene : Мельпоме́на, му́за траге́дии
  Polyhymnia : Полиги́мния, му́за свяще́нных
  ги́мнов
  Terpsichore : Терпсихо́ра, му́за та́нцев
  Thalia : Та́лия, му́за коме́дии
  Urania : Ура́ния, му́за астроно́мии
musette : мюзе́т/волы́нка
Museum of Contemporary Art (New York) : Нью-
-Йо́ркский музе́й совреме́нного иску́сства
music hall : мю́зик-хо́лл
musical : мю́зикл
Muslim : мусульма́нин; мусульма́нский
Muslim League : Мусульма́нская ли́га
Musset, Alfred de : А́льфред де Мюссе́
Mussolini, Benito : Бени́то Муссоли́ни *see also*
  Duce

MUTATIS MUTANDIS

mutatis mutandis : внеся необходи́мые измене́ния

Mutter Courage und ihre Kinder (Brecht) : «Мама́ша Кура́ж и её де́ти»

Mycenae : Мике́ны

Mycenaean : мике́нский

My Fair Lady : «Моя́ прекра́сная ле́ди»

Mysteries of Udolpho, The (Radcliffe) : «Удо́льфские та́йны»

Mythe de Sisyphe, Le (Camus) : «Миф о Сизи́фе»

N

Naaman (bibl.) : Нееман

nabob : набоб

Naboth the Jezreelite (bibl.) : Навуфей
иезраилитянин

Nabucco (Verdi) : «Набукко»/«Навуходоносор»

Nachdruck : ударение

Nachsommer (Stifter) : «Бабье лето»

Nachtstücke (Hoffmann) : «Ночные рассказы»

nadir : надир

Nagy, Imre : Имре Надь

Nahum (bibl.) : «Книга Пророка Наума»

Naipaul, V.S. : В.С. Нейпал

Naked and the Dead, The (Mailer) : «Нагие и
мёртвые»

Naked Maja, The (Goya) : «Маха обнажённая»

Nanking : Нанкин

Nansen, Fridtjof : Фритьоф Нансен

Nantes : Нант

Naomi (bibl.) : Ноеммннь

Naphtali (bibl.) : Неффалим

Napierian logarithm (math.) : Неперов логарифм

Naples : Неаполь (м.)

Naples, Kingdom of (hist.) : Неаполитанское
королевство

Napoléon Bonaparte : Наполеон Бонапарт

Napoli *see* **Naples**

napolitaine, à la : по-неаполитанскому

Narcissus (myth.) : Нарцисс

Narziss und Goldmund (Hesse) : «Нарцисс и
Гольдмунд»

NASA : НАСА/Национальное управление по
аэронавтике и исследованию космического
пространства

Naseby, battle of : битва при Нейзби

Nash, Ogden : Óгден Нэш

Nashville (US) : Нáшвилл

Nasser, Gamal Abdel : Гáмаль Áбдель Нáсер

Nat King Cole : Нэт Кинг Кóул

Natal : Натáль (f.)

Nathan (bibl.) : Нафáн

Nathan der Weise (Lessing) : «Натáн Мýдрый»

Nathanael (bibl.) : Нафанаúл

National Gallery (London, Washington) : Национáльная галерéя

National Guard (US) : национáльная гвáрдия

National Maritime Museum (Greenwich) : Национáльный морскóй музéй, Грúнвич

National Portrait Gallery (London) : Национáльная портрéтная галерéя

National Rifle Association (US) : Национáльная оружéйная ассоциáция

NATO : НАТО/Организáция Североатлантúческого договóра

Natural History Museum (London) : Британский музéй естéственной истóрии

natural selection : естéственный отбóр

Nausée, La (Sartre) : «Тошнотá»

Nausicaa (myth.) : Навсикáя

navarin (cul.) : рагý из барáнины с рéпой и морkóвью

Navarino, battle of : Наварúнское сражéние

Navarra : Навáрра

nawab : навáб

Naxos : Нáксос

Nazarene : назареянин/назареянка; назарéтский (of Nazareth); назарéйский (Nazarene)

Nazareth : Назарéт

Nazi : нацúст; нацúстский

NBC : Эн-Би-Си («Нéшонал бродкáстинг кóмпани»)

Neanderthal Man (prehist.) : неандертáлец

neapolitan sixth (mus.) : неаполитáнский секстакóрд

Nebelwerfer : хими́ческий миномёт

Nebraska : Небра́ска

Nebuchadnezzar (bibl.) : Навуходоно́сор

nécessaire : несессе́р

Nefertiti : Нофрета́ри

négligé : неглиже́

Negri, Ada : А́да Не́гри

Nehemiah (bibl.) : «Кни́га Нееми́и»

Nehru, Jawaharlal : Джавахарла́л Не́ру

Nelson, Horatio : Гора́цио Не́льсон

nem. con. : без возраже́ний

Nemean Games (myth.) : Неме́йские и́гры

Nemesis (myth.) : Немеси́да/Немези́да

Neo-Kantianism (philos.) : неокантиа́нство

Neolithic : неоли́т; неолити́ческий

Neoplatonism (philos.) : Неоплатони́зм

Neo-Thomism (philos.) : Неотоми́зм

ne plus ultra : совершенство/до кра́йних преде́лов

Neptune (astron., myth.) : Непту́н

Nereids (myth.) : Нереи́ды

Nero, Emperor : Кла́вдий Це́зарь Неро́н

Nerva : Марк Кокце́й Не́рва

Nessus, shirt of (myth.) : плащ Не́сса

Nestor : Не́стор

Nestroy, Johann : Иога́нн Не́строй

Netherlands : Нидерла́нды

Neubrandenburg : Нёйбранденбург

Neue Sachlichkeit (art) : но́вая веще́ственность

Neufchâtel (cul.) : нешате́ль (m.)

Neurath, Otto : О́тто Не́йрат

Nevada : Нева́да

névé : фирн; фи́рновый снег

New Brunswick : Нью-Бра́нсуик

New Deal (hist.) : но́вый курс

New England : Но́вая А́нглия

New Essays on the Human Understanding (Leibniz) :
   «Но́вые о́пыты о челове́ческом ра́зуме»

Newfoundland : Ньюфаундле́нд

New Grub Street (Gissing) : «Новая Граб-Стрит»/ «Му́ченики пера́»

New Hampshire : Нью-Хэ́мпшир

New Jersey : Нью-Дже́рси

Newman, Cardinal : кардина́л Нью́мен

New Mexico : Нью-Ме́ксико

New Orleans : Но́вый Орлеа́н

New South Wales : Но́вый Ю́жный Уэ́льс

Newsweek : «Нью́суи́к»

New Testament : Но́вый заве́т го́спода на́шего Иису́са Христа́

Newton, Isaac : Иса́ак Нью́тон

Newtonian reflector : систе́ма рефле́ктора Нью́тона

Newton's law of gravity : зако́н тяготе́ния Нью́тона

Newton's laws of motion : зако́ны меха́ник Нью́тона

Newton's rings : ко́льца Нью́тона

'New World' Symphony (Dvořák) : Симфо́ния «Из Но́вого Све́та»

New York : Нью-Йо́рк

New York City Ballet : «Нью-Йо́рк си́ти ба́лле»

New York Times : «Нью-Йо́рк Таймс»

New Yorker : «Нью-Йо́ркер»

Ney, Marshal : ма́ршал Ней

Niagara Falls : Ниага́рский водопа́д (waterfall); Ниага́ра-Фолс (Canadian/US town)

Nibelungenlied : «Пе́сня о Нибелу́нгах»

Nice : Ни́цца

Nicholas Nickleby (Dickens) : «Жизнь и приключе́ния Никола́са Ни́клби»

Nicodemus : Никоди́м

Nicomachean Ethics (Aristotle) : «Никома́хова э́тика»

Niebuhr, Barthold : Ба́ртольд Ни́бур

Nielsen, Carl : Карл Ни́льсен

Niels Klim's Subterranean Journey (Holberg) : «Подзе́мное стра́нствие Ни́льса Кли́ма»

Niemöller, Martin : Ма́ртин Нимёллер

Niersteiner (vin.) : нирштейн

Nietzsche, Friedrich : Фри́дрих Ни́цше

Nigger of the Narcissus, The (Conrad) : «Негр с «Нарци́сса»

Night Watch, The (Rembrandt) : «Ночно́й дозо́р»

Nightingale, Florence : Фло́ренс На́йтингейл

nihil obstat : нет препя́тствий (опубликова́нию)

Nikolai, Otto : О́тто Никола́и

nil desperandum : отча́иваться не от чего́

Nile, River : Нил

nimbostratus (meteor.) : сло́исто-дождевы́е

Nîmes : Ним

Nineveh : Нине́вия

Niobe (myth.) : Нио́ба

Nirvana : нирва́на

Nivôse *see* **Calendar, French Revolutionary**

Nixon, Richard : Ри́чард Ни́ксон

nizam : низа́м

Nkrumah, Kwame : Author Нкру́ма

Kwame

NMR (nuclear magnetic resonance) : ЯМР (я́дерный магни́тный резона́нс)

Noah : Ной

Noah's ark : Но́ев Ковче́г

Nobel, Alfred : А́льфред Но́бель

Nobel prize : Но́белевская пре́мия

noblesse oblige : положе́ние обя́зывает

Noël : Рождество́

Noeud de Vipères, Le (Mauriac) : «Клубо́к змей»

No Laughing Matter (Angus Wilson) : «Нешу́точное де́ло»

Nolde, Emil : Эми́ль Но́льде

nolens volens : во́лей-нево́лей

noli me tangere : не тронь меня́

nom de guerre : псевдони́м

nom de plume : псевдони́м

non compos mentis : не в своём уме́

nones (eccles.) : девя́тый час

Noh drama : но

non sequitur : нелоги́чный вы́вод

Nordrhein-Westphalen : Се́верный Рейн-Вестфа́лия

NORMA

Norma (Bellini) : «Но́рма»

Norman Conquest (hist.) : норма́ндское завоева́ние А́нглии

Normandy : Норма́ндия

North and South (Mrs Gaskell) : «Се́вер и юг»

Northanger Abbey (Austen) : «Норте́нгерское абба́тство»

North Atlantic Treaty Organization *see* **NATO**

North Carolina : Се́верная Кароли́на

North Dakota : Се́верная Дако́та

North of Boston (Frost) : «К се́веру от Бо́стона»

Northumbria : Норту́мбрия

North-West Territories (Canada) : Се́веро-За́падные террито́рии

nostalgie de la boue (lit.) : «тоска́ по гря́зи»

Nostredame, Michel de (Nostrodamus) : Мише́ль де Нострода́м (Нострода́мус)

Nostromo (Conrad) : «Ностро́мо»

nota bene : нотабе́не

Notes of the Fatherland : «Оте́чественные запи́ски»

Notre-Dame de Paris : Собо́р Пари́жского богома́тери

notturno (mus.) : ноктю́рн

Nourritures terrestres, Les (Gide) : «Я́ства земны́е»

nouveau riche : «нувори́ш»

nouveau roman : но́вый рома́н

Nouvelle Héloïse, La (Rousseau) : «Но́вая Эло́иза»

Novalis : Нова́лис (Фри́дрих фон Ха́рденберг)

Nova Scotia : Но́вая Шотла́ндия

Novelas ejemplares (Cervantes) : «Назида́тельные нове́ллы»

Novelle : по́весть/нове́лла

Noyades (hist.) : потопле́ния

NSDAP (National Socialist German Workers Party) (hist.) : Национа́л-социалисти́ческая рабо́чая па́ртия Герма́нии

Nuclear Non-Proliferation Treaty : Догово́р о нераспростране́нии я́дерного ору́жия

Nuclear Test Ban Treaty : Догово́р о запре́те испыта́ний я́дерного ору́жия

Numbers (bibl.) : «Четвёртая кни́га Моисе́ева. Чи́сла»

Nuremberg Trials (hist.) : Нюрнбе́ргский проце́сс

Nürnberg : Ню́рнберг

Nutcracker, The (Tchaikovsky) : «Щелку́нчик»

Nyasaland (hist.) : Нья́саленд

O

Oak Ridge (US) : Ок Ридж

Oath of the Horatii, The (David) : «Кля́тва Гора́циев»

Obadiah (bibl.) : «Кни́га проро́ка Авди́я»

obbligato (mus.) : облига́то

Oberammergau : Обера́ммергау

Oberon (Weber) : «Оберо́н»

obiter dictum : случа́йное замеча́ние

objet d'art : предме́т иску́сства

oboe d'amore : гобо́й д'аму́р

Occam/Ockham, William of : Уи́льям О́ккам

Occam's razor (philos.) : бри́тва О́ккама

occultism : оккульти́зм

Oceanides (myth.) : Океани́ды

Octavian *see* **Augustus**

odalisque : одали́ска

Odelsting (Norwegian Parliament) : О́дельстинг

'Ode to Joy' (Schiller, Beethoven) *see* **'An die Freude'**

'Ode to the West Wind' (Shelley) : «О́да За́падному Ветру́»

Oder—Neisse Line (hist.) : ли́ния О́дра-Ни́са

Odin (myth.) : О́дин

Odysseus : Одиссе́й

Odyssey (Homer) : «Одиссе́я»

Oedipus : Эди́п

Oedipus at Colonus (Sophocles) : «Эди́п в Коло́не»

Oedipus complex (psych.) : Эди́пов ко́мплекс

Oedipus Rex (Sophocles) : «Царь Эди́п»

Offenbach, Jacques : Жак Оффенба́х

Officers and Gentlemen (Waugh) : «Офице́ры и джентльме́ны»

Of Human Bondage (Maugham) : «Бре́мя страсте́й челове́ческих»

Of Mice and Men (Steinbeck) : «О мыша́х и лю́дях»

ogham : огами́ческое письмо́; огами́ческий алфави́т

O. Henry *see* **Henry, O.**

Ohio : Ога́йо

ohm : ом

Ohm's law (phys.) : зако́н О́ма

Oise, River : Уа́за

Oklahoma : Оклахо́ма

Oklahoma City : Оклахо́ма-Си́ти

Oktoberfest : октя́брьские наро́дные гуля́ния

Olbers' paradox (astron.) : парадо́кс О́льберса

Old Curiosity Shop, The (Dickens) : «Ла́вка
  дре́вностей»

Old Man and the Sea, The (Hemingway) : «Стари́к и
  мо́ре»

Old Men at the Zoo, The (Angus Wilson) : «Старики́
  в зоопа́рке»

Old Testament : Кни́ги Ве́тхого заве́та

Olduvai Gorge (anthrop.) : уще́лье Олдова́й

'Old Vic' Theatre (London) : «Олд Ви́к»

Old Wives' Tale, The (Bennett) : «По́весть ста́рых
  жён»

Oligocene (geol.) : олигоце́новая эпо́ха

Oliver Twist (Dickens) : «Приключе́ния О́ливера
  Тви́ста»

Olives, Mount of : гора́ Элео́нская

Olivier, Laurence : Ло́ренс Оливье́

oloroso (vin.) : олоро́со

Olympia : Оли́мпия

Olympiad : олимпиа́да

Olympian : олимпи́ец; олимпи́йский

Olympic Games : олимпи́йские и́гры

Olympus, Mount : Оли́мп

Omar Khayyám : Ома́р Хайя́м

ombudsman : о́мбудсма́н

Omega *see* **Alpha and Omega**

omertà : ко́декс молча́ния (среди́ престу́пников)

Omphale (myth.) : Омфа́ла

O'NEILL, EUGENE

O'Neill, Eugene : Юджи́н О'Ни́л

On ne badine pas avec l'amour (de Musset) : «С любо́вью не шу́тят»

Ontario : Онта́рио

Ontario, Lake : о́зеро Онта́рио

On the Road (Kerouac) : «На доро́ге»

op art : «оп-арт»/«опти́ческое иску́сство»

OPEC : ОПЕК (Организа́ция стран-экспортёров не́фти)

Open Sesame : «Сеза́м, отвори́сь!»

opera buffa/opéra bouffe : о́пера-бу́фф

opéra comique : коми́ческая о́пера/опере́тта

Opiuchus (astron.) : Змеено́сец

oracle : ора́кул

Orange Free State : Ора́нжевое Свобо́дное госуда́рство (hist.); Ора́нжевая прови́нция

ora pro nobis : моли́сь за нас

Ordeal of Gilbert Penfold, The (Waugh) : «Испыта́ние Джи́льберта Пе́нфолда»

Ordeal of Richard Feverel, The (Meredith) : «Испыта́ние Ри́чарда Фе́вереля»

Ordovician (geol.) : ордови́кский пери́од

Oregon : Орего́н

Oresteia (Aeschylus) : «Оресте́я»

Orestes (myth.) : Оре́ст

Orfeo et Euridice (Gluck) : «Орфе́й и Евриди́ка»

Orff, Carl : Карл Орф

Organization of Petroleum Exporting Countries *see* **OPEC**

Organon (Aristotle) : «Органо́н»

oriflamme (hist.) : орифла́мма

Origin of Species, The (Darwin) : «Происхожде́ние ви́дов путём есте́ственного отбо́ра»

Orion (astron.) : Орио́н

Orion's Belt (astron.) : Трапе́ция Орио́на

Orlando Furioso (Ariosto) : «Неи́стовый Рола́нд»

Orleanist (hist.) : орлеани́ст/орлеани́стка; орлеани́стский

Orléans : Орлеа́н

Ormuzd (relig.) : Орму́зд

Orpheus : Орфе́й

Orpheus Descending (Tennessee Williams) : «Орфе́й спуска́ется в ад»

Orphism (art) : орфи́зм

Ortega y Gasset, José : Хосе́ Орте́га-и-Гасе́т

Orthodox Church, Greek : Гре́ческая правосла́вная це́рковь

Orwell, George : Джордж О́руэлл (Э́рик Блер)

Osiris (myth.) : Оси́рис

Ossa *see* **Pelion**

Ossian : Оссиа́н

Ostade, Adriaan van : Адриа́н ван Оста́де

ostinato (mus.) : остина́то

Ostpolitik (hist.) : Остполити́к/восто́чная поли́тика

Ostrogoths : остго́ты

o, tempora, o mores! : «о времена́, о нра́вы!»

Othello (Shakespeare) : «Оте́лло»

ottava rima (ling.) : окта́ва/восьмисти́шие

Ottawa : Отта́ва

Ottoman empire : Осма́нская импе́рия

oubliette : подзе́мная тюрьма́

Our Man in Havana (Greene) : «Наш челове́к в Гава́не»

Our Mutual Friend (Dickens) : «Наш о́бщий друг»

outrance, à : до го́рького конца́

outré : утри́рованный

ouverture : уверти́ора

ouzo (vin.) : у́зо

Ovid : Пу́блий Ови́дий Назо́н

Oviedo : Овье́до

Owen, Robert : Ро́берт О́уэн

Owen, Wilfred : Уи́лфред О́уэн

Oxford Movement : Оксфо́рдское движе́ние

Oxford University : Оксфо́рдский университе́т

Oxford University Press : «О́ксфорд юниве́рсити пресс»

OXYMORON

oxymoron : оксю́морон

Oxyrhynchus historian : Оксири́нхский исто́рик

P

pace : не в оби́ду (кому́)
padre : оте́ц/па́дре
padrone : хозя́ин/владе́лец
Padua : Па́дуя
paella (cul.) : паэ́лья
Pagliacci, I (Leoncavallo) : «Пая́цы»
paillasse : соло́менный тюфя́к
Paine, Thomas : То́мас Пейн
Painter's Studio, The (Courbet) : «Ателье́»
Palaeocene (geol.) : палеоце́новая эпо́ха
palaeolithic (geol.) : палеоли́т; палеолити́ческий
Palaeozoic (geol.) : палеозо́йская э́ра
palaestra : пале́стра
palazzo : дворе́ц
Palestine : Палести́на
Palestine Liberation Organization *see* **PLO**
Palestrina, Giovanni : Джова́нни Палестри́на
Palladian (archit.) : палла́диев/палладиа́нский
Palmerston, Henry : Ге́нри Па́льмерстон
Palm Sunday : ве́рбное воскресе́нье
Palomar *see* **Mount Palomar Observatory**
Pamela (Richardson) : «Па́мела, или
  Вознаграждённая доброде́тель»
pampas : па́мпы
Pan (myth.) : Пан
panache : щегольство́
Panama Canal Zone : зо́на Пана́мского кана́ла
Pandora's box (myth.) : я́щик Пандо́ры
Panegyricus (Pliny the Younger) : «Панеги́рик»
panem et circenses : «хле́ба и зре́лищ»
Pangaea (prehist.) : Панге́я
Pan Tadeusz (Mickiewicz) : «Пан Таде́уш»
panzer : та́нковый
Papal States (hist.) : Па́пская о́бласть

paparazzo : свётский фотохроникёр

papier collé : клёйкая бумага

papier mâché : папьé-машé

Paradise Lost (Milton) : «Потéрянный рай»

Paradise Regained (Milton) : «Возвращённый рай»

parador : парадóр

par avion : авиапóчтой

Pardo Bazán, Emilia : Эмилия Пáрдо Басáн

par excellence : по преимуществу

parfait (cul.) : пломбир

pari passu : равномéрно и одноврéменно

Paris : Париж

Paris (myth.) : Парис

Paris Commune (hist.) : Парижская Коммуна

Parisien : парижáнин

Parisienne : парижáнка

Parliament of Fowls, The (Chaucer) : «Птичий парлáмент»

Parmenides (Plato) : «Парменид»

Parmesan/*parmigiano* : пáрмский; пармезáн

Parmigianino, Francesco : Франчéско Пармиджанино

Parnassians (lit.) : парнáсцы

Parnassus, Mount : Парнáс

parole (ling.) : речь (f.)

parsec (astron.) : парсéк

Parsee : фарси; фáрский/фарсийский

Parthenon : Парфенóн

Parthian Empire : Парфянское цáрство

Parthian shot : Парфянская стрелá

parti pris : предвзятое мнéние

partita (mus.) : партита

parvenu(e) : парвеню

Parzifal/Perceval (Arthur.) : Парсифáль

Parzifal (Wagner) : «Парцифáль»

Pascal, Blaise : Блез Паскáль

Pascal's triangle (math.) : треугóльник Паскáля

Pascoli, Giovanni : Джованни Пáсколи

Pas-de-Calais : Па-де-Кале́

pas de deux : па-де-де́

pasha : паша́

paso doble : пасодо́бль

Pasquier Chronicles, The (Duhamel) see *Chronique des Pasquier, La*

pasquinade (lit.) : па́сквиль (m.)

passacaglia (mus.) : пассака́лья

Passage to India, A (Forster) : «Пое́здка в Йндию»

Passau : Пасса́у

passé : старомо́дный; вы́цветший

passe-partout : отмы́чка (passkey); паспарту́ (picture mounting)

passim : там и ся́м/в ра́зных места́х/повсю́ду

Passion, The Greater (Dürer) : «Больши́е стра́сти»

Passion, The Little (Dürer) : «Ма́лые стра́сти»

Passion Week : Страстна́я неде́ля

pasta : те́сто

Pasteur, Louis : Лу́и Пастёр

pastiche : паро́дия (imitation); пасти́чио (mixture of styles)

pastis : ани́совый ликёр

pastorale : пастора́ле

'Pastoral' Symphony (Beethoven) : «Пастора́льная» симфо́ния

patchouli (perfume) : пачу́ли

pâté (cul.) : паштѐт

pâté de foie gras (cul.) : печёночный паштѐт

paterfamilias : оте́ц семе́йства

Paternoster ('Our Father') : моли́тва «о́тче наш»

paternoster (lift/elevator) : патерно́стер

patetico (mus.) : патети́чно/взволно́ванно

Pathans (hist.) : пата́ны

'Pathétique' Sonata (Beethoven) : «Патети́ческая» сона́та

Pathet Lao (hist.) : Патѐт-Ла́о

Path to the Nests of Spiders, The (Calvino) : «Тропи́нка к пау́чьим гнёздам»

PÂTISSERIE

pâtisserie : кондитерская

patois : местное наречие/патуа

Paton, Alan : Áлан Пейтон

patricians (hist.) : патриции

Patroclus : Патрокл

Paul (bibl.) : Павел

Paul et Virgine (Bernadin de St Pierre) : Поль и Виргиния

Pauli, Wolfgang : Вóльфганг Паули

Pauli exclusion principle (sci.) : принцип Паули

Pauling, Linus : Линус Паулинг

pavan (dance) : павана

Pavane pour une infante défunte (Ravel) : «Павана на смерть инфанты»

Pavese, Cesare : Чезáре Павéзе

Pax Romana : мир, навязанный римской империей

pax vobiscum : «мир вам»

pazos de Ulloa, Los (Pardo Bazán) : «Родовые замки Ульóа»

Pearl Fishers, The (Bizet) see *Pêcheurs des Perles, Les*

Pearl Harbour (hist.) : Пёрл-Хáрбор

Peau de chagrin, La (Balzac) : «Шагрéневая кóжа»

peccavi : «я грешил»

Pêcheurs des Perles, Les (Bizet) : «Искáтели жéмчуга»

Peder Paars (Holberg) : «Пéдер Порс»

Peel, Robert : Рóберт Пиль

Peer Gynt (Grieg) : «Пер Гюнт»

Pegasus (myth.) : Пегáс

peignoir : пеньюáр

Peking see **Beijing**

Peking Man (anthrop.) : синáнтроп

Pelagian : пелагиáнский

Pelagius : Пелáгий

Peleus (myth.) : Пелéй

Pelias (myth.) : Пéлий

Pelion to heap Pelion upon Ossa (myth.) : «нагромоздить Пелиóн на Óссу»

Pelléas et Mélisande (Debussy) : «Пеллеа́с и Мелиза́нда»

Peloponnese : Пелопонне́с

Peloponnesian Wars : Пелопонне́ские во́йны

pelota : пело́та

penchant : скло́нность (+ к)

PEN Club : междунаро́дная ассоциа́ция писа́телей

Penelope (myth.) : Пенело́па

Pennsylvania : Пенсильва́ния

Pensées, Les (Pascal) : «Мы́сли»

Penseroso, Il (Milton) see *Il Penseroso*

pensieroso (mus.) : заду́мчиво

pentameter (vers.) : пента́метр

Pentateuch (bibl.) : пятикни́жие

Pentecost, day of : день пятидеся́тницы

Pentecostalists (relig.) : пятидеся́тники

Penthesilea (Kleist) : «Пентесиле́я»

per annum : в год

per aspera ad astra : че́рез те́рнии к звёздам

per capita : на ду́шу

Perceval ou Le Conte de Graal (Chrétien de Troyes) : «Персева́ль или По́весть о Граа́ле»

per diem : в день

Père Goriot, Le (Balzac) : «Оте́ц Го́рио»

Peregrine Pickle (Smollett) : «Приключе́ния Пе́регрина Пи́кля»

Peregrino en su patria (Lope de Vega) : «Стра́нник в своём оте́честве»

Père Lachaise Cemetery (Paris) : кла́дбище Пер-Лаше́з

Perez de Cuellar : Пе́рес де Куэ́льар

perfect cadence (mus.) : по́лная/соверше́нная каде́нция

Pericles (Shakespeare) : «Пери́кл»

Périgueux : Периге́

Periodic law (chem.) : периоди́ческий зако́н

peripeteia (lit.) : перепети́я/неожи́данный поворо́т

per mensem : в ме́сяц

153

PERMIAN

Permian (geol.) : пе́рмский пери́од

perpetuum mobile : ве́чное движе́ние; ве́чный дви́гатель/перпе́туум мо́биле

Perpignan : Перпинья́н

per se : само́ по себе́

Persephone (myth.) : Персефо́на

Persepolis : Персе́поль (m.)

Perseus (myth.) : Персе́й

Persians (Aeschylus) : «Пе́рсы»

Persistence of Memory, The (Dali) : «Постоя́нство па́мяти»

persona (non) grata : персо́на (нон) гра́та

Persuasion (Austen) : «Убежде́ние»

Perth : Перт

Perugia : Перу́джа

Pestalozzi, Johann : Иога́нн Песталоцци

Peste, La (Camus) : «Чума́»

Pétain, Marshal : ма́ршал Петэ́н

pétanque : игра́ в шары́

Peter I (bibl.) : «Пе́рвое посла́ние Петра́»

Peter II (bibl.) : «Второ́е посла́ние Петра́»

Peter and Paul Fortress (St Petersburg) : Петропа́вловская кре́пость

Peter Grimes (Britten) : «Пи́тер Гра́ймс»

Peter Pan (Barrie) : «Пи́тер Пэн»

Peter Schlemihl (Chamisso) : «Необыча́йная исто́рия Пе́тера Шле́миля»

Peter the Hermit (hist.) : Пётр Амье́нский, Пусты́нник

petit bourgeois : ме́лкий буржуа́

petit four (cul.) : петифу́р/десе́ртное пече́нье

petit mal : лёгкий припа́док эпиле́псии

petit point : ме́лкая вы́шивка

Petrarch, Francesco : Франче́ско Петра́рка

Petrarchan sonnet : соне́т в мане́ре Петра́рки

Petrarchism (lit.) : подража́ние Петра́рке

pfeffernuss : ма́ленький кру́глый пря́ник

pfennig : пфе́нниг

Pfitzner, Hans : Ганс Пфи́цнер

pH : pH (водоро́дный показа́тель)

Phaedo (Plato) : «Федо́н»

Phaeton (myth.) : Фаэто́н

Phantasien über die Kunst (Tieck) : «Фанта́зии об иску́сстве»

Pharaoh : Фарао́н

Pharisees (bibl.) : фарисе́и

Pharos : Фа́рос

Pharsalia (Lucan) : «Фарса́лия»

Phèdre (Racine) : «Фе́дра»

Phenomenology of the Mind (Hegel) : «Феномено-ло́гия ду́ха»

Phi Beta Kappa : Фи-Бе́та-Ка́ппа

Phidias : Фи́дий

Philadelphia : Филаде́льфия

Philémon et Baucis (Gounod) : «Филемо́н и Бавки́да»

Philip (bibl.) : Фили́пп

Philip of Macedon : Фили́пп Македо́нский

Philippi : Фили́ппы

Philippians (bibl.) : Посла́ние к Филиппи́йцам»

Philippines : Филиппи́ны

philistine : фили́стерский/обыва́тельский

Philistines (bibl.) : филистимля́не

Philoctetes (myth.) : Филокте́т

Philosophical Fragments (Kierkegaard) : «Филосо́фские кро́хи»

Philosophy of Right (Hegel) : «Филосо́фия пра́ва»

Phinias Finn (Trollope) : «Фи́ниас Финн»

Phinias Redux (Trollope) : «Фи́ниас возвращённый»

Phobos (astron.) : Фо́бос

Phoebe (myth.) : Фе́ба

Phoebus (myth.) : Феб

Phoenicia : Финики́я

Phoenician : финики́ец; финики́йский

Phoenix (US) : Фе́никс

Phoney War (hist.) : «стра́нная война́» (без вое́нных де́йствий)

Phrygia : Фри́гия

Phrygian cap : фриги́йский колпа́к

Phrygian mode (mus.) : фриги́йский лад

Physiker, Die (Dürrenmatt) : «Фи́зики»

pi : пи

Piaget, Jean : Жан Пиаже́

pianissimo (mus.) : пиани́ссимо

piano (mus.) : пиа́но

piano quartet : фортепья́нный кварте́т

piano quintet : фортепья́нный квинте́т

piano trio : фортепья́нное три́о

piastre : пиа́стр

piazza : пло́щадь (f.)

picador : пикадо́р

Picasso, Pablo : Па́бло Пика́ссо

pickelhaube (hist.) : острове́рхая ка́ска

Pickwick Papers (Dickens) : «Посме́ртные запи́ски Пикви́кского клу́ба»

pièce de résistance : са́мое выдаю́щееся; основно́е блю́до (cul.)

pied-à-terre : вре́менное жили́ще

Piedmont : Пьемо́нт

pied noir : «черноно́гий»/алжи́рец европе́йского происхожде́ния

Pied Piper of Hamelin, The (Browning) : «Кра́сочный волы́нщик из Гамели́на»

Piero della Francesca : Пье́ро де́лла Франче́ска

Piero di Cosimo : Пье́ро ди Ко́зимо

Pierrot : Пьеро́

Piers the Plowman (Langland) : «Виде́ние о Петре́ Па́харе»

pietà : пиета́

Pietà (Michelangelo) : «Опла́кивание Христа́»

Pigeon Feathers (Updike) : «Пе́рья го́лубя»

pilaff (cul.) : плов

Pilgrimage of Grace (hist.) : Благода́тное пало́мничество

Pilgrim Fathers (hist.) : Отцы́ Пало́мники

Pilgrim's Progress (Bunyan) : «Путь паломника/
Путешéствие пилигрима»

Pillars of Hercules : геркулéсовы столпы́

Pillars of Society (Ibsen) : «Столпы́ óбщества»

Pinakothek Museum (Munich) : Пинакотéка

pince-nez : пенснé

Pindar : Пи́ндар

Pinochet, Augusto : Аугу́сто Пиночéт Угáрте

pinot (vin.) : пинó

pique : досáда

piqué (fabric) : пикé

piquet (card game) : пикéт

Pirandello, Luigi : Луи́джи Пирандéлло

pirouette : пируэ́т

Pisa, Leaning tower of : пáдающая бáшня Пи́зы/
Пизáнская бáшня

Pisano : Никкóло и Андрé Пизáно

Pisces (zod.) : Ры́бы

Pissarro, Camille : Ками́ль Писсаррó

piste : трáсса

Pit and the Pendulum, The (Poe) : «Колóдец и
мáятник»

Pithecanthropus (anthrop.) : питекáнтроп

Pittsburgh : Пи́тсбург

più (mus.) : бóлее

più mosso (mus.) : живéе

Pius, Pope : пáпа Пий

Pizarro, Francisco : Франси́ско Писáрро

pizzicato (mus.) : пиццикáто

placebo : плацéбо/безврéдное лекáрство

place d'armes (milit.) : учéбный плац

plagal cadence (mus.) : плагáльная кадéнция

Plague, The (Camus) see Peste, La

Plaid Cymru : Плайд Ки́мру

Plain Tales from the Hills (Kipling) : «Просты́е
рассказы с гор»

Planck's constant (sci.) : постоя́нная Плáнка

Plantagenet (hist.) : Плантагенéт

PLAT DU JOUR

plat du jour : дежу́рное блю́до

Plate, River : Ла-Пла́та

Plato : Плато́н

Platonism : платони́зм

Platt-Deutsch (ling.) : нижненеме́цкий

Plautus : Тит Ма́кций Плавт

Playboy of the Western World, The (Synge) : «Удало́й молоде́ц — го́рдость За́пада»

plaza : пло́щадь (f.)

plebs : плебе́и

Pléiade (lit.) : Плея́да

Pleiades (astron., myth.) : Плея́ды

Pleistocene (geol.) : плейстоце́новая эпо́ха

Pliny the Elder : Пли́ний Ста́рший

Pliny the Younger : Пли́ний Мла́дший

Pliocene (geol.) : плиоце́новая эпо́ха

PLO (Palestine Liberation Organization) : ООП (Организа́ция освобожде́ния Палести́ны)

Plotinus : Плоти́н

Plough (astron.) *see* **Ursa Major**

Plumed Serpent, The (Lawrence) : «Перна́тый змий»

plus ça change, plus c'est la même chose : «чем бо́льше переме́н, тем бо́льше всё остаётся по-ста́рому»

plus royaliste que le roi : быть бо́льше рояли́стом, чем сам коро́ль

Plutarch : Плута́рх

Pluto (astron., myth.) : Плуто́н

Pluviôse *see* **Calendar, French Revolutionary**

p.m. (post meridiem) : пополу́дни

poco a poco (mus.) : ма́ло-пома́лу

Poe, Edgar Allan : Э́дгар А́ллан По

Poema del cante jondo (Lorca) : «Ка́нте хо́ндо»

Poema de mío Cid (Pardo Bazán) : «Поэ́ма о моём Си́де»

Poètes maudits, Les (Verlaine) : «Про́клятые поэ́ты»

Poetical Sketches (Blake) : «Поэти́ческие набро́ски»

Poet Laureate : придво́рный поэ́т

Pohjola's Daughter (Sibelius) : «Дочь Похьёлы»

poilu (hist.) : пуалю/солда́т-фронтови́к

Poincaré, Henri : Анри́ Пуанкаре́

Point Counter Point (Huxley) : «Контрапу́нкт»

point d'appui : то́чка опо́ры

pointillism (art) : пуантили́зм

Poirot Investigates (Christie) : «Пуаро́ рассле́дует»

Poisson distribution (math.) : распределе́ние Пуассо́на

Poitiers : Пуатье́

polder : по́льдер/обвало́ванная низи́на

Pole Poppenspäler (Storm) : «По́ле-Ку́кольник»

polka : по́лька

Pollock, Jackson : Дже́ксон По́ллок

Pollux (myth.) : Поллу́кс

polonaise (dance) : полоне́з

Polyclitus : Поликле́т из А́ргоса

Polyeucte (Corneille) : «Полие́кт»

Polyhymnia *see* **Muses, the**

Polyneices (myth.) : Полини́к

Polyphemus (myth.) : Полифе́м

Pompeii : Помпе́и

Pompey : Гней Помпе́й

Pompidou Centre (Paris) : Центр Помпиду́

pomposo (mus.) : помпе́зно

Pons Asinorum (philos.) : ка́мень (m.) преткнове́ния

ponticello (mus.) : подста́вка

pontifex (relig.) : понти́фик

Pontine Marshes : Помти́нские боло́та

Pontius Pilate : По́нтий Пила́т

Pont l'Évêque (cul.) : понлеве́к

Poorhouse Fair, The (Updike) : «Я́рмарка в богаде́льне»

pop art : «поп-арт»

Pope, the : Ри́мский па́па

Pope, Alexander : Алекса́ндр Поп

Popular Front (hist.) : Наро́дный фронт

Poquelin, Jean-Baptiste *see* **Molière**

PORGY AND BESS

Porgy and Bess (Gershwin) : «Пóрги и Бесс»

Porphyrogenitus (hist.) : Багрянорóдный/ порфирорóдный

portamento (mus.) : портамéнто

Porte étroite, La (Gide) : «Тéсные вратá»

porte-monnaie : портмонé/кошелёк

Porter, Cole : Кол Пóртер

Porter, William Sydney *see* **Henry, O.**

Porto : Пóрту

Portrait of a Lady (James) : «Жéнский портрéт»

Portrait of Dorian Gray (Wilde) : «Портрéт Дориáна Грéя»

Portrait of the Artist as a Young Man (Joyce) : «Портрéт худóжника в ю́ности»

Port-Royal : Пор-Роя́ль (m.)

Poseidon (myth.) : Посейдóн

poseur/poseuse : позёр

poste restante : «до вострéбования»

Post-Impressionism : постимпрессиони́зм

Postmodernism : постмодерни́зм

postscriptum : постскри́птум

Potato Eaters, The (Van Gogh) : «Едоки́ картóфеля»

Potiphar (bibl.) : Потифáр

Potomac, Army of the (hist.) : Потомáкская áрмия

pot-pourri : попурри́ (medley of tunes); смесь из цветóв и благовóнных трав

Potsdam Conference : Потсдáмская конферéнция

potter's field (bibl.) : земля́ горшéчника

Poulenc, Francis : Фрáнсис Пýленк

Pound, Ezra : Э́зра Пáунд

pourboire : чаевы́е

poussin (cul.) : цыплёнок

Poussin, Nicolas : Николá Пуссéн

Powell, Anthony : Э́нтони Пóуэлл

Power and the Glory, The (Greene) : «Власть и слáва»

PR (Proportional Representation) : пропорционáльная систéма представи́тельства

Prado (Madrid) : Пра́до
praefecti (hist.) : префе́кты
Praetorian Guard : Преториа́нцы
praetors (hist.) : пре́торы
Pragmatic Sanction (hist.) : прагмати́ческая са́нкция
Prägnanz (psych.) : ме́ткость
Prague : Пра́га
Prairial *see* **Calendar, French Revolutionary**
praline (cul.) : прали́на
Praxiteles : Праксите́ль
Precambrian (geol.) : докембри́йская э́ра
precession of the equinoxes : прецессия
равноде́нствий
Précieuses ridicules, Les (Molière) : «Смешны́е
жема́нницы»
préciosité : прецио́зность
precipitato (mus.) : преципита́то
précis : конспе́кт
predikant : свяще́нник
préfecture : префекту́ра
première (theat.) : премье́ра
Pre-Raphaelites : прерафаэли́ты/Бра́тство
прерафаэли́тов
Presbyterianism : пресвитериа́нство
Presidential Address : президе́нтское Посла́ние
Presley, Elvis : Э́львис Пре́сли
prestissimo (mus.) : прести́ссимо
presto (mus.) : пре́сто
preux chevalier : богаты́рь
Prévert, Jacques : Жак Преве́р
Prévost d'Éxiles : Прево́ д'Экзи́ль
Priam (myth.) : Приа́м
Priapus (myth.) : Приа́п
Pride and Prejudice (Austen) : «Го́рдость и
предубежде́ние»
Pride's Purge (hist.) : Пра́йдова чи́стка
prie-dieu : скаме́ечка для моли́твы
prima donna : примадо́нна

161

prime (eccles.) : пе́рвый канони́ческий час

Prime of Miss Jean Brodie, The (Spark) : «Мисс Джин Бро́ди в расцве́те лет»

primus inter pares : пе́рвый ме́жду ра́вными

Prince and the Pauper, The (Twain) : «Принц и ни́щий»

Prince Edward Island : О́стров Принс-Эдуа́рд

Princess and the Pea, The (Andersen) : «Принце́сса на горо́шине»

Princeton University : При́нстонский университе́т

Principe, Il (Machiavelli) : «Князь»/«Госуда́рь»

Principia Mathematica (Newton) : «Нача́ла»

Principia Philosophiae (Descartes) : «Нача́ла филосо́фии»

Prinz Friedrich von Homburg (Kleist) : «Принц Фри́дрих Гомбу́ргский»

Prisoner of Chillon, The (Byron) : «Шильо́нский у́зник»

prix Goncourt : Гонку́ровская пре́мия

pro bono publico : для по́льзы о́бщества

proconsuls (hist.) : проко́нсулы

procrustean bed (myth.) : Прокру́стово ло́же

Procrustes (myth.) : Прокру́ст

Procyon (astron.) : Процио́н

prodigal son (bibl.) : блу́дный сын

pro et contra : за и про́тив

profession de foi : изложе́ние свои́х взгля́дов

Professor Unrat (H. Mann) : «Учи́тель Гнус»

profiterole (cul.) : профитро́ль (m.)

pro forma : профо́рма

Prohibition (hist.) : Запреще́ние

prolepsis (lit.) : проле́псис

prologomenon : введе́ние

Promessi sposi, I (Manzoni) : «Обручённые»

Promethean fire : Промете́ев ого́нь

Prometheus : Промете́й

Prometheus Bound (Browning) : «Прико́ванный Промете́й»

Prometheus Unbound (Shelley) : «Освобождённый
  Прометей»

Promised Land : обетованная земля

pronunciamento : военный мятеж/
  пронунсиам(ь)енто

propter hoc : в таком случае

pro rata : в соответствии

prosit! : «за ваше здоровье!»

Protagoras : Протагор

protégé(e) : протеже

Protestantism : протестантство

Proteus (myth.) : Протей

Proust, Marcel : Марсель Пруст

Provençal : провансальский

proverbe dramatique (lit.) : маленькая пьеса,
  построенная на поговорке

Proverbs (bibl.) : «Книга Притчей Соломоновых»

Prozeß, Der (Kafka) : «Процесс»

Prussia : Пруссия

psalm : псальма

psalmist : псалмопевец

Psalms (bibl.) : «Псалтирь»

Psyche (myth.) : Психея

Psycho (film) : «Психоз»

Puccini, Giacomo : Джакомо Пуччини

Puget, Pierre : Пьер Пюже

Puglia : Апулия

Pugwash Conferences : Пагуошские конференции

Pulitzer Prize : Пулицеровская премия

pulsar (astron.) : пульсар (пульсирующий источник
  радиоизлучения)

pumpernickel (cul.) : вестфальский ржаной хлеб

pundit : эксперт

Punic Wars : Пунические войны

Punjab : Пенджаб

purée (cul.) : пюре

Purgatory : чистилище

Puritani, I (Bellini) : «Пуритане»

PURITANS, THE
Puritans, The (Scott) : «Пуритáне»
putsch : путч
Pygmalion (Shaw) : «Пигмалиóн»
Pylades (myth.) : Пилáд
Pyongyang : Пхенья́н
Pyrenees : Пиренéи
pyrrhic : пирри́хий
Pyrrhic victory : Пи́ррова побéда
Pythagoras : Пифагóр Самóсский
Pythagoras' theorem : теорéма Пифагóра
Pythagoreanism : пифагорéизм
Pythian : пифи́йский

Q

QED (*quod erat demonstrandum*) : что и тре́бовалось
  доказа́ть

qua : в ка́честве (+ gen.)

Quadragesima (eccles.) : пе́рвое воскресе́нье Поста́

quadrille : кадри́ль (f.)

quaestors (hist.) : кве́сторы

Quai d'Orsay : Министе́рство иностра́нных дел
  Фра́нции

Quakers (Society of Friends) : ква́керы/О́бщество
  друзе́й

quasar (quasi-stellar object) : кваза́р (квазизвёздный
  объе́кт)

Quaternary (geol.) : четверти́чная э́ра

quatrain (lit., mus.) : катре́н/четверости́шие

quaver (mus.) : восьма́я но́та

Quebec : Квебе́к

Québécois : жи́тель/жи́тельница Квебе́ка;
  квебе́кский; францу́зский язы́к в Квебе́ке

Queen Mab (Shelley) : «Короле́ва Маб»

Queen's (New York) : Куи́нс

Queensland : Кви́нсленд

Quellenforschung (lit.) : иссле́дование
  первоисто́чников

Quentin Durward (Scott) : «Кве́нтин До́рвард»

Quevedo, Francisco : Франси́ско Кеве́до-и-Вилье́гас

quid pro quo : возмеще́ние

Quiet American, The (Greene) : «Ти́хий америка́нец»

Quimper : Кемпе́р

Quinquagesima (eccles.) : сыропу́ст

quintet (mus.) : квинте́т

Quintilian : Марк Фа́бий Квинтилиа́н

Quirinus : Квири́н

quis custodiat ipsos custodies? : кто охраня́ет
  охрани́телей?

QUI S'EXCUSE S'ACCUSE

qui s'excuse s'accuse : кто опра́вдывается, тот себя́ и улича́ет

Quisling, Vidkun : Ви́дкун Кви́слинг

quixotic : донкихо́тский

Qumran : Кумра́н *see also* **Dead Sea Scrolls**

quodlibet (mus.) : кводли́бет

quondam : бы́вший

quorum : кво́рум

quo vadis? : куда́ идёшь?

Qur'an *see* **Koran**

R

Raabe, Wilhelm : Вильгéльм Рáабе
rabbi : раввúн
Rabbit Run (Updike) : «Крóлик, бегú»
Rabelais, François : Франсуá Раблé
Rachel (bibl.) : Рахúль
Racine, Jean : Жан Расúн
raconteur : расскáзчик
raconteuse : расскáзчица
Radcliffe Library (Oxford) : библиотéка Рэдклиффа
Radcliffe, Ann : Áнна Рáдклиф
'Radetzky' March (J. Strauss) : «Радéцкий» марш
Raft of the Medusa, The (Géricault) : «Плот Медýзы»
Ragnarok (myth.) : рагнарёк
ragtime : регтáйм
Rahmenerzählung (lit.) : обрамлÿюшее повествовáние
Rainbow, The (Lawrence) : «Рáдуга»/«Семьÿ Брэнгуэ́нов»
Rain, Steam and Speed (Turner) : «Дождь, пар и скóрость»
Raising of Lazarus, The (Piombo) : «Воскрешéние Лáзаря»
raison d'être : разýмное основáние
raisonneur : резонёр
raj : радж
raja : рáджа
Rake's Progress, The (Hogarth) : «Карьéра мóта»
Raleigh (US) : Рóли
Raleigh, Walter : Уóлтер Рéйли/Рэ́ли/Рóли
rallentando (mus.) : замедлÿя
Ramadan (relig.) : Рамазáн/Рамадáн
Rambler, The : «Рассéянный»
Rameau, Jean Philippe : Жан Филúпп Рамó

RAMESES

Rameses : Рамсéс

ranchero : ранчéро

Rapallo, Treaty of : Рапáлльский договóр

Rape of Europa, The (Titian) : «Похищéние Эврóпы»

Rape of the Lock, The (Pope) : «Похищéние лóкона»

Raphael : Рафаэ́ль (Раффаэ́ло Сáнти)

rappel : спуск по верёвке

rapport : взаимопонимáние

rapprochement : сближéние

rara avis : чýдо

Rasselas (Johnson) : «Расселас, принц Абиссúнский»

Rastafarian : растафáри; относя́щийся к кýльту растафáри

ratafia : домáшняя настóйка

ratatouille (cul.) : рататýй

Rathaus : рáтуша

Räuber, Die (Schiller) : «Разбóйники»

Ravel, Maurice : Мóрис Равéль

Reagan, Ronald : Рóнальд Рéйган

Realms of Being (Santayana) : «Цáрство бытия́»

Realpolitik : реалистúческая полúтика

Realschule : реáльное учúлище

Réaumur scale : шкалá Реомю́ра

Rebecca (bibl.) : Ревéкка

Rebelión de las masas, La (Ortega y Gasset) : «Восстáние масс»

réchauffé : затáсканный

recherché : изы́сканный (elegant, refined); рéдкостный (rare)

recitando (mus.) : декламúруя

recitativo (mus.) : речитатúв

Reclining Nude (Modigliani) : «Большáя обнажённая»

Reconquista (hist.) : Реконкúста

reculer pour mieux sauter : взять разгóн, чтóбы лýчше пры́гнуть

Red and the Black, The (Stendhal) see *Rouge et le Noir, Le*

168

Red and the Green, The (Murdoch) : «Алое и зелёное»

Red Badge of Courage, The (Crane) : «Алый знак доблести»

Redgauntlet (Scott) : «Редгонтлет»/«Квитанция после смерти»

Red Guards (hist.) : красные охранники

Red Sea (bibl.) : Чёрмное море

red shift (astron.) : красное смещение

Redshirts (hist.) : «красные рубашки»/ гарибальдийцы

reductio ad absurdum : сведение к абсурду/ доведение до нелепости

Red Vineyard at Arles (Van Gogh) : «Красные виноградники в Арле»

Reformation (hist.) : Реформация

regardant (herald.) : смотрящий назад

Regency (archit., hist.) : в стиле эпохи Регентства

Regents of the Old Men's Alms House (Hals) : «Регенты приюта для престарелых»

Regulus (astron.) : Регул

Rehoboam (bibl.) : Ровоам

Reichstag (hist.) : рейхстаг

Reichswehr (hist.) : рейхсвер

Reign of Terror (hist.) : эпоха Террора якобинской диктатуры

Reineke Fuchs (Goethe) : «Рейнеке-Лис»

Reisebilder (Heine) : «Путевые картины»

relativity, general theory of : общая теория относительности

relativity, special theory of : специальная теория относительности

religioso (mus.) : религиозно

Remarque, Erich Maria : Эрих Мария Ремарк

Rembrandt : Рембрандт ван Рейн

Remedia Amoris (Ovid) : «Средства от любви»

Renaissance : Возрождение

Renate (Storm) : «Рената»

RENDER UNTO CAESAR

render unto Caesar that which is Caesar's :
«Ке́сареву Ке́сарево»

rendezvous : рандеву́

René (Chateaubriand) : «Рене́, и́ли После́дствия
страсте́й»

Rennes : Ренн

Renoir, Pierre : Пьер Огю́ст Ренуа́р

rentier : рантье́

repêchage (sport) : вытя́гивание

répétiteur (mus.) : репети́тор

reprise (mus.) : репри́за

Republican Party : Республика́нская па́ртия

Republic, The (Plato) : «Госуда́рство»

Requiem aeternam : Поко́й ве́чный

Resistance (hist.) : движе́ние Сопротивле́ния

Respighi, Ottorino : Отторри́но Респи́ги

Restoration (hist.) : Реставра́ция

résumé : резюме́

retoucheur (art) : ретушёр

Return of the King, The (Tolkien) : «Возвраще́ние
короля́»

Return of the Native, The (Hardy) : «Возвраще́ние на
ро́дину»

Return of the Prodigal Son, The (Rembrandt) :
«Возвраще́ние блу́дного сы́на»

Reuben (bibl.) : Руви́м

Reuters : Ре́йтерс

Rêve de d'Alembert, Le (Diderot) : «Сон д'Алембе́ра»

reveille : подъём

Revelation, Book of : «Открове́ние Иоа́нна
Богосло́ва»

Revolutionary Étude (Chopin) : «Революцио́нный
этю́д»

Reykjavik : Рейкья́вик

Reynolds, Joshua : Джо́шуа Ре́йнолдс

Rhea (myth.) : Ре́я

Rhein, River : Рейн

Rheingold, Das (Wagner) : «Зо́лото Ре́йна»

Rheinland-Pfalz : Рейнланд-Пфальц

Rhine (wine) : рейнвейн

Rhine, Confederation of the (hist.) : Рейнский союз

Rhineland : Рейнская область

Rhode Island : Род-Айленд

Rhodes, Cecil : Сесил Родс

Rhodos : Родос

Rhône, River : Рон

Rhône Culture (prehist.) : ронская культура

Ribera, Jusepe de : Хусепе де Рибера

ricercar (mus.) : ричеркар

Richard II (Shakespeare) : «Ричард II»

Richard III (Shakespeare) : «Ричард III»

Richard the Lionheart : Ричард I Львиное Сердце

Richardson, Samuel : Сэмюэл Ричардсон

Richelieu, Cardinal : Кардинал Ришелье

Richter, Johann Paul *see* **Jean Paul**

Richter scale : шкала Рихтера

Richthofen, Baron von : барон фон Рихтофен

Riders to the Sea (Synge) : «Скачущие к морю»

Riemannian geometry : геометрия Римана

Rienzi (Wagner) : «Риенци»

Riesling (vin.) : рислинг

rigaudon (rigadoon) (dance) : ригодон

Rigel (astron.) : Ригель

Rigoletto (Verdi) : «Риголетто»

rigor mortis : трупное окоченение

Rijksmuseum (Amsterdam) : Рейксмюсеум

Riksdag (Swedish Parliament) : Риксдаг

Riksmål (ling.) : риксмол

Rilke, Reiner Maria : Райнер Мария Рильке

Rimbaud, Arthur : Артур Рембо

Rime of the Ancient Mariner, The (Coleridge) see
Ancient Mariner, Rime of the

Ring and the Book, The (Browning) : «Кольцо и
книга»

Ring des Nibelungen, Der (Wagner) : «Кольцо
Нибелунга»

Ring Round the Moon (Anouilh, Christopher Fry) see
 Invitation au Château, L'

Rio de Janeiro : Рио-де-Жанейро

ripieno (mus.) : рипиено

Rip Van Winkle : Рип Ван Винкль

Rise and Fall of the City of Mahagonny (Brecht, Weill)
 see Aufstieg und Fall der Stadt Mahagonny, Der

Risorgimento (hist.) : Рисоргименто

risotto (cul.) : ризотто

risqué : рискованный

rissole (cul.) : слоёный пирожок

ritardando (mus.) : ритардандо

ritenuto (mus.) : ритенуто

Rite of Spring, The (Stravinsky) : «Весна священная»

ritornello (mus.) : ритурнель (f.)

Rivals, The (Sheridan) : «Соперники»

Rivera, Diego : Диего Ривера

Riviera : Ривьера/Лазурный берег

RNA (ribonucleic acid) : РНК (рибонуклеиновая
 кислота)

Roads to Freedom, The (Sartre) see *Chemins de la
 Liberté, Les*

Road to Wigan Pier , The (Orwell) : «Дорога в
 Уайган»

Robbe-Grillet, Alain : Ален Роб-Грийе

Robert the Bruce : Роберт Брюс

Robespierre : Робеспьер

Robinson Crusoe (Defoe) : «Робинзон Крузо»

Rob Roy (Scott) : «Роб Рой»

Rockefeller Centre (New York) : Рокефеллеровский
 центр

Rockies : Скалистые горы

rococo : рококо; в стиле рококо

rodeo : родео

Roderick Hudson (James) : «Родрик Хадсон»

Roderick Random (Smollett) : «Приключения
 Родрика Рэндома»

Rodin, Auguste : Огюст Роден

rodomontade : фанфаро́нство

roentgen : рентге́н

Rogation (eccles.) : проце́ссия и моле́бен об урожа́е

Roi d'Ys, Le (Lalo) : «Коро́ль го́рода Ис»

roi soleil (hist.) : «коро́ль-со́лнце»

Rois Fainéants (hist.) : лени́вые короли́

Rokeby Venus (Velásquez) see Cupid and Venus

Romains, Jules : Жюль Роме́н

roman-à-clef : зашифро́ванный рома́н/рома́н-
-аллего́рия

roman-à-thèse : иллюстрати́вный рома́н

Roman Catholic Church : Ри́мская католи́ческая
  це́рковь

Romancero gitano (Lorca) : «Цыга́нский романсе́ро»

Roman de la Rose : «Рома́н о ро́зе»

roman-feuilleton : роман с продолже́нием (в
  журна́ле)

roman—fleuve : многото́мный роман/ «роман-река́»

roman-policier : детекти́вный рома́н

Romans, Epistle to the (bibl.) : «Посла́ние к
  ри́млянам»

Romansh (ling.) : реторома́нский (язы́к)

Romany : цыга́н; цыга́нский

romanza (mus.) : рома́нс

Rome, Treaty of : Ри́мский догово́р

Romeo and Juliet (Shakespeare) : «Ро́мео и
  Джулье́тта»

Romeo und Julia auf dem Dorfe (Keller) : «Се́льские
  Ро́мео и Ю́лия»

Romersholm (Ibsen) : «Ро́мерсхольм»

Römische Elegien (Goethe) : «Ри́мские эле́гии»

Rommel, Erwin : Э́рвин Ро́ммель

Romney, George : Джордж Ро́мни

Romulus and Remus : Ро́мул и Рем

Roncevalles : Ронсева́ль

rondeau (lit.) : рондо́

rondo (mus.) : ро́ндо

Room with a View, A (Forster) : «Ко́мната с ви́дом»

Roosevelt, Franklin D. : Фра́нклин Д. Ру́звельт

Roosevelt, Theodore : Те́одор Ру́звельт

Rorschach test (psych.) : о́пыт Рорша́ха

Rosenkavalier, Der (R. Strauss) : «Кавале́р роз»

Roses, Wars of the : Война́ А́лой и Бе́лой роз

Rosetta Stone : Розе́ттский ка́мень

Rossetti, Dante Gabriel : Да́нте Габрие́л Россе́тти

Rossetti, Gabriele : Габрие́ле Россе́тти

Rosicrucians : розенкре́йцерство

Rossini, Gioacchino : Джоакки́но Росси́ни

Rostand, Edmond : Эдмо́н Роста́н

Rothschild family : Ро́тшильды

rotisserie : ла́вка торго́вца жа́реным мя́сом

rotten boroughs (hist.) : «гнилы́е месте́чки»

Roualt, Georges : Жорж Руо́

roué : развра́тник

Rouen : Руа́н

Rouen Cathedral (Monet) : «Руа́нский собо́р»

Rouge et le Noir, Le (Stendhal) : «Кра́сное и чёрное»

roulade (mus.) : рула́да

Roundheads (hist.) : «круглоголо́вые»

Round the World in Eighty Days (Verne) : «Вокру́г
све́та в 80 дней»

Rousseau, Henri (Le Douanier) : Анри́ Руссо́
(Тамо́женник)

Rousseau, Jean Jacques : Жан Жак Руссо́

Roussillon (vin.) : руссильо́н

routier : придоро́жный рестора́н

Royal Albert Hall (London) : «Ро́йял А́льберт-холл»

Royal Ballet (London) : «Ро́йял ба́лле»

Royal Canadian Mounted Police : Короле́вская
кана́дская ко́нная поли́ция

Royal Court Theatre (London) : «Ро́йял Ко́рт»

Royal Festival Hall (London) : «Ро́йял фе́стивал-
-холл»

Royal Opera House (London) : Короле́вская о́пера

Royal Shakespeare Theatre (Stratford) : Короле́в-
вский шекспи́ровский теа́тр

Royal Society (UK) : Лóндонское королéвское óбщество

Rubáiyát : рубаи́/четверости́шие

Rubáiyát of Omar Khayyam, The (Fitzgerald) : «Рубайáт Омáра Хайя́ма»

rubato (mus.) : рубáто

Rubens, Peter Paul : Пи́тер Пáуль Рýбенс

Rubicon, River : Рубикóн

Rückert, Friedrich : Фри́дрих Рю́ккерт

Rudolf of Habsburg : Рудóльф I

Ruhrgebiet : Рýрская óбласть

Ruiz (Quevedo) : «Хуáн Руи́с, протопресви́тер»

rumba : рýмба

Rumpelstiltskin : Рýмпельштильцхен

Rump Parliament (hist.) : «охвóстье» Дóлгого парлáмента

Runyon, Damon : Дáмон Руньóн

rupee : рýпия

ruse de guerre : воéнная хи́трость

Ruskin, John : Джон Рéскин

Russell, Bertrand : Бéртран Рáссел

Ruth (bibl.) : «Кни́га Руфь»

Rutherford, Ernest : Э́рнест Рéзерфорд

Ruy Blas (Hugo) : «Рюй Блаз»

Ruysdael, Jakob van : Я́коб ван Рéйсдал

Rydberg constant (sci.) : постоя́нная Ри́дберга

S

SA *(Sturmabteilung)* **(nat. soc.)** : штурмовы́е
отря́ды (СА)

Saarbrücken : Саарбрю́ккен

Saarland : Са́арская о́бласть

Sabaoth : Савао́ф

Sabines (hist.) : Саби́ны/сабиня́не

Sabine Women, The (David) : «Сабиня́нки»

Sachsen *see* Saxony

sacré bleu! : чёрт возьми́!

Sacré Coeur (Paris) : Собо́р Сакре-Кёр

Sacred and Profane Love (Titian) : «Любо́вь земна́я и
небе́сная»

Sadam Hussein : Сада́м Хусе́йн

Sadat, Anwar : А́нвар Сада́т

Sadducees (bibl.) : саддуке́и

Sade, Marquis de : марки́з де Сад

Sadlers Wells (London) : Сэ́длерс-Уэ́ллс

Sagittarius (zod.) : Стреле́ц

sahib : сахи́б/саги́б

Saigon : Сайго́н

St Basil's Cathedral (Moscow) : Храм Васи́лия
Блаже́нного

St Elmo's fire : огни́ Эльма

Saint Étienne : Сент Этье́н

Saint-Exupéry, Antoine de : Антуа́н де Сент-
-Экзюпери́

St Helena : о́стров св. Еле́ны

St Isaac's Cathedral (St Petersburg) : Исаа́киевский
собо́р

St Jerome in his Study (Dürer) : «св. Иерони́м»

Saint Joan (Shaw) : «Свята́я Иоа́нна»

St John Passion (J.S. Bach) : «Стра́сти по Иоа́нну»

St John's (Canada) : Сент-Джонс

Saint-Just : Сен-Жюст

St Louis (US) : Сент-Лу́ис

St Matthew Passion (J.S. Bach) : «Стра́сти по Матфе́ю»

St Paul (US) : Сент-Пол

St Paul's Cathedral (London) : собор св. Па́вла

Saint-Saëns, Charles Camille : Шарль Ками́ль Сен-Санс

Saint-Simon : Сен-Симо́н

Sainte-Beuve, Charles : Шарль Огюсте́н Сент-Бёф

sake : саке́

Saladin : Салади́н/Сала́х ад-Ди́н

Salamanca : Салама́нка

Salamis : Салами́н

Salammbô (Flaubert) : «Саламбо́»

Salazar, António de : Анто́ниу ди Салаза́р

Salem : Се́йлем

Salic law (hist.) : Сали́ческий зако́н

Salinger, J.D. : Джеро́м Де́йвид Сэ́линджер

Salisbury Cathedral (Constable) : «Собо́р в Со́лсбери с реки́»

Sallust : Гай Саллю́стий Крисп

Salome (R. Strauss) : «Саломе́я»

Salpêtrière, La (Paris) : Сальпетрие́р

SALT (Strategic Arms Limitation Talks) : Перегово́ры по ограниче́нию стратеги́ческих наступа́тельных вооруже́ний

Salt Lake City (US) : Солт-Лейк-Си́ти

Salt Water Ballads (Masefield) : «Морски́е пе́сни»

saltarello (mus.) : сальтаре́лла

Salvation Army : А́рмия спасе́ния

Salzburg : За́льцбург

Salzburger grosse Welttheater : За́льцбургский большо́й теа́тр жи́зни

Samaritan (bibl.) : самаря́нин *see also* **Good Samaritan**

Sampling-Officers of the Cloth-Makers' Guild, The/The Syndics (Rembrandt) : «Старе́йшины суко́нного це́ха»/«Си́ндики»

SAMSON

Samson (bibl.) : Самсо́н

Samson Agonistes (Milton) : «Самсо́н-боре́ц»

Samson et Dalila (Saint-Saëns) : «Самсо́н и Дали́ла»

Samuel (bibl.) : Самуи́л

Samuel I (bibl.) : «Пе́рвая кни́га Царств»

Samuel II (bibl.) : «Втора́я кни́га Царств»

samurai : самура́й

San Andreas Fault (geol.) : сдвиг Сан Андре́ас

Sancho Panza : Са́нчо Па́нсо

Sanctuary (Faulkner) : «Святи́лище»

Sanctus : Са́нктус

Sand, George : Жорж Санд (Авро́ра Дюпе́н/ Дюдева́н)

San Diego : Сан-Дие́го

San Francisco : Сан-Франци́ско

Sang des autres (de Beauvoir) : «Чужа́я кровь»

sang-froid : хладнокро́вие

sangria (vin.) : сангри́я

Sanhedrin : синедрио́н

sansculotte : санкюло́т

sans-culottide (hist.) : [дополни́тельный день францу́зского революцио́нного календаря́]

Sanskrit : Санскри́т

sans peur et sans reproche : «бесстра́шный и безупре́чный»

Santa Cruz de Tenerife : Са́нта-Кру́с-де-Тенери́фе

Santa Fe : Са́нта-Фе́

Santander : Сантанде́р

Santayana, George : Джордж Сантая́на

Santiago : Сантья́го

Saône, River : Со́на

Sapir—Whorf hypothesis (ling.) : гипоте́за Се́пира- -У́орфа

Sapphic ode : сапфи́ческая строфа́

Sappho : Сапфо́

saraband : сараба́нда

Saracen : сараци́н

Sarai/Sarah (bibl.) : Са́ра/Са́рра

Sarajevo : Сара́ево
Sarawak : Сарава́к
Sardinia : Сарди́ния
Sargasso Sea : Сарга́ссово мо́ре
Sargent, John Singer : Джон Си́нгер Са́рджент
Saroyan, William : Уи́льям Саро́ян
Sartor Resartus (Carlyle) : «Са́ртор Реса́ртус»
Sartre, Jean-Paul : Жан Поль Сартр
Saskatchewan : Саска́чеван
Satan : сатана́
satire bernesque (lit.) : шутли́вая сати́ра
Saturn (astron., myth.) : Сату́рн
Saturn Devouring One of His Children (Goya) :
  «Сату́рн»
Saturnalia : сатурна́лии
satyr : сати́р
sauce hollandaise : соу́с из яи́чных желтко́в и ма́сла
  с лимо́нным со́ком
sauerkraut : ки́слая капу́ста
Saul (Handel) : Савл
Saul of Tarsus (bibl.) : Савл Тарсяни́н
Saussure, Ferdinand de : Фердина́нд де Соссю́р
sauté (cul.) : жа́реный
Sauterne (vin.) : соте́рн
sauve qui peut! : «спаса́йся кто мо́жет!»
sauvignon (vin.) : совиньо́н
savant(e) : учёный
savoir-faire : уме́ние
Savonarola, Girolamo : Джироламо Савонаро́ла
Savoy : Саво́йя
Saxons (hist.) : са́ксы
Saxony : Саксо́ния
Scala di seta, La (Rossini) : «Шёлковая ле́стница»
scald (lit.) *see* skald
scampi (cul.) : ска́мпи/креве́тки
Scarlatti, Alessandro : Алесса́ндро Скарла́тти
Scarlatti, Domenico : Доме́нико Скарла́тти
schadenfreude : злора́дство

SCHEHERAZADE

Scheherazade : Шехереза́да

Schelling, Friedrich : Фри́дрих Шёллинг

scherzo (mus.) : ске́рцо

Schiele, Egon : Эго́н Ши́ле

Schiller, Friedrich : Фри́дрих Ши́ллер

schilling (Aust.) : ши́ллинг

Schimmelreiter, Der (Storm) : «Вса́дник на бе́лом коне́»

Schlacht in Loener Bruch (Droste-Hülshoff) : «Би́тва Ле́нской расще́лине»

Schlafwandler, Die (Broch) : «Луна́тики»

Schlegel, Friedrich : Фри́дрих Шле́гель

schleppend (mus.) : затя́жно

Schleswig-Holstein : Шле́звиг-Гольште́йн

Schlieffenplan (hist.) : План Шли́фена

Schliemann, Heinrich : Ге́нрих Шли́ман

Schloß, Das (Kafka) : «За́мок»

schmaltz : сентимента́льщина

Schmidt, Helmut : Ге́льмут Шмидт

Schmidt telescope : телеско́п Шми́дта

schnapps : шнапс

schnauzer : жесткошёрст(н)ый пи́нчер

schnitzel : шни́цель (m.)

Schnitzler, Arthur : Арту́р Шни́тцлер

Schoenberg, Arnold : Арнольд Шёнберг

Schönbrunn (Vienna) : дворе́ц Шёнбрунн

schöne Müllerin, Die (Schubert) : «Прекра́сная ме́льничиха»

School for Scandal, The (Sheridan) : «Шко́ла злосло́вия»

School of Athens (Raphael) : «Афи́нская шко́ла»

Schopenhauer, Arthur : Арту́р Шопенга́уэр

Schrödinger wave equation (sci.) : уравне́ние Шрёдингера

Schubert, Franz : Франц Шу́берт

Schumacher, Kurt : Курт Шу́махер

Schumann, Robert : Ро́берт Шу́ман

Schuschnigg, Kurt von : Курт фон Шу́шниг

Schutzstaffel **(nat. soc.)** *see* **SS**

schwärmerei : увлечéние

schwarze Spinne, Die (Gotthelf) : «Чёрный пау́к»

Schwarzschild radius (sci.) : ра́диус сфéры Шва́рцшильда

Schwarzwald : Шва́рцвальд

schweigsame Frau, die (R. Strauss) : «Молчали́вая жéнщина»

Schweitzer, Albert : Альбéрт Швéйцер

Schwerin : Швéрин

Science Museum (London) : Нау́чный музéй

scintillante (mus.) : блестя́ще

Scipio Africanus : Сципио́н Африка́нский

Sciron (myth.) : Скиро́н

Scorpio (zod.) : Скорпио́н

Scott, Walter : Ва́льтер Скотт

Scream, The (Munch) : «Крик»

scribes (bibl.) : кни́жники

Scrooge : скря́га Скрудж

Scylla and Charybdis : Сци́лла и Хари́бда

Scythians : ски́фы

SD *(Sicherheitdienst)* **(nat. soc.)** : слу́жба безопа́сности

SDI (Strategic Defence Initiative) : Инициати́ва по стратеги́ческой оборо́не

Sea of Galilee (bibl.) : мо́ре Галилéйское

Seasons, The (Haydn) : «Временá го́да»

SEATO (South East Asia Treaty Organisation) : СЕАТО (Организа́ция догово́ра Юго-Восто́чной А́зии

Seattle : Сиэ́тл

Sea-Wolf, The (London) : «Морско́й волк»

Sebastiano del Piombo : Себастья́но дель Пьо́мбо

Second Coming : Второ́е пришéствие Христа́

Second Mrs Tanqueray, The (Pinero) : «Втора́я ми́ссис Тéнкерей»

Secret of Edwin Drood, The (Dickens) : «Тáйна Э́двина Дру́да»

see Naples and die : «посмотри́ на Неа́поль и мо́жешь умере́ть»

Seghers, Hercules : Геркю́лес Се́герс

Segovia : Сего́вия

seigneur : сенье́р

Seilbahn : кана́тная доро́га

Seine, River : Се́на

Sein und Zeit (Heidegger) : «Бытие́ и вре́мя»

Sei personaggi in cerca d'autore (Pirandello) : «Шесть персона́жей в по́исках а́втора»

Sejm (Polish Parliament) : Сейм

Seleucid dynasty (hist.) : Сельджуки́ды

Seljuks (hist.) : Сельджу́ки

Semele : Семе́ла

semibreve (mus.) : по́лная но́та

sémillon (vin.) : семильо́н

semiquaver (mus.) : шестна́дцатая но́та

Semiramide (Rossini) : «Семирами́да»

Semiramis : Семирами́да

Semitic : семи́тский

semper fidelis : «всегда́ ве́рный»

Senate : сена́т

Seneca : Лу́ций Анне́й Се́нека

Sennacherib : Сеннахири́м

se non è vero, è ben trovato : е́сли э́то и не пра́вда, то хорошо́ приду́мано

Señor : сенье́р

Sense and Sensibility (Austen) : «Ра́зум и чувстви́тельность»

Sentimental Journey through France and Italy, A (Sterne) : «Сентимента́льное путеше́ствие по Фра́нции и Ита́лии»

Seoul : Сеу́л

Sephardim (hist.) : сефа́рды

sepoy : сипа́й

Septimus Severus : Септи́мий Севе́р

Septuagesima (eccles.) : пе́рвое из трёх воскресе́ний до Вели́кого Поста́

Seraglio, Il (Mozart) see Entführung aus dem Serail, Die

seraphim : серафи́м

Serapionsbrüder, Die (Hoffmann) : «Серапио́новы бра́тья»

seriatim : по пу́нктам

Sermon on the Mount (bibl.) : Нагóрная Прóповедь

Sessions, Roger : Рóджер Сешнс

Seth (bibl.) : Сиф

Seurat, Georges : Жорж Сёра

Seven against Thebes (Aeschylus) : «Сéмеро прóтив Фив»

Seven Lamps of Architecture, The (Ruskin) : «Семь свéточей архитекту́ры»

Seven Pillars of Wisdom (T.E. Lawrence) : «Семь столпóв му́дрости»

Seventh Day Adventists : Цéрковь Адвенти́стов Седьмóго Дня

Seven Wonders of the World : Семь чудéс свéта
  The Colossus of Rhodes : Колóсс родóсский
  The Hanging Gardens of Babylon : Вися́чие сады́ в Вавилóне
  The Pharos of Alexandria : Маяк в Алексáндрии
  The Pyramids of Egypt : Еги́петские пирами́ды
  The Statue of Jupiter by Phidias : Стату́я Зéвса
  The Temple of Diana at Ephesus : Храм Артеми́ды в Эфéсе
  The Tomb of Mausolus : Гробни́ца Мавзóла

Seven Years War : семилéтняя войнá

Severed Head, A (Murdoch) : «Отру́бленная головá»

Severn, River : Сéверн

Severus Alexander : Алексáндр Севéр

Sévigné, Madame de : Мадам де Севиньé

Seville : Севи́лья

Sèvres porcelain : сéрвский фарфóр

Sexagesima (eccles.) : мясопу́ст

sext (eccles.) : шестóй час

Seyfert galaxies (astron.) : галáктики Сéйферта

SFORZANDO

sforzando (mus.) : сфорцáндо

sfumato (art) : сфумáто

Shadrach, Meshach and Abednego (bibl.) : Седрáх, Мисáх и Авденáго

Shakers (relig.) : шéйкеры

Shakespeare, William : Уи́льям Шекспи́р

Shams ud-din Muhammad *see* **Hafiz**

Shang dynasty : Инь (f.)/Шан

Shanghai : Шанхáй

Shape of Things to Come, The (Wells) : «О́блик грядýщего»

shari'ah (relig.) : шариáт

Shaw, George Bernard : Джордж Бéрнард Шóу

Sheba, Queen of : цари́ца Сáвская

sheikh : шейх

shekel : шéкель/си́кель (m.)

Shelley, Mary : Мэ́ри Уóлстенкрафт Шéлли

Shelley, Percy Bysshe : Пéрси Биш Шелли

Shem, Ham and Japhet (bibl.) : Сим, Хам и Иафéт

Sheridan, Richard : Ри́чард Бри́нсли Шéридан

Sherpa : шéрпа

She Stoops to Conquer (Goldsmith) : «Ночь оши́бок, и́ли Униже́ние пáче гóрдости»

Shiah : шии́зм

shibboleth : шиб(б)олéт

Shiites : шии́ты

Shiloh (bibl.) : Силóм

Shintoism : синтои́зм

Shirley (Charlotte Brontë) : «Шéрли»

shish kebab : шашлы́к

Shiva/Siva : Ши́ва

shogun (Jap.) : сёгýн

Shortest Way with the Dissenters, The (Defoe) : «Кратчáйший путь распрáвы с диссéнтерами»

Shoshone : шошóны

Shrove Tuesday : послéдний день Мáсленицы

SI (Système International d'Unités) : Междунарóдная систéма едини́ц

Sibelius, Jean : Ян Сибе́лиус

Sibylline books : Сиви́ллины кни́ги

Sibyls (myth.) : Сиви́ллы

sic : так!

Sicherheitsdienst **(nat. soc.)** *see* **SD**

Sicilia : Сици́лия

Sicilian octave (mus.) : сицилиа́на

Sicilian Vespers, The (Verdi) *see* **Vespri Siciliani, I**

sic transit gloria mundi : «так прохо́дит земна́я сла́ва»

Sidon : Сидо́н

Siege of Corinth, The (Rossini) : «Оса́да Кори́нфа»

Siegfried (Wagner) : Зи́гфрид

Siegfried Line (hist.) : ли́ния Зи́гфрида

Sieg Heil! : «Sieg Heil!»/«да здра́вствует побе́да!»

sierra : сье́рра

Sierra Nevada : Сье́рра-Нева́да

siesta : сие́ста/полу́денный о́тдых

signified (ling.) : означа́емый

signifier (ling.) : означа́ющий

Sign of Four, The (Conan Doyle) : «Знак четырёх»

Signora : синьо́ра

Signore : синьо́р

Signorina : ба́рышня

Sigurd (myth.) : Си́гурд

Sikh : сикх; си́кхский

Sikhism : сикхи́зм

si la jeunesse savait, si la vieillesse pouvait : «ка́бы мо́лодость да зна́ла, ка́бы ста́рость да могла́»

Silas (bibl.) : Си́ла

Silas Marner (George Eliot) : «Са́йлес Ма́рнер»

Silken Ladder, The (Rossini) *see* **Scala di seta, La**

Silurian (geol.) : силури́йский перио́д

Simeon (bibl.) : Симео́н

Simon of Cyrene (Bibl.) : кирине́янин, по и́мени Симо́н

Simon the Canaanite/Zelotes *see* **Disciples, the Twelve**

SIMON

Simon, who is called Peter *see* **Disciples, the Twelve**

Simon Boccanegra (Verdi) : «Симо́н Бокканéгра»

Simplicissimus : «Симплици́ссимус»

Sinai, Mount : гора́ Сина́й

sinanthropus (anthrop.) : сина́нтроп *see also* **Peking Man**

Sindbad : Синдба́д

sine die : на неопределённый срок/без указа́ния дня

sine qua non : непремéнное усло́вие

Sinn Fein : Шин фéйн

Sioux : сиу́

Sir Charles Grandison (Richardson) : «Исто́рия сэ́ра Ча́рльза Гра́ндисона»

Sirens (myth.) : сирéны

Sirius (astron.) : Си́риус

sirocco (meteor.) : сиро́кко

SIS (Secret Intelligence Service) : Та́йная развéдывательная слу́жба

Sister Carrie (Dreiser) : «Сестра́ Кéрри»

Sistine Chapel : Сиксти́нская капéлла

Sistine Madonna (Raphael) : «Сиксти́нская мадо́нна»

Sisyphean task : Сизи́фов труд

Sisyphus (myth.) : Сизи́ф

Six Characters in Search of an Author (Pirandello) *see* *Sei personaggi in cerca d'autore*

skald (lit.) : скальд

Sketch Book, The (Irving) : «Кни́га эски́зов»

Sketches by Boz (Dickens) : «О́черки Бо́за»

Skinner box (psych.) : ски́ннеровский я́щик

Skylab : «Ска́йлеб»

Slaughter of the Innocents (Tintoretto) : «Избиéние младéнцев»

Slavophiles (hist.) : славянофи́лы

Sleeper Awakes, The (Wells) : «Когда́ спя́щий проснётся»

Sleipnir (myth.) : Слéйпнир

Sluter, Claus : Кла́ус Слю́тер

Smetana, Bedrich : Бéдржих Смéтана

186

Smith, Adam : А́дам Смит

Smith, Joseph : Ио́зеф Смит

Smithsonian Institute : Смитсо́новский институ́т

Smollett, Tobias : Тоба́йас Смо́ллетт

Smuts, Jan : Ян Смэтс

Snorri Sturluson : Сно́рри Сту́рлусон

Snow, C.P. : Чарльз Пе́рси Сно́у

snowman, abominable *see* **yeti**

Snow Queen, The (Andersen) : «Сне́жная короле́ва»

Snow White and the Seven Dwarves : «Белосне́жка и семь гно́мов»

Snowy River Project (Australia) : проэ́кт Сно́уи-
-Ри́вер

Soave (vin.) : соа́ве

sobriquet : кли́чка

Social Darwinism : социа́льный дарвини́зм

Society of Friends *see* **Quakers**

Society of Jesus *see* **Jesuits**

Socrates : Сокра́т

Socratic irony : сокра́това иро́ния

Sodom and Gomorrah : Содо́м и Гомо́рра

Sofia : Софи́я

Sohrab and Rustam (Arnold) : «Со́раб и Ру́стем»

soi-disant : так называ́емый

soigné : хо́леный

soirée : ве́чер

Solar System : Со́лнечная систе́ма

Soldier's Pay (Faulkner) : «Солда́тская награ́да»

solfeggio : сольфе́джио/сольфе́джо

solitaire : солитёр (diamond); солите́р (card game)

Solomon (bibl.) : Соломо́н

Somme, River : Со́мма

Somme, battle of the : сраже́ние на Со́мме

sommelier : слу́жащий рестора́на, ве́дающий
ви́нами

sonata : сона́та

Sonata de estío (Valle-Inclán) : «Сона́та ле́та»

Sonata de otoño (Valle-Inclán) : «Сона́та о́сени»

SONATINA

sonatina : сонатина

son et lumière : звук и свет

Sonette an Orpheus, Die (Rilke) : «Сонеты к Орфею»

Song of Roland see Chanson de Roland

Song of Solomon (bibl.) : «Книга Песни Песней Соломона»

Songs of Experience (Blake) : «Песни опыта»

Songs of Innocence (Blake) : «Песни невинности»

Songs Without Words (Mendelssohn) see Lieder ohne Worte

Sonnambula, La (Bellini) : «Сомнамбула»

Sons and Lovers (Lawrence) : «Сыновья и любовники»

Sons of Israel : Сыны Израилевы

Sophia : София

Sophocles : Софокл

sorbet : фруктовое мороженое

Sorbonne : Сорбонна

Sorcerer's Apprentice, The (Dukas) : «Ученик чародея»

sordino (mus.) : сурдина

Sorrows of Young Werther, The (Goethe) see Leiden des jungen Werthers, Die

sostenuto (mus.) : состенуто

sotto voce : вполголоса

soubrette (theatr.) : субретка

soufflé (cul.) : суфле

souffleur : суфлёр

souk : рынок на открытом воздухе

soupçon : капелька

South Africa, Republic of : Южно-Африканская республика

South Carolina : Южная Каролина

South Dakota : Южная Дакота

Southey, Robert : Роберт Саути

Soweto : Соуэто

spaghetti : спагетти

spaghetti western : итальянский вестерн

Spanish Succession, War of the : война за
  Испанское наследство
Spark, Muriel : Мюриэл Спарк
Sparta : Спарта *see also* **Lacedaemon**
Spartacus : Спартак
SPD (Sozialdemokratische Partei Deutschlands) :
  Социал-демократическая партия (Западной)
  Германии
Spectator, The : «Спектейтор»
Spengler, Oswald : Освальд Шпенглер
Spenser, Edmund : Эдмунд Спенсер
Spica (astron.) : Спика
Spiegel, Der : «Шпигель»
Spielraum (philos.) : свобода действий
Spinoza, Benedict : Бенедикт Спиноза
Spire, The (Golding) : «Шпиль»
spiritoso (mus.) : живо
Spiritualists : спиритисты
Spohr, Louis : Людвиг (Луи) Шпор
spondee (vers.) : спондей
SS *(Schützstaffel)* **(nat.soc.)** : эсэсовские отряды/
  эсэсовцы
Staatskapelle (Dresden) : Дрезденская
  государственная капелла
Stabat Mater : «Стабат Матер»
Stabat Mater dolorosa : «Мать скорбящая стояла»
staccato (mus.) : стаккато
Staël, Anne Louise Germaine, Madame de : Анна
  Луиза Жермена де Сталь
Stahlhelm (hist.) : Стальной шлем
Stanford University : Станфордский университет
Star Chamber (hist.) : Звёздная палата
Stations of the Cross : хождение по мукам
status quo : статус-кво/существующее положение
steady state (astron., sci.) : стационарное состояние
Steinbeck, John : Джон Стейнбек
Steiner, Rudolf : Рудольф Штейнер
Stendhal : Стендаль (Анри Мари Бейль)

STENTOR

Stentor : Сте́нтор

Stephen (bibl.) : Стефа́н

Steppenwolf (Hesse) : «Степно́й волк»

Stern : «Штерн»

Sterne, Lawrence : Ло́ренс Стерн

stet : оставить!

Stevenson, Robert Louis : Ро́берт Лью́ис Сти́венсон

Stifter, Adalbert : Адальбе́рт Шти́фтер

Stiller (Frisch) : «Шти́ллер»

Stimmen der Völker in Liedern (Herder) : «Голоса́ наро́дов в пе́снях»

Stine (Fontane) : «Сти́на»

Stockhausen, Karlheinz : Карлге́йнз Што́кхаузен

Stockholm : Стокго́льм

Stoicism : стоици́зм

Stokowski, Leopold : Леопо́льд Стоко́вский

Stonehenge : Стоунхе́ндж

Stone Mason's Yard (Canaletto) : «Двор каменотёса»

Storm and Stress *see* **Sturm und Drang**

Storm, Theodor : Теодо́р Шторм

Storting (Norwegian Parliament) : Сто́ртинг

Stowe, Harriet Beecher : Га́рриет Би́чер-Сто́у

Strabo : Страбо́н

Stradivari, Antonio : Анто́нио Страдива́ри

Stradivarius (stringed instrument) : страдива́риус/ страдива́рий

Strangers and Brothers (Snow) : «Чужи́е и бра́тья»

Strasb(o)urg : Стра́сбург

Strategic Arms Limitation Talks *see* **SALT**

Strategic Defence Initiative *see* **SDI**

Stratford-on-Avon : Стра́тфорд на Э́йвоне

stratocumulus (meteor.) : сло́йсто-кучевы́е облака́

stratus (meteor.) : сло́йстые облака́

Strauss, Johann : Иога́нн Штра́ус

Strauss, Richard : Ри́хард Штра́ус

Streetcar Named Desire, A (Tennessee Williams) : «Трамва́й «Жела́ние»

strepitoso (mus.) : бу́рно

stretto (mus.) : стре́тто

Strindberg, Johan August : Ю́хан А́вгуст
  Стри́ндберг

stringendo (mus.) : ускоря́я

string quartet : стру́нный кварте́т

string quintet : стру́нный квинте́т

string trio : стру́нное три́о

structuralism : структу́рная лингви́стика

strudel (cul.) : штру́дель (m.)

Stuart dynasty : дина́стия Стю́артов

stucco : штукату́рка под мра́мор

stuka (hist.) : пики́рующий бомбардиро́вщик

Stunden-Buch, Das (Rilke) : «Часосло́в»

Sturluson see Snorri Sturluson

Sturmabteilung (nat. soc.) see SA

Sturm und Drang (lit.) : «бу́ря и на́тиск»

Stuttgart : Шту́тгарт

Stygian : стиги́йский

style indirect libre : несо́бственно-пряма́я речь

Styron, William : Уи́льям Ста́йрон

Styx, River (myth.) : Стикс

subahdar : субада́р

subdominant (mus.) : субдомина́нта

sub judice : [тяжба] всё ещё не решена́

submediant (mus.) : субмедиа́нта

sub specie eternitatis : с то́чки зре́ния ве́чности

succès fou : бе́шеный успе́х

Such Darling Dodos (Wilson) : «Миле́йшие До́до»

Süddeutsche Zeitung : «Зю́ддойче ца́йтунг»

Sudetenland : Суде́тская о́бласть

Suë, Eugène : Евге́ний Сю

Suetonius : Гай Тра́нквилл Свето́ний

Suevi (hist.) : све́вы

Suez Canal : Суэ́цкий кана́л

Sufi : суфи́сты

Sufism : суфи́зм

suggestio falsi : непряма́я ложь

Suharto : Суха́рто

SUI GENERIS

sui generis : в своём ро́де

Suleiman the Magnificent : Сулейма́н
Великоле́пный

Sullivan, Arthur *see* **Gilbert and Sullivan**

Sully Prudhomme, René : Рене́ Сюлли́-Прюдо́м

sultan : султа́н

Sumer : Шуме́р

Sumerians : шуме́ры

Summa contra Gentiles (Aquinas) : «Су́мма про́тив
язы́чников»

Summa Theologiae (Aquinas) : «Су́мма теоло́гии»

summum bonum : велича́йшее бла́го

Sunday Express : «Са́нди экспре́сс»

Sunflowers (Van Gogh) : «Подсо́лнечники»

Sung dynasty : Сун

Sunni : сунни́зм/сунни́ты

Sun Yat-sen : Сунь Ят-се́н

super-ego : сверх-я́

Superior, Lake : о́зеро Ве́рхнее

supernova (astron.) : сверхно́вая звезда́

Suppliants, The (Aeschylus) : «Проси́тельницы»

Sûreté : «Сюрте́ женера́ль»

surrealism : сюрреали́зм

Surrender of Breda, The (Velázquez) : «Сда́ча Бре́ды»

sursum corda : горе́ се́рдца!

survival of the fittest : выжива́ние наибо́лее
приспосо́бленных

sutra (relig.) : су́тра

Svevo, Italo : И́тало Све́во

Swan Lake (Tchaikovsky) : «Лебеди́ное о́зеро»

Swan of Tuonela, The (Sibelius) : «Туоне́льский
ле́бедь»

Swan Song (Galsworthy) : «Лебеди́ная песнь»

swastika : сва́стика

Swedenborg, Emanuel : Эммануэ́ль Сведенбо́рг

Swift, Jonathan : Джо́натан Свифт

Swinburne, Algernon : А́лджернон Чарльз
Су́инберн

Sydney : Сидней

Symphony of a Thousand (No. 8), (Mahler) :
Симфония тысячи участников»

synagogue : синагога

synecdoche (lit.) : синекдоха

Synge, J.M. : Джон Миллингтон Синг

Synoptic Gospels : синоптическое евангелие

Syracuse : Сиракузы

Syrinx (myth.) : Сиринга

système D (le systéme débrouille) : смекалка/
находчивость

Système International d'Unités *see* **SI**

System of Transcendental Idealism, The (Schelling) :
«Система трансцендентального идеализма»

syzygy (astron.) : сизигия

Szymanowski, Karol : Кароль Шимановский

T

tabernacle (bibl.) : скѝния
table d'hôte : табльдо́т
tables/tablets of stone (bibl.) : скрижа́ли ка́менные
tabula gratuloria : поздрави́тельный спи́сок
tabula rasa : «tabula rasa»/чи́стый лист
tacet (mus.) : (дли́тельная) па́уза
Tacitus : Пу́блий Корне́лий Таци́т
taedium vitae : отвраще́ние к жи́зни
Tafelmusik : засто́льная му́зыка
Taft—Hartley Act (hist.) : зако́н Та́фта-Ха́ртли
tagliatelle (cul.) : дли́нная лапша́
Tagore, Rabindranath : Рабиндрана́т Таго́р
Taine, Hippolyte : Ипполи́т Тэн
Taiwan : Тайва́нь (m.)
Taj Mahal : Тадж-Маха́л
Tale of a Tub, A (Swift) : «Ска́зка о бо́чке»
Tale of Two Cities, A (Dickens) : «По́весть о двух
городах»
Tales from the Vienna Woods (J. Strauss) : «Ска́зки
ве́нского ле́са»
Tales of a Traveller (Irving) : «Расска́зы
путеше́ственника»
Tales of Hoffmann, The (Offenbach) : «Ска́зки
Го́фмана»
Tales of the Grotesque and Arabesque (Poe) :
«Гроте́ски и арабе́ски»
Tales of Unrest (Conrad) : «Расска́зы о непоко́е»
Tallahassee (US) : Таллаха́сси
Talleyrand, Charles : Шарль Талейра́н
Talmud : Талму́д
Tamberlaine the Great/Tamerlane : Тамерла́н
Вели́кий/Тиму́р
Taming of the Shrew, The (Shakespeare) :
«Укроще́ние стропти́вой»

Tancredi (Rossini) : «Танкре́д»

Tang dynasty : Тан

Tanganyika (hist.) : Танганьи́ка

Tanglewood Tales (Hawthorne) : «Та́нглвудские расска́зы»

Tannhäuser (Wagner) : «Танге́йзер»

Tantalus (myth.) : Танта́л

tant pis : тем ху́же

Tanzania : Танза́ния

Taoiseach : премье́р-мини́стр Ирла́ндии

Taoism : даоси́зм

Tao te ching : «Да́о-дэ-цзи́н»

Tapiola (Sibelius) : «Тапио́ля»

tarantella : таранте́лла

tarot : таро́к/таро́т

Tarpeian Rock (Rome) : Тарпе́йская скала́

Tarquin : Таркви́ний

Tarragona : Тарраго́на

Tarsus (bibl.) : Тарс

Tartarin de Tarascon (Daudet) : «Необыча́йные приключе́ния Тартаре́на из Тараско́на»

Tartarus (myth.) : Та́ртар

tartine (cul.) : тарти́нка

Tartuffe ou l'Imposteur (Molière) : «Тарти́оф»

Tasso *see* **Torquato Tasso**

Tate Gallery (London) : Тейт галере́я

Taurus (zod.) : Теле́ц

taxe de séjour : су́точная пла́та

Taylor series (math.) : ряд Те́йлора

Taylorism : Тейлори́зм

Teheran : Тегера́н

Teheran Conference (hist.) : Тегера́нская конфере́нция

Teilhard de Chardin, Pierre : Пьер Тейя́р де Шарде́н

Tel Aviv : Тель-Ави́в

Telemachus (myth.) : Телема́х

téléphérique : подвесна́я (кана́тная) доро́га

TÉMÉRAIRE, THE FIGHTING

Téméraire, The Fighting (Turner) *see* **Fighting Téméraire, The**

Tempest, The (Giorgione) : «Гроза́»

Tempest, The (Shakespeare) : «Бу́ря»

Temple of Diana at Ephesus *see* **Seven Wonders of the World**

tempo di marcia (mus.) : в те́мпе ма́рша

tempo primo (mus.) : первонача́льный темп

Temptation of St Anthony, The (Bosch) : «Искуше́ние св. Анто́ния»

tempus fugit : «вре́мя лети́т»

Tenant of Wildfell Hall, The (Anne Brontë) : «Аренда́тор Ва́йлдфелл-Го́лла»

Ten Commandments : Де́сять за́поведей

Tendenzroman *see* *roman à thèse*

Tender is the Night (Fitzgerald) : «Ночь нежна́»

Teniers, David : Дави́д Те́нирс

Tennessee : Те́ннесси

Tennyson, Alfred : Альфре́д Те́ннисон

tepee : вигва́м

tequila : теки́ла

terce : девятичасова́я у́тренняя моли́тва

Terence : Пу́блий Тере́нций

terminus ad quem : ме́сто назначе́ния

Terpsichore *see* **Muses, the**

terracotta : террако́та

terra firma : про́чная земля́/су́ша

terra incognita : незнако́мая о́бласть

Terre, La (Zola) : «Земля́»

Terre des hommes (Saint-Exupéry) : «Плане́та люде́й»

Tertiary (geol.) : трети́чная э́ра

Tertullian : Квинт Септи́мий Тертуллиа́н

Teruel : Теру́эль

terza rima (vers.) : трёхсти́шие

terzetto (mus.) : терце́т

Teseide (myth.) : Тесеи́да

tesla coil (sci.) : трансформа́тор Те́сла

tessitura (mus.) : тесситу́ра

Tess of the D'Urbervilles (Hardy) : «Тэсс из рóда д'Эрбевѝллей»

Testament (Villon) : «Большóе завещáние»

tête-à-tête : тет-а-тéт/разговóр с глáзу на глáз

tête-bêche (philat.) : валéтом

Tethys (prehist.) : Тéтис

tetrameter (vers.) : тетрáметр

Teutonic Knights : Тевтóнский óрден

Texas : Техáс

Thackeray, William Makepeace : Уѝльям Мéйкпис Тéккерей

Thales : Фалéс

Thalia *see* Muses, the

Thames, River : Тéмза

Thanatos (myth.) : Тáнатос

Thanksgiving Day : День благодарéния

Thatcher, Margaret : Мáргарет Тэтчер

That Uncertain Feeling (Amis) : «Это неопределѐнное чýвство»

thé dansant : вечерѝнка с тáнцами

Thebes : Фѝвы

Themis (myth.) : Фемѝда

Themistocles : Фемистóкл

theodicy : теодицéя

Theodosius : Феодóсий Велѝкий

Theogony (Hesiod) : «Теогóния»

Theophilus (bibl.) : Феóфил

Theosophical Society : Теосóфское óбщество

Thérèse Desqueroux (Mauriac) : «Терéза Дескейрý»

Thermidor *see* Calendar, French Revolutionary

Thermopylae : Фермопѝлы

Theseus (myth.) : Тесéй

Thesmophoriazusae (Aristophanes) : «Жéнщины на прáзднике Фесмофóрий»

Thessalonians I (bibl.) : «Пéрвое послáние к Фессалоникѝйцам»

Thessalonians II (bibl.) : «Вторóе послáние к Фессалоникѝйцам»

THESSALY

Thessaly : Фессáлия

Thibault, Les (Martin du Gard) : «Семья Тибó»

Thiers, Louis : Луи́ Тьер

Thieving Magpie, The (Rossini) see *Gazza Ladra, La*

Thinker, The (Rodin) : «Мысли́тель»

Third Estate see *tiers état*

Third Reich : трéтий рейх

thirty pieces of silver (bibl.) : три́дцать срéбреников

Thirty Years War : тридцатилéтняя войнá

Thomas (bibl.) : Фомá

Thomas, Dylan : Ди́лан Тóмас

Thomas à Becket : Тóмас Бéкет

Thomas à Kempis : Фомá Кемпи́йский

Thomson, William : Уи́льям Тóмсон see also
Kelvin, Lord

Thor (myth.) : Тор

Thoreau, Henry : Гéнри Тóро

Thorwaldsson, Eirik : Эйрик Тóрвальдсон

Thousand and One Nights : «Ты́сяча и однá ночь»

Thrace : Фрáкия

Three-Cornered Hat, The (de Falla) : «Треугóлка»

Three Men in a Boat (Jerome) : «Трóе в (однóй)
лóдке (не считáя собáки)»

Three Men on the Bummel (Jerome) : «Трóе на
велосипéде»

Three Musketeers, The (Dumas) see *Trois
Mousquetaires, Les*

Threepenny Opera, The (Brecht, Weill) see
Dreigroschenoper

Through the Looking-glass (Carroll) : «В Зазеркáлье»

Thucydides : Фукиди́д

Thus Spake Zarathustra (Nietzsche, R. Strauss) see
Also sprach Zarathustra

Tianamen Square (Beijing) : плóщадь Тяньаньмы́нь

Tiber, River : Тибр

Tiberius, Emperor : Клáвдий Нерóн Тибéрий

Tieck, Ludwig : Лю́двиг Тик

Tiepolo, Giovanni : Джовáнни Батти́ста Тьéполо

tierce : те́рция (mus.); девятичасова́я у́тренняя
  моли́тва (eccles.) *see also* **terce**

Tierra del Fuego : О́гненная Земля́

tiers état : тре́тье сосло́вие

Tigris, River : Тигр

Till Eulenspiegel (R. Strauss) : «Тиль Уленшпи́гель»

Timaeus (Plato) : «Тиме́й»

timbre : тембр

Timbuctu : Тимбукту́

Time Machine, The (Wells) : «Маши́на вре́мени»

Time of Hope (Snow) : «Пора́ наде́жд»

Time of Troubles (hist.) : «Сму́тное вре́мя»

Times, The : «Таймс»

Timon of Athens (Shakespeare) : «Тимо́н Афи́нский»

Timothy I (bibl.) : «Пе́рвое посла́ние к Тимофе́ю»

Timothy II (bibl.) : «Второ́е посла́ние к Тимофе́ю»

Tinderbox, The (Andersen) : «Де́вочка со спи́чками»

Tin Drum, The (Böll) see **Blechtrommel, Die**

Tin Soldier, The (Andersen) : «Сто́йкий оловя́нный
  солда́тик»

Tintoretto, Jacopo : Я́копо Тинторе́тто

Tippett, Michael : Ма́йкл Ти́ппит

tirailleur (hist.) : стрело́к

Tiresias (myth.) : Тире́сий

Tirso de Molina : Ти́рсо де Моли́на

Titania (myth.) : Тита́ния

Titanic : Тита́ник

Titans (myth.) : тита́ны

Titian : Тициа́н

Titus : «Посла́ние к Ти́ту»

Titus, Emperor : Фла́вий Веспасиа́н Тит

Titus Andronicus (Shakespeare) : «Тит Андро́ник»

Tobacco Road (Caldwell) : «Таба́чная доро́га»

Tobit (Apocrypha) : «Тоби́т»

toccata (mus.) : токка́та

Tocqueville, Alexis de : Але́ксис де Токви́ль

Tod des Vergil, Der (Broch) : «Смерть Верги́лии»

Tod in Venedig, Der (T. Mann) : «Смерть в Вене́ции»

TOD UND VERKLÄRUNG

Tod und Verklärung (R. Strauss) : «Смерть и просветле́ние»

toga : то́га

Togliatti, Palmiro : Пальми́ро Толья́тти

To Have and to Have Not (Hemingway) : «Име́ть и не име́ть»

Tojo, Emperor : импера́тор Тодзи́о

Toledo : Толе́до

Tolkien, J.R.R. : Джон Ро́нальд Ру́эл То́лкин

Tombeau de Couperin, Le (Ravel) : «Гробни́ца Ку́перена»

Tom Brown's Schooldays (Hughes) : «Шко́льные го́ды То́ма Бра́уна»

Tom Jones, A Foundling (Fielding) : «Исто́рия То́ма Джо́нса, найдёныша»

Tom Sawyer (Twain) : «Том Со́йер»

tomahawk : томага́вк

tone poem (mus.) : симфони́ческая поэ́ма

tonic (mus.) : то́ника

tonic sol-fa (mus.) : сольфе́джио/сольфе́джо

Tonio Kröger (T. Mann) : «То́нио Кре́гер»

Tonkin, Gulf of : Тонки́нский зали́в

tonneau : бо́чка

Tono Bungay (Wells) : «То́но-Бе́нге»

Torah : то́ра

torero : торе́ро

Tories : то́ри

Torino *see* **Turin**

Toronto : Торо́нто

Torquato Tasso (Goethe) : «Торква́то Та́ссо»

Torquemada, Tomas : Тома́с Торквема́да

Torte (cul.) : торт

tortilla (cul.) : пло́ская кукуру́зная лепёшка

Tosca (Puccini) : «То́ска»

Toscanini, Arturo : Арту́ро Тоскани́ни

Totentanz : пля́ска сме́рти

To the Lighthouse (Woolf) : «К маяку́»

touché! : «туше́!»

Toulon : Тулóн

Toulouse : Тулýза

Toulouse-Lautrec, Henri de : Анри́ де Тулýз-
-Лотрéк

tour de force : настоя́щий пóдвиг

Tour de France : «Тур де Фрáнс»

tour d'horizon : обзóр

tournedos (cul.) : говя́жье филé

Tours : Тур

Toussaint L'Ouverture : Туссéн-Лувертю́р

tout compris : без дополни́тельных расхóдов

tout court : прóсто-нáпросто

Tower of London : Тáуэр

Toynbee, Arnold : Арнóлд Тóйнби

Tractatus Logico-Philosophicus (Wittgenstein) :
«Лóгико-филосóфский трактáт»

Trades Union Congress *see* TUC

Trafalgar, battle of : Трафальгáрское сражéние

trahison des clercs : предáтельство учёных

Trajan, Emperor : Марк У́льпий Трая́н

tranche de vie : «кусóк жи́зни»/сцéна, вы́хваченная
из жи́зни

transcendental meditation : трансцендентáльная
медитáция

Transfiguration (relig.) : Преображéние

Transfiguration, The (Raphael) : «Преображéние»

Transsiberian Railway : Транссиби́рская
Магистрáль

Transvaal : Трансвáаль

Trappists (relig.) : траппи́сты

Trasimene, Lake : Трази́менское óзеро

trattoria : ресторáн/тракти́р

Travels with a Donkey (Stevenson) : «Путешéствия с
ослóм»

Traviata, La (Verdi) : «Травиáта»

Treasure Island (Stevenson) : «Óстров сокрóвищ»

Treatise of Human Nature (Hume) : «Трактáт о
человéческой прирóде»

TREATISE ON PAINTING

Treatise on Painting (Leonardo) : «Тракта́т о
  жи́вописи»
trebuchet (hist.) : требюше́
Treitschke, Heinrich von : Ге́нрих фон Тре́йчке
tremolando (mus.) : дрожа́ще
tremolo (mus.) : тре́моло
Trent, Council of (hist.) : Триде́нтский Собо́р
Trentino-Alto-Adige : Тренти́но-А́льто-Ади́же
triage : сортиро́вка
Trial, The (Kafka) see *Prozeß, Der*
Triassic (geol.) : триа́совый пери́од
tribune (Rom.) : трибу́н
tricolour : францу́зский триколо́р/национа́льный
  флаг Франции
tricoteuses (hist.) : «вяза́льщицы»
Trieste : Трие́ст
Trinitarians : тринита́рии
Trinity : Тро́ица
Trinity Sunday : Тро́ицын день
Triple Alliance (hist.) : Тро́йственный сою́з
Tristan und Isolde (Wagner) : «Триста́н и Изо́льда»
Tristram Shandy, Life and Opinions of (Sterne) :
  «Жизнь и мне́ния Три́страма Ше́нди»
Triton (myth.) : Трито́н
Triumph of Caesar (Mantegna) : «Триу́мф Це́заря»
Troades (myth.) : Троя́нки
trochaic (vers.) : хореи́ческий
trochee (vers.) : хоре́й
Troilus (myth.) : Тро́йл
Troilus and Cressida (Chaucer) : «Тро́йл и Кресси́да»
Trois contes (Flaubert) : «Три по́вести»
Trois Mousquetaires, Les (Dumas) : «Три
  мушкетёра»
Trojan Horse : Троя́нский конь
Trojan War : Троя́нская война́
Trollope, Anthony : Э́нтони Тро́ллоп
trompe-l'oeil : изображе́ние, создаю́щее иллю́зию
  реа́льности (art); опти́ческая иллю́зия

troubadour : трубаду́р

troupe : тру́ппа

trousseau : прида́ное

'Trout' quintet (Schubert) : фортепья́нный квинте́т «Форе́ль»

trouvaille : нахо́дка

Trovatore, Il (Verdi) : «Трубаду́р»

Troy : Тро́я

Troy, siege of : оса́да Тро́и

Troyat, Henri : Анри́ Труайя́

Troyens, Les (Berlioz) : «Троя́нцы»

Troyens à Carthage, Les (Berlioz) : «Троя́нцы в Карфаге́не»

Truman, Harry : Га́рри Тру́мэн

Truman Doctrine (hist.) : доктри́на Тру́мэна

Trumpet-Major, The (Hardy) : «Ста́рший труба́ч драгу́нского полка́»

Trygve Lie : Трю́гве Ли

tsunami : цуна́ми

TUC (Trades Union Congress) : Конгре́сс тредюнио́нов

Tudor, House of : Тюдо́ры

Tuileries (Paris) : Тюильри́

Turandot (Puccini) : «Турандо́т»

Turin : Тури́н

Turing machine (math.) : маши́на Тью́ринга

Turkish bath : Туре́цкая ба́ня

Turner, J.M.W. : Джо́зеф Мэ́ллорд Уи́льям Тёрнер

Turn of the Screw, The (Britten, James) : «Поворо́т винта́»

Tuscany : Тоска́на

Tuscany (hist.) : Ту́сция

Tusculan Disputations (Cicero) : «Тускула́нские бесе́ды»

Tussaud's, Madame (London) : Мада́м Тюссо́

Tutenkhamen : Тутанхамо́н

tutoiement : обраще́ние на «ты»

TUTTI

tutti (mus.) : ту́тти

tutti-frutti (cul.) : моро́женое с ра́зными фру́ктами

Twain, Mark : Марк Твен (Сэ́мюэл Ле́нгхорн Кле́менс)

Twelfth Night (Shakespeare) : «Двена́дцатая ночь»

twelve-tone scale (mus.) : додекафо́ния

Twentieth-Century Fox : «20-век Фокс»

Twenty Thousand Leagues under the Sea (Verne) : «20 000 лье под водо́й»

Twilight of the Gods, The (Wagner)   *see* *Götterdämmerung*

Two Gentlemen of Verona (Shakespeare) : «Два веро́нца»

Two Towers, The (Tolkien) : «Две кре́пости»

Tyre : Тир

U

Übermensch (philos.) : сверхчелове́к
Über naive und sentimentalische Dichtung (Schiller) :
  «О наи́вной и сентимента́льной поэ́зии»
ubique : повсю́ду
U-boat : подво́дная ло́дка
Uccello, Paolo : Па́оло Учче́лло
Uffizi Gallery (Florence) : Галере́я Уффи́ци
UFO : НЛО (неопо́знанный лета́ющий объе́кт)
Ugly Duckling, The (Andersen) : «Га́дкий утёнок»
UHF (ultra-high frequency) : УВЧ (ультравысо́кие
  частоты́)
Uitlander : уи́тлендер
Ulbricht, Walter : Ва́льтер У́льбрихт
Ulster : О́льстер
ultima Thule : кра́йний преде́л
ultra vires (leg.) : вне компете́нции
Ulysses (Joyce) : «Ули́сс»
Ulysses deriding Polyphemus (Turner) : «Ули́сс и
  Полифе́м»
Umbria : У́мбрия
umlaut : умля́ут
UN : ООН (Организа́ция Объединённых На́ций)
Unamuno, Miguel : Миге́ль де Унаму́но
Uncle Tom's Cabin (Beecher Stowe) : «Хи́жина дя́ди
  То́ма»
Unconditional Surrender (Waugh) : «Безогово́рочная
  капитуля́ция»
Under Milk Wood (Thomas) : «В моло́чном лесу́»
Under the Greenwood Tree (Hardy) : «Под де́ревом
  зелёным»
Under the Net (Murdoch) : «Под се́тью»
Under Western Eyes (Conrad) : «Глаза́ми за́пада»
Und sagte kein einziges Wort (Böll) : «И не сказа́л ни
  еди́ного сло́ва»

205

UNESCO

UNESCO : ЮНЕСКО (Организа́ция Объединённых На́ций по вопро́сам образова́ния, нау́ки и культу́ры)

'Unfinished' symphony (Schubert) : «Неоко́нченная» симфо́ния

UNICEF : Де́тский фонд ООН

Unionist Party (Northern Ireland) : Юниони́стская па́ртия

Unitarians (relig.) : Унита́рии

United Arab Emirates : Объединённые Ара́бские Эмира́ты

United Nations *see* **UN**

United Press International : «Юна́йтед пресс интерне́шенл»

United Reformed Church : Объединённая Реформа́тская це́рковь

Untergang des Abendlandes (Spengler) : «Зака́т Евро́пы»

Untermensch : «недочелове́к»

Untertan, Der (H. Mann) : «Верноподданный»

Upanishad (relig.) : Упаниша́д

Updike, John : Джон А́пдайк

Uppsala : У́псала

Urania *see* **Muses, the**

Uranus (astron., myth.) : Ура́н

Urdu : Урду́

Uriah the Hittite (bibl.) : У́рий Хеттея́нин

Ursa Major (astron.) : Больша́я Медве́дица

Ursa Minor (astron.) : Ма́лая Медве́дица

Urtext (lit.) : первонача́льный текст

Utah : Ю́та

U Thant : У Тан

Uther Pendragon (Arthur.) : У́тер Пендра́гон

Utopia (More) : «Уто́пия»

Utrillo, Maurice : Мори́с Утри́лло

V

V 1 (hist.) : Фа́у-1
V 2 (hist.) : Фа́у-2
vade-mecum : вадеме́кум/путеводи́тель
vair (herald.) : бе́личий
vale : проща́й
Valencia : Вале́нсия
Valerius Maximus : Вале́рий Ма́ксим
Valéry, Paul : Поль Валери́
Valhalla : Вальха́лла/Вальга́лла
Valkyries (myth.) : валькири́и
Valkyries, The (Wagner) *see Walküre, Die*
Valladolid : Вальядоли́д
Valle d'Aosta : Ва́лле д'Ао́ста
Valle-Inclán, Ramon : Рамо́н Мари́я дель Ва́лье-
-Инкла́н
Valley of Fear, The (Conan Doyle) : «Доли́на у́жаса»
Valley of the Kings : Доли́на фарао́нов
Valois, Ninette de : Нине́т де Валуа́
valpolicella (vin.) : вальполиче́лла
Valses nobles et sentimentales (Ravel) : «Благо-
ро́дные и сентимента́льные ва́льсы»
Valse triste (Sibelius) : «Гру́стный вальс»
Vanburgh, John : Джон Ва́нбру
Vandals (hist.) : ванда́лы
Van der Waal's force (sci.) : Ван-Дер-Ва́альсова
си́ла
Van de Velde, Willem : Ви́ллем ван де Ве́лде
Van Dyck, Anthony : Анто́нис ван Дейк
Van Eyck, Jan : Ян ван Эйк
Van Gogh, Vincent : Винсе́нт Ван Гог
vanitas vanitatum : суета́ суе́т
Vanity Fair (Thackeray) : «Я́рмарка тщесла́вия»
Vanity of Human Wishes (Johnson) : «Тщета́
челове́ческих жела́ний»

Van't Hoff's law (sci.) : зако́н Вант-Го́ффа

Varèse, Edgar : Э́дгар Варе́з

Vasco da Gama : Ва́ско да Га́ма

Vatican : Ватика́н

vaudeville : водеви́ль (m.)

Vaughan Williams, Ralph : Ралф Во́ан-Уи́льямс

VDQS (vin délimité de qualité supérieure) : вино гаранти́рованного ка́чества

Vedanta (philos.) : Веда́нта

VE day : День побе́ды над Герма́нией

Vega (astron.) : Ве́га

vehmgericht *see* **Femgericht**

Velázquez, Diego : Дие́го Вела́скес

vendange (vin.) : сбор виногра́да

Vendée : Ванде́я

Vendémiaire *see* **Calendar, French Revolutionary**

Venetian School (art) : Венециа́нская шко́ла

veni, vidi, vici : «пришёл, уви́дел, победи́л»

Venice : Вене́ция

Venn diagram : диагра́мма Ве́нна

Ventôse *see* **Calendar, French Revolutionary**

Venturi tube (sci.) : трубка́ Венту́ри

Venus (astron., myth.) : Вене́ра

Venus and Cupid (Velásquez) : «Вене́ра с зе́ркалом»

Venus de Milo : Афроди́та Мило́сская

Vénus d'Ille, La (Mérimée) : «Вене́ра И́лльская»

Venus of Urbino (Titian) : «Вене́ра Урби́нская»

verbatim : сло́во в сло́во

Verdi, Giuseppe : Джузе́ппе Ве́рди

Verdun : Верде́н

Verfremdungseffekt : остране́ние/эффе́кт отчужде́ния

Verga, Giovanni : Джованни Ве́рга

Vergeltungswaffe (hist.) : ору́жие возме́здия *see also* **V 1, V 2**

Verhaeren, Émile : Эми́ль Верха́рн

Verklärte Nacht (Schönberg) : «Просветлённая ночь»

Verlaine, Paul : Поль Верле́н

Vermeer, Jan : Ян Вермéр Дéльфтский
vermicelli (cul.) : вермишéль (f.)
Vermont : Вермóнт
Verne, Jules : Жюль Верн
vernier (scale) : верньéр
vernissage (art) : вернисáж/покáз картúн чáстной
  коллéкции
Veronese, Paolo : Пáоло Веронéзе
Verrocchio, Andrea del : Андрéа дель Веррóккьо
Versailles : Версáль (m.)
Versailles, Treaty of : Версáльский мúрный договóр
vers libre : верлúбр/свобóдный стих
Versuch einer Kritik aller Offenbarung (Fichte) :
  «Óпыт крúтики всячеcкого откровéния»
Verwandlung, Die (Kafka) : «Превращéние»
Verwoerd, Hendrik : Хéндрик Фервýрд
Vespasian, Emperor : Тит Флáвий Веспасиáн
vespers (eccles.) : вечéрня
Vespri Siciliani, I (Verdi) : «Сицилúйская вечéрня»
Vesta (myth.) : Вéста
VHF (very high frequency) : ОВЧ (óчень высóкие
  частотьí)
Via Crucis : крéстный путь
via dolorosa : скóрбный путь
Viardot-Garcia, Pauline : Полúна Виардó-Гарсúа
vibrato (mus.) : вибрáто
Vicar of Wakefield, The (Goldsmith) : «Векфúльдский
  свящéнник»
vice : вмéсто
vice versa : наоборóт
Vichy (hist.) : «Вишú»
Vichy water : минерáльная водá вишú
Vichyssois : вишúст; вишúйский
Vico, Giovanni Battista : Джамбаттúста Вúко
Victor Emanuel : Вúктор Эммануúл
victor ludorum : победúтель (m.)
Victoria and Albert Museum (London) : музéй
  Виктóрии и Альбéрта

VICTORY OF SAMOTHRACE

Victory of Samothrace : «Ни́ка Самофраки́йская»

videlicet see viz.

Vienna : Ве́на

Vienna Circle (philos.) : Ве́нский круг

Vienna, Congress of : Ве́нский конгре́сс

Vienna Philarmonic Orchestra : Ве́нский
филармони́ческий орке́стр

Vietcong : Вьетко́нг

Viet Minh : Вьетми́нь

View from the Bridge, A (Miller) : «Вид с моста́»

View of Delft (Vermeer) : «Вид Де́льфта»

vignette : карти́нка; эски́з

Vigny, Alfred de : Альфре́д де Ви́ньи

vigoroso (mus.) : энерги́чно

Viking : ви́кинг; древнескандина́вский

Vile Bodies (Waugh) : «Омерзи́тельные тела́»

Villa-Lobos, Heitor : Эйто́р Ви́ла-Ло́бос

villanelle (lit., mus.) : вилланэ́лла/пасту́шеская
поэ́зия

Villette (Charlotte Brontë) : «Вилье́т»

Villiers de l'Isle Adam : Вилье́ де Лиль-Ада́н

Villon, François : Франсуа́ Вийо́н

vin d'appellation contrôlée : вино́ прове́ренной ма́рки

vin délimité de qualité supérieur see VDQS

vin du pays : ме́стное ма́рочное вино́

vinaigrette (cul.) : запра́вка для сала́тов

vingt-et-un : карто́чная игра́ в очко́

Vinland : Ви́нланд

vin mousseux : шипу́чее вино́

viola da gamba : вио́ла да га́мба

viola d'amore : вио́ла д'аму́р

virago : вира́дж

virement : перечисле́ние

Virgil : Пу́блий Верги́лий Маро́н

Virgin Mary : де́ва Мари́я

Virgin and Child with St Anne, The (Leonardo) : «св.
А́нна с Мари́ей и младе́нцем Христо́м»

Virginia : Вирги́ния

Virginians, The (Thackeray) : «Вирги́нцы»

Virgo (zod.) : Де́ва

vis-à-vis : визави́

Vishnu : Ви́шну

Visigoths (hist.) : вестго́ты

Vision of Judgment, The (Byron) : «Виде́ние суда́»

Vita de' campi, La (Verga) : «Се́льская честь»

vivat! : вива́т!

viz. : и́менно

vizier : визи́рь (m.)

VJ day : день побе́ды над Япо́нией

Vlad the Impaler : Влад Це́пеш

voie sacrée (hist.) : Свяще́нная доро́га

Volapük (ling.) : волапю́к

vol-au-vent (cul.) : волова́н

Vol de nuit (Saint-Exupéry) : «Ночно́й полёт»

Volksdeutsche (nat. soc.) : «фольксдо́йче»

Volkslied : наро́дная пе́сня

Volksmärchen : наро́дная ска́зка

Volkswagen : фольксва́ген

Volpone (Jonson) : «Вольпо́не»

volt : вольт

Voltaire : Вольте́р (Франсуа́ Мари Аруэ́)

volte-face : ре́зкая переме́на взгля́дов

Vonnegut, Kurt : Курт Во́ннегут

voodoo : вуду́

voortrekker (hist.) : южноафрика́нский переселе́нец

Vorster, Balthazar : Бальтаза́р Фо́рстер

Vosges : Воге́зы

Vouvray (vin.) : вувре́

Vow of Louis XIII (Ingres) : «Обе́т Людови́ка XIII»

vox populi — vox dei : «глас наро́да — глас бо́жий»

vraisemblance : правдоподо́бие

Vulcan (myth.) : Вулка́н

W

Wacht am Rhein : «Стра́жа на Рейне»

Wackenroder, Wilhelm : Вильге́льм Ва́ккенродер

Wagner, Richard : Ри́хард Ва́гнер

Wagnerian : ва́гнеровский

wagon-lit : спа́льный ваго́н

Wahlverwandtschaften, Die (Goethe) : «Избира́тельное сро́дство»

Wailing Wall (Jerusalem) : Стена́ пла́ча

Waiting for Godot (Beckett) : «В ожида́нии Годо́»

Walden, or Life in the Woods (Thoreau) : «Уо́лден, и́ли Жизнь в лесу́»

Waldensians (hist.) : вальде́нсы

Waldheim, Kurt : Курт Вальдха́йм

Walküre, Die (Wagner) : «Валькирия»

Wallensteins Tod (Schiller) : «Смерть Валлен-
  шта́йна»

Wallonia : Валло́ния

Walloon : валло́нец; валло́нский

Wall Street : Уо́лл-Стрит

Wall Street Journal : «Уо́лл-стрит джо́рнал»

Walpole, Horace : Хо́рас Уо́лпол

Walpurgisnacht : вальпу́ргиева ночь; ша́баш ведьм

Walter von der Vogelweide : Ва́льтер фон дер
  Фо́гельвейде

Walton, William : Уи́льям Уо́лтон

'**Wanderer' Fantasy (Schubert)** : Фанта́зия
  «Скита́лец»

Wanderer, kommst du nach Spa? (Böll) : «Стра́нник,
  когда́ ты придёшь в Спа?»

'**Wanderers, The' (art)** : «Передви́жники»

Wanderings of Oisin, The : «Стра́нствия Оссиа́на»

Wanderjahr : год стра́нствований

wanderlust : любо́вь к путеше́ствиям

Wankel rotary engine : дви́гатель Ва́нкеля

Warhol, Andy : Э́нди Уо́рхол

War of Independence : Война́ за незави́симость

War of the Worlds, The (Wells) : «Война́ ми́ров»

Warsaw Pact : Варша́вский догово́р

Warwick the Kingmaker (hist.) : Уо́рвик (Уо́рик) «де́латель короле́й»

Washington : Вашингто́н

Washington, George : Джордж Вашингто́н

Washington Post and Times-Herald : «Ва́шингтон пост и Таймс-ге́ральд»

Washington Square (James) : «Ва́шингтон-сквер»

Washington University : Вашингто́нский университе́т

Wasps, The (Aristophanes) : «О́сы»

Waste Land, The (T.S. Eliot) : «Беспло́дная земля́»

Watergate : Уо́ртергейт

Waterlilies (Monet) : «Кувши́нки»

Waterloo, battle of : сраже́ние при Ватерло́о

Water Music (Handel) : «Му́зыка на воде́»

watt : ватт

Watteau, Antoine : Антуа́н Ватто́

Wat Tyler Rebellion (hist.) : восста́ние Уо́та Та́йлера

Waugh, Evelyn : И́влин Во

Waverley (Scott) : «Уэ́верли»

Way of All Flesh, The (Butler) : «Путь вся́кой пло́ти»

Way of the World, The (Congreve) : «Путь све́тской жи́зни»

Webb, Sidney and Beatrice : Си́дней и Беатри́са Вебб

Weber, Carl Maria von : Карл Мари́я фон Ве́бер

Webern, Anton : Анто́н Ве́берн

Webster, Daniel : Даниель Уэ́бстер

Wedgwood, Josiah : Джоза́йя Уэ́джвуд/Ве́джвуд

Weill, Kurt : Курт Вейль/Вайль

Weimar Republic (hist.) : Ве́ймарская респу́блика

Weinstube : ви́нный погребо́к

Weizmann, Chaim : Ха́им Ве́йцман

Weizsäcker, Carl : Карл Вéйцзэккер

Well of Moses (Sluter) : «Колóдец Моисéя»

Welles, Orson : Óрсон Уэ́ллс

Wellington, Duke of : Вéллингтон (Áртур Уэ́лсли)

Wellington (New Zealand) : Уэ́ллингтон

Wells, H.G. : Гéрберт Джордж Уэ́ллс

Wells Fargo : Уэ́льс-Фáрго

Welsh (ling.) : валлúйский язы́к

Welt als Wille und Vorstellung, Die (Schopenhauer) :
«Мир как вóля и представлéние»

Weltanschauung : мировоззрéние

Weltpolitik : всемúрная полúтика

Weltschmerz : мировáя скорбь

Wesen des Christentums, Das (Feuerbach) :
«Сýщность христиáнства»

Wesley, John : Джон Уэ́сли

Wessex Poems (Hardy) : «Стихú Уэ́ссекса»

western (film) : вéстерн

Westernisers (hist.) : зáпадники

Westinghouse : «Вéстинггауз»

Westminster, Statutes of (hist.) : Вестмúнстерские
статýты

Westminster Abbey (London) : Вестмúнстерское
аббáтство

West-östlicher Divan (Goethe) : «Зáпадно-востóчный
дивáн»

Westphalia, Peace of : Вестфáльский мир

West Point ((US) : Уэст Пойнт

West Side Story (Bernstein) : «Вестсáйдская истóрия»

West Virginia : Зáпадная Виргúния

Westward Ho! (Kingsley) : «Эй, к зáпаду!»/«Хрáбрый
искáтель приключéний Эмúас Лей из Берýффа»

Wheatstone bridge (sci.) : мост Уúтстона

Where Angels Fear to Tread (Forster) : «Кудá боя́тся
ступúть áнгелы»

Whigs (hist.) : вúги

Whistler, James : Джеймс Уúстлер

White Fang (London) : «Бéлый клык»

Whitehorse (Canada) : Уайтхо́рс

White Peacock, The (Lawrence) : «Бе́лый павли́н»

Whitman, Walt : Уо́лт Уи́тмен

Whitsun *see* **Pentecost**

Who's Afraid of Virginia Woolf? (Albee) : «Кто бои́тся Вирджи́нии Вулф?»

Wieland, Christoph : Кри́стоф Ви́ланд

Wiener schnitzel : шни́цель (m.) по-ве́нски

Wiesbaden : Висба́ден

wigwam : вигва́м

Wild Duck, The (Ibsen) : «Ди́кая у́тка»

Wilde, Oscar : О́скар Уа́йльд

Wilder, Thornton : То́рнтон Уа́йлдер

Wilhelm Meisters Lehrjahre (Goethe) : «Го́ды уче́ния Вильге́льма Ме́йстера»

Wilhelm Meisters Wanderjahre (Goethe) : «Го́ды стра́нствий Вильге́льма Ме́йстера»

Wilhelmshaven : Вильгельмсха́фен

Wilhelmstrasse (hist.) : Министе́рство иностра́нных дел (в Герма́нии)

Wilhelm Tell (Schiller) : «Вильге́льм Телль»

William of Orange : Вильге́льм I Ора́нский

William the Conqueror : Вильге́льм I Завоева́тель

William Tell (Rossini, Schiller) *see* *Guillaume Tell*, *Wilhelm Tell*

Williams, Tennessee : Те́ннесси Уи́льямс (То́мас Ла́нир)

Wilson, Angus : Э́нгус Уи́лсон

Wilson, Harold : Га́рольд Ви́льсон

Wilson, Woodrow : Ву́дро Ви́льсон

Wind in the Willows, The (Grahame) : «Ветеро́к в и́вах»

Windsor Forest (Pope) : «Уиндзо́рский лес»

Winnie-the-Pooh (Milne) : «Ви́нни-Пу́х»

Winnipeg : Ви́ннипег

Winter of our Discontent (Steinbeck) : «Зима́ трево́ги на́шей»

Winterreise, Die (Schubert) : «Зи́мний путь»

Winter's Tale, A (Shakespeare) : «Зи́мняя ска́зка»

Wisconsin : Виско́нсин

Wisconsin University : Виско́нсинский университе́т

Wise Men, the Three *see* **Magi**

Wissenschaft der Logik (Hegel) : «Нау́ка ло́гики»

Wissenschaftslehre (Fichte) : «Наукоуче́ние»

witenagemot (hist.) : Уитенагемо́т

Wittgenstein, Ludwig : Лю́двиг Витгенште́йн

Witwatersrand : Витва́терсранд

Wives and Daughters (Gaskell) : «Жёны и дочери»

Wizard of Oz, The : «Волше́бник страны́ Оз»

Wohltemperierte Klavier, Das (J.S. Bach) : «Хорошо́ темпери́рованный клави́р»

Wolf, Hugo : Гу́го Вольф

Wolf-Ferrari, Ermanno : Эрма́нно Вольф-Ферра́ри

Wolfram von Eschenbach : Во́льфрам фон Э́шенбах

Wolsey, Cardinal : кардина́л Уо́лси

Woman in White, The (Collins) : «Же́нщина в бе́лом»

Woman of No Importance, A (Wilde) : «Же́нщина, не стоя́щая внима́ния»

Women in Love (Lawrence) : «Влюблённые же́нщины»

Women of Trachis (Sophocles) : «Трахи́нянки»

Woodlanders, The (Hardy) : «В краю́ лесо́в»

Woodstock : Ву́дсток

Woolf, Virginia : Вирджи́ния Вулф

Wordsworth, William : Уи́льям Во́рдсворт

Works and Days (Hesiod) : «Тру́ды и дни»

World Wide Web : «Web»/[«Всеми́рная Паути́на»]

Worms, Concordat of (hist.) : Во́рмский конкорда́т

Worms, Edict of (hist.) : Во́рмский эди́кт

Wo warst du, Adam? (Böll) : «Где ты был, Ада́м?»

Wozzeck (Berg) : «Во́ццек»

Wren, Christopher : Кри́стофер Рен

Wright, Frank Lloyd : Фрэнк Ллойд Райт

Wright Brothers : Бра́тья Уи́льям и О́рвил Райт

Wrong Set, The (Wilson) : «Не тот набо́р»

wunderkind (psych.) : вундерки́нд

wurst : колбаса́
Würzburg : Вю́рцбург
Wuthering Heights (Emily Brontë) : «Грозово́й
перева́л»
Wyclif, John : Джон Уи́клиф
Wyoming : Вайо́минг

X

x : икс
Xanthippe : Ксанти́ппа
Xenophon : Ксенофо́нт
Xerxes : Ксеркс
X-rays : рентге́новские лучи́

Y

y : и́грек
Yahveh : Я́хве
Yale University : Йе́льский университе́т
Yalta Conference : Кры́мская (Ялти́нская)
конфере́нция
Yamamoto, Admiral : адмира́л Ямамо́то
Yangtse, River : Янцзы́
Yankee : я́нки
Yeats, William Butler : Уи́льям Ба́тлер Йе́йтс
(Йи́тс)
Yellowknife (Canada) : Йе́ллоунайф
Yellowstone, River : Йе́ллоустон
Yellowstone National Park : Йеллоусто́нский
национа́льный парк
Yerkes Observatory (US) : Йе́рксская астроном-
и́ческая обсервато́рия
yeti : сне́жный челове́к/йе́ти
Yggdrasil (myth.) : и́ггдрасиль (m.)
Yiddish : и́диш; на языке́ и́диш
yin yang : инь ян
YMCA : Христиа́нская ассоциа́ция молоды́х люде́й
yodel : петь с перели́вами
yoga : йо́га
Yom Kippur (relig.) : йом-киппу́р
Yorkists (hist.) : Йо́рки
Yosemite National Park (US) : Йосе́митский национ-
на́льный парк
Younger Edda, The (Sturluson) : Мла́дшая э́дда
Young Men's Christian Association *see* YMCA
Young Turks (hist.) : младоту́рки
Ypres, battle of : сраже́ние за И́прский вы́ступ
Ysaye, Eugène : Эже́н Иза́и
Yukon Territory : Юко́н

Z

zabaglione (cul.) : го́голь-мо́голь (m.)

Zacchaeus (bibl.) : Закхе́й

Zadok (bibl.) : Са́док

Zamora : Замо́ра

Zaragoza : Сараго́са

Zarathustra : Зарату́стра *see also* **Zoroaster**

Zauberberg, Der (T. Mann) : «Волше́бная гора́»

Zauberflöte, Die (Mozart) : «Волше́бная фле́йта»

Zebulun (bibl.) : Завуло́н

Zechariah (bibl.) : «Кни́га Проро́ка Захарии»

Zeit, Die : «Цайт»

Zeitgeist : дух вре́мени

Zen buddhism : будди́йская се́кта «дзен»

Zeno of Citium : Зено́н из Китио́на

Zeno of Elea : Зено́н Эле́йский

Zeno's paradox (philos.) : зено́нова апори́я

Zephaniah (bibl.) : «Кни́га Проро́ка Софо́нии»

Zephyr (myth.) : Зефи́р

zerbrochene Krug, Der (Kleist) : «Разби́тый кувши́н»

zeugma (lit.) : зе́вгма

Zeus : Зевс

Zhou Enlai : Чжо́у Энь-ла́й

Zigeunerbaron, Der (J. Strauss) : «Цыга́нский баро́н»

Ziggurat : Зиккура́т

Zimmerwald conference (hist.) : Циммерва́льдская конфере́нция

Zionism : сиони́зм

zögernd (mus.) : нереши́тельно

Zola, Émile : Эми́ль Золя́

Zollverein (hist.) : тамо́женный сою́з

Zoroaster : Зоро́астр *see also* **Zarathustra**

zouave : зуа́в

zucchetto : ермо́лка

zucchini (cul.) : кабачки́

Zuckmayer, Carl : Карл Цу́кмайер
zugzwang (chess) : цу́гцванг
Zuider Zee : Зёйдер-Зе́
Zulu : зулу́с; зулу́сский
Zurich : Цю́рих
Zweig, Stefan : Стефа́н Цвейг
zwieback (cul.) : суха́рь (m.)
Zwingli, Ulrich : У́льрих Цви́нгли
zwischenspiel (mus.) : интерме́дия

BIBLIOGRAPHY

The following sources were consulted during the compilation of this dictionary:

Abrams, M.H., *A Glossary of Literary Terms*, fifth edition, Fort Worth, 1988.

Ashukin, N.S. and Ashukina M.G., *Krylatye slova*, Moscow, 1955.

Babkin, A.M. and Medvedev, I.I., *Slovar' inoiazychnykh vyrazhenii i slov*, 3 volumes, Moscow, 1995.

Bliss, Alan Joseph, *A Dictionary of Foreign Words and Phrases in Current English*, London, 1966.

Boardman, John, Griffin, J., Murray O. (eds.), *The Oxford History of the Classical World*, Oxford, 1986.

Bol'shaia Sovetskaia Entsiklopediia, 30 volumes, Moscow, 1970-78.

Bol'shoi entsiklopedicheskii slovar', Moscow, 1991.

Borowski, E.J. and Borwein, J.M., *Collins Dictionary of Mathematics*, second edition, London, 1989.

Brereton, Geoffrey, *A Short History of French Literature*, London, 1961.

Brokgauz, F.A. and Efron, I.A., *Entsiklopedicheskii slovar'*, 86 volumes, St Petersburg, 1890-1907.

Cairns, Christopher, *Italian Literature*, London, 1977.

Chambers Biographical Dictionary, Edinburgh, 1971.

Chilvers, Ian, *The Oxford Concise Dictionary of Art and Artists*, second edition, Oxford, 1996.

Cuddon, J.A., *A Dictionary of Literary Terms*, Penguin Books, 1982.

Ehrlich, Eugene (ed.), *The Penguin Dictionary of Foreign Terms and Phrases*, London, 1990.

Esposito, John L., *The Oxford Encyclopedia of the Mod-*

ern Islamic World, Oxford, 1995.

Eti zagadochnye anglichanki, Moscow, 1992.

Ezhegodnik Bol'shoi Sovetskoi Entsiklopedii, Moscow, 1970-90.

Friche, V.M. *et al* (eds.), *Literaturnaia entsiklopediia*, 11 volumes (incomplete), Moscow, 1929-39.

Gak, V.G. and Ganshina, K.A., *Novyi frantsuzsko-russkii slovar'*, Moscow, 1995.

Garland, Henry and Mary, *The Oxford Companion to German Literature*, second edition, London, 1986.

Gerhart, Genevra, *The Russian's World, Life and Language*, New York, 1974.

Graves, Robert, *The Greek Myths*, London, 1964.

The Great Soviet Encyclopedia, New York, 1973-83.

Harvey, Sir Paul and Heseltine, J.E., *The Oxford Companion to French Literature*, London, 1959.

Hirsch, E.D., *Cultural Literacy. What Every American Needs to Know*, Vintage Books, New York, 1987.

Jones, Colin D.H., *The Cambridge Illustrated History of France*, Cambridge, 1994.

Kabakchi, V.V., *Angliiskii iazyk mezhkul'turnogo obshcheniia*, St Petersburg, 1993.

Kinder, Hermann and Hilgemann, Werner, *The Penguin Atlas of World History*, volume 1, London, 1978; volume 2, updated edition, London, 1995.

Krylatye slova, po tolkovaniiu S. Maksimova, Moscow, 1955.

Lamzin, V.I. and Smirnova, N.A., *Atlas istorii srednikh vekov*, revised edition, Moscow, 1996

Lexikon der deutschen Literatur, Munich, 1958.

Lodge, David, *The Modes of Modern Writing*, London, 1977.

Macdonald A.M. (ed.), *Chambers Twentieth Century Dictionary*, new edition, Edinburgh, 1983.

Martin, George, *The Opera Companion*, London, 1984.

Mednikova, E.M. and Apresian, Iu.D., (eds.), *Novyi bol'shoi anglo-russkii slovar'*, 3 volumes, Mosow, 1993.

Metelinskii, E.M. (ed.), *Mifologicheskii slovar'*, Moscow, 1992.

Nemetsko-russkii slovar', Moscow, 1995.

The New Collins Concise Dictionary of the English Language, London, 1983.

The New Encyclopaedia Britannica, fifteenth edition, 1994.

The Oxford Dictionary for Writers and Editors, Oxford, 1981.

The Oxford Dictionary of Quotations, second edition, London, 1953.

The Oxford Russian Dictionary, revised edition, Oxford, 1997.

Ozhegov, S.I., *Slovar' russkogo iazika*, sixteenth edition, Moscow, 1984.

Pankratova, V.A., *Opernye libretto*, Moscow, 1962.

Pfeffer, J. Alan, *Deutsches Sprachgut im Wortschatz der Amerikaner und Engländer*, Tübingen, 1987.

Phythian, B. A., *A Concise Dictionary of Foreign Expressions*, London, 1982.

Rao, G. Subba, *Indian Words in English*, Oxford, 1954.

Reber, Arthur S., *The Penguin Dictionary of Psychology*, second edition, London, 1995.

Room, Adrian (ed.), *Brewer's Dictionary of Phrase and Fable*, fifteenth edition, London, 1996.

Scholes, Percy A., *The Oxford Companion to Music*, tenth edition, Oxford, 1970.

Serjeantson, Mary S., *A History of Foreign Words in English*, London, 1961.

Shteinpress, B.S. and Iampol'skii, I.M., *Entsiklopedicheskii muzikal'nyi slovar'*, Moscow, 1959.

Slovar' ateista, Moscow, 1975.

Slovar' inostrannykh slov, Moscow, 1996.

Slovar' sokrashchenii russkogo iazyka, Moscow, 1963.

Slovar' sovremennogo russkogo literaturnogo iazyka, 15 volumes, Moscow, 1950-65.

Slovar' sovremennogo russkogo literaturnogo iazika, 6

volumes, Moscow, 1991-94.

Slovar' udarenii dlia rabotnikov radio i televideniia, Moscow, 1970.

Solzhenitsyn, A., *Russkii slovar' iazykovogo rasshireniia*, Moscow, 1990.

Speake, Jennifer (ed.), *A Dictionary of Philosophy*, London, 1979.

Speake, Jennifer (ed.), *The Oxford Dictionary of Foreign Words and Phrases*, Oxford, 1997.

Stamm, James R., *A Short History of Spanish Literature*, New York, 1967.

Stewart, W.J. and Burgess, Robert, *Collins Dictionary of Law*, Glasgow, 1996.

Surkov, A.A. *et al* (eds.), *Kratkaia literaturnaia entsiklopediia*, 9 volumes, Moscow, 1962-78.

Teatral'naia entsiklopediia, 5 volumes, Moscow, 1961-67.

Teed, Peter, *The Oxford Dictionary of Twentieth-Century History*, Oxford, 1992.

Timofeev, L.I. and Turaev, S.V., *Slovar' literaturovedcheskikh terminov*, Moscow, 1974.

Urdang, Laurence and Abate, Frank R., *Loanwords Index*, Detroit, 1983.

Uvarov, E.B. and Isaacs, Alan (eds.), *The Penguin Dictionary of Science*, seventh edition, London, 1993.

Zor'ko, G.F., Maizel, B.N. and Skvortsova, N.A., *Novyi ital'iansko-russkii slovar'*, Moscow, 1995.